P9-ARP-441

"Abu-Jamal's writing tends to be forceful, outraged, and humorous, but he also engages in the bombastic approaches of another era . . . [T]he author offers powerful columns on diverse subjects ranging from the plight of black farmers to the crushing of dissent after 9/11. Some remain all too relevant—e.g., those decrying systemic police brutality as seen in flashpoints from Rodney King to Ferguson or the rise of racial disparities in drug sentencing. Abu-Jamal meditates on central figures in the black political narrative, ranging from Dr. Martin Luther King Jr. to Trayvon Martin . . . As a collection that spans from 1982 to 2014, these topical essays testify to the effects of incarceration on mind and spirit. While his prose has sharpened over time, Abu-Jamal remains enraged and pessimistic about an America that, in his view, remains wholly corrupt: '[Blacks] know from bitter experience that while Americans may say one thing, they mean something quite different.'"

—*Kirkus Reviews*

"Hope and the seeds of revolution can come from the depths of isolation. Writing from his cell on death row, where he was held in solitary confinement for nearly 30 years, Abu-Jamal has long been a loud and clear voice for all who suffer injustice, racism, and poverty. Edited by Fernandez, this selection of 100 previously unpublished essays includes a foreword by Cornel West."

—Evan Karp, *SF Weekly*

"The power of his voice is rooted in his defiance of those determined to silence him. Magically, Mumia's words are clarified, purified by the toxic strata of resistance they must penetrate to reach us. Like the blues. Like jazz."

—John Edgar Wideman

"Mumia refuses to allow his spirit to be broken by the forces of injustice; his language glows with an affirming flame."

—Jonathon Kozol

"Mumia is a dramatic example of how the criminal justice system can be brought to bear on someone who is African American, articulate, and involved in change in society. The system is threatened by someone like Mumia. A voice as strong and as truthful as his—the repression against him is intensified."

—Sister Helen Prejean, author of *Dead Man Walking*

"Brilliant in its specificity and imperative, Mumia Abu-Jamal's work is about why multitudes of people don't overcome. It rings so true because he has not overcome."

—*LA Weekly*

"Expert and well-reasoned commentary on the justice system . . . His writings are dangerous."

—*The Village Voice*

"Uncompromising, disturbing . . . Abu-Jamal's voice has the clarity and candor of a man whose impending death emboldens him to say what is on his mind without fear of consequence."

—*The Boston Globe*

"Abu-Jamal, a gifted and controversial Philadelphia journalist, [has an] ever-lucid voice and humanistic point of view. [His essays are] eloquent and indelible."

—*Booklist* (starred review) for *All Things Censored*

"Like the most powerful critics in our society—Herman Melville . . . to Eugene O'Neil—Mumia Abu-Jamal forces us to grapple with the most fundamental question facing this country: what does it profit a nation to conquer the whole world and lose its soul?"

—Cornel West

WRITING ON THE WALL

WRITING ON THE WALL

SELECTED PRISON WRITINGS OF MUMIA ABU-JAMAL

Foreword by Cornel West
Edited by Johanna Fernández

Open Media Series | City Lights Books

Library of Congress Cataloging-in-Publication Data
Abu-Jamal, Mumia.
[Works. Selections]
 Writing on the wall : selected prison writings of Mumia Abu-Jamal /
foreword by Cornel West ; edited by Johanna Fernández.
    pages cm. — (City Lights Books open media series)
 Includes bibliographical references and index.
 ISBN 978-0-87286-675-1 (paperback)
 ISBN 978-0-87286-655-3 (ebook)
1. Civil rights—United States—History—21st century. 2. Justice,
Administration of—United States—History—21st century. 3. United
States—Politics and government—History—21st century. 4. United
States—Social conditions—History—21st century. I. Fernández,
Johanna. II. Title.

 JC599.U5A346 2015
 323.0973—dc23

                          2014048024

City Lights Books
Open Media Series
www.citylights.com

Each generation must discover its mission,
fulfill it or betray it, in relative opacity.
—Frantz Fanon

Contents

REVOLUTIONARY LOVE
AND THE PROPHETIC TRADITION

By Cornel West

Based on conversations
with Johanna Fernández in September 2014

The first opportunity I had to stand publicly with my dear brother and comrade, the revolutionary Mumia Abu-Jamal, was in the 1990s at the Philadelphia gathering of the National Association of Black Journalists, when the organization was scheduled to take a vote on whether to support Mumia. At that meeting, I delivered an impassioned indictment of the refusal of Black journalists to support Mumia unequivocally. For Mumia is not just an outstanding writer and journalist, he is a living expression of the best of the Black prophetic tradition.

For many years, I had known of Mumia as someone who is a truth teller, a witness bearer, who exposes lies. In 1985, when the MOVE organization became known to the world after that vicious bombing ordered by Philadelphia's first Black mayor, Wilson Goode, I had already developed great respect for Mumia's journalism, including his writings on MOVE's travails with the power structure of the City of Brotherly Love.

Although I had not had the opportunity to interact with Mumia personally, he had been the subject of numerous discussions in the National Black United Front, to which I belonged alongside Reverend Herbert D. Daughtry and his House of the Lord Pentecostal Church in Brooklyn. Mumia was included in our meditations as one of the living figures in the Black community who is part of both our revolutionary and our prophetic traditions.

In the 1990s, the voice of Mumia Abu-Jamal emerges in a special context. On the one hand, that decade is a period of reaction, because the class war against poor and working people is becoming more intense. Progressive movements are more dispersed and shattered than before, and the Black Freedom movement, under vicious attack, begins to lose its vitality. At this moment we begin to hear more from Mumia Abu-Jamal in the public sphere, a rare voice telling the truth from the vantage point of the wretched of the earth. Then he takes the next vital steps, offering a global analysis and calling for a local praxis.

During this period, I was blessed to stand with Mumia in court in Philadelphia, where Judge Albert Sabo, the judge in his original trial, now presided over a Jim Crow appellate process in his case. I remember clearly that Judge Sabo walked into the courtroom with a rigid, bigoted disposition. In contrast, Mumia entered the courtroom with a smile that announced that he was unbroken and "*ona Move*." Mumia was stronger than we were. I walked out of there a freer Black man by seeing him. I walked out of there more dedicated, more full of conviction by seeing his conviction, his dedication and his love in the face of the lies coming at him.

It was not until Chris Hedges recently took Jim Cohen and me to the prison in Frackville, Pennsylvania, that I first spent time with Mumia face to face. That kind of meeting, which allowed human contact, was possible only because Mumia had been transferred from Death Row to the general prison population. I was deeply moved. When somebody has been through what Mumia has been through, you think they'd be down and out, downtrodden, just barely making it. But again, Mumia walked out with this smile, this tenacity, this style, this unbelievable determination and just sheer spirit.

It was clear to me that the John Coltranes, the Curtis Mayfields, the Charlie Birds, the Gil Scott Herons—all the cultural artists whose works articulate the struggle of our spiritual survival—were at work in the sparkle in his eyes. In the presence of that wonderful juxtaposition of ferocity and tenderness, I began to leap intellectually, to consider that there's David Walker in him. There's Harriet Tubman in him. There's Garvey in him, there's a whole lot of Malcolm X and Fanny Lou Hamer in him. What I witnessed was that Mumia Abu-Jamal is rooted in the Black tradition that produced him, that he is ready for battle. And steeped in this tradition, he has the organic ability to draw life into his own spirit from the social, political, existential and economic analyses that he has mastered. And for me, that is the mark of a prophetic figure in our tradition.

I've always said that he is the freest man on death row, and in mind, soul and spirit, he continues to be one of the freest men imprisoned in the early part of the 21st century.

Not many people could undergo what he underwent and still have what I call a militant tenderness, a subversive sweetness and a radical gentleness in his demeanor, in his voice, in his singing and in his writing. In place of bitterness, he radiates gentleness and tenderness.

The lack of bitterness in the face of oppression is a sign of spiritual mastery.

Young people today on the frontlines of organizing need the revolutionary love that Mumia Abu-Jamal has. They're also going to need the revolutionary memory, never forgetting the great freedom fighters, the Frederick Douglasses, the Ella Bakers, the Martins. And they're going to need revolutionary analysis. And all of it—the revolutionary love, revolutionary memory and revolutionary analysis—is at work in every page written by Mumia Abu-Jamal.

What the young folk might not have is the deep Black culture and history out of which brother Mumia emerges. Mumia is not just a great public intellectual, he is an old-school jazz man who has the elegance of what I call "earned self-togetherness." That's hard to get. That only happens in particular historical moments, like the period after World War II, when people steeped in a rich Black Southern culture move to the urban centers, but they're still connected to deep roots of love and self-affirmation at the level of body and memory.

Young people today are not rooted in that experience. They're third-generation urban. They've grown up in a period of social breakdown, massive unemployment, a crack epidemic, obsession with commodification, and all of this presents them with difficult challenges. It's not a put-down of young people to say that.

But Mumia Abu-Jamal is part of that cultural continuum of struggle that shaped urban Black people between 1950 and about 1980. And the fact that he continues on with tremendous courage and vision and a sacrifice that is beyond description, all of that is a mighty tribute both to him and to the people, the culture and the traditions that produced him.

The Black prophetic tradition is the principled and creative response to being terrorized, traumatized and stigmatized. In the United States, the oppression of generations of Black families and communities is systemic. It has taken the form of white supremacism, enslavement, disenfranchisement, and the terrorism of the Jim Crow and Jane Crow justice system. Oppression is also meted out at the level of the individual. It can take the form of being hated and despised and spat upon. It can take the form of convincing us to hate ourselves, hate our bodies, hate the shape of our noses and lips and so forth. The Black prophetic tradition keeps track of these different forms of oppression. It responds with vision rooted in an analysis of the problem. It spurs praxis through organization and mobilization.

And sometimes it takes the form of an isolated voice, like that of the great David Walker. Sometimes it is a voice that goes back into the belly of the beast over and over again, like Harriet Tubman, to rescue Black life. Sometimes it's about creating a mass movement, as in the example of Marcus Garvey. Sometimes, as with the great W.E.B. Du Bois and

Paul Robeson, it articulates a global, international analysis, but always based in an understanding of American terror visited upon Black people.

The Black prophetic tradition refuses to view Black people's conditions simply as a Negro problem. It identifies these conditions as catastrophes visited on Black people by a system, and it responds with compassion and with a deep knowledge that our sacrifice serves a cause bigger than ourselves.

It's impossible to read any of Mumia's texts without seeing profound visions of freedom, not just for Black folks, but for everybody. Mumia's outlook always includes all the wretched of the earth, no matter what color or country or gender or sexual orientation. Mumia Abu-Jamal's voice is always on the side of those who are fighting against domination, and that is one the highest functions of Black prophetic activity.

We've got rich traditions in the Dominican Republic, rich traditions in Jamaica, rich traditions in Barbados and so forth. But the African American experience is distinct. It's the experience of existing within the most powerful empire in the history of the world, dealing with empire's in-your-face violence and hatred, while still talking seriously about revolutionary love, revolutionary memory, revolutionary analysis. Our truth tellers like brother Mumia pay a tremendous price for their courage, actions and speech.

Many of our precious everyday people pay a tremendous price, too, whether they're part of the movement or not. But the ones who say, "Let's shatter the sleepwalking. Let's awaken the people. Let's expose the lies. Let's courageously bear witness"—those are on the way to the cross, or torment at the hands of the FBI or CIA or DHS. That's just the way things operate in America. We've seen it over and over again, from the repression suffered by the abolitionists through to Garvey and Martin and Malcolm, right up to today. Fanny Lou was viciously attacked and under surveillance. Numerous attempts were made to marginalize Ella Baker. Vicki Garvin and Paul

Robeson were under house arrest for almost a decade. Du Bois was handcuffed when he was 83 years old in February 1951. We can go on and on and on, up to the current moment.

In Black journalism, probably the greatest figure before Mumia Abu-Jamal was Ida B. Wells-Barnett, an American whose level of courage we lack the language to describe. She had a bounty on her head when she was run out of Memphis, Tennessee. She went to T. Thomas Fortune's *New York Globe* newspaper, which embraced her. Then her supporters had to get her out of the country to England, because her life was threatened after three of her friends had been lynched in Memphis.

The risk-all level of courage she demonstrated by writing about American terrorism in the South, particularly the subject of lynchings—something that Booker T. Washington and Du Bois failed to highlight—is rarely seen today among journalists of any stripe. She was also the first Black journalist to write for a white newspaper when she published in the *Chicago Tribune*, a historically important crossing of the color line.

Ida B. Wells was a great crusader for justice, and a radical reformer. Mumia Abu-Jamal, however, is not a reformer: he's a revolutionary. And he's not writing for pay or tenure. He's writing for the people. That means that he's actually engaging in a completely unfettered analysis of systems of domination—capitalism, imperialism, patriarchy and so forth—and calling for a new world that requires fundamental transformation, a revolutionary transformation of the status quo. See, Ida, whom we love deeply, didn't go that far. But Mumia Abu-Jamal does. He builds on Ida B. Wells and others.

A profound crisis of Black professionals becomes apparent when you look critically, the way Mumia does, at Black intellectuals and Black elected officials within America's power structure today. We could say that there has been a *reniggerization* of the Black professional class. They've got money, position, power, but most of them are scared, intimidated and afraid. That's what niggerization does to Black people: *keeps . . . us . . . afraid.*

Mumia Abu-Jamal is one of the most deniggerized Black people alive today. He looks terror in the face. He keeps fighting, keeps swinging, keeps writing, keeps loving. Even when he was on death row all those years, Mumia Abu-Jamal was not afraid. T. Thomas Fortune was not afraid. Ida B. Wells was not afraid. Most of our Black professionals, journalists, those in the academy and so forth, *are* scared. Their career, their position, their access to power—they've succumbed to all the trappings and paraphernalia of status. But thank God we've got a new generation of young people emerging, and Ferguson is just one sign of it. There are entire communities of people who are definitely not afraid. They've had enough.

The challenge going forward will be learning from Mumia Abu-Jamal and others about how to take your rage and transform it into righteous indignation, how to combine it with a subversive memory, personal integrity and moral tenacity, and then direct it against the indignities of daily injustice and structures of domination. If you don't have the memory and a sense of history, you're not going to have the vision you need. If you don't have integrity, people are going to buy off your movement, and if you don't have tenacity, you're going to run out of gas. So you aren't going to be a long-distance runner like brother Mumia, whose voice and writings instill us, year after year, with all we need to run long, to run together, to run with love, which is what it takes to win.

Love is the dominant force that allows us to sustain ourselves and to resist forces of domination. Given the ubiquitous commodification in society, where everything and everybody seems to be up for sale, if you don't have a deep love, you'll sell out. I'm talking about love for the people, which Mumia Abu-Jamal embodies—a profound, revolutionary, community-building love. A love that sees the business-as-usual suffering, impoverishment, war and dehumanization as a call to rise up.

If Mumia could hold on and voice that call for all these years inside the nightmare and never cave in, then we have no excuses for ever caving in, giving up or selling out when it comes to the sacred needs of the everyday people we should be willing to live and die for. Mumia is a special brother, and his writings are a wake-up call. He is a voice from our prophetic tradition, speaking to us here, now, lovingly, urgently. Black man, old-school jazz man, freedom fighter, revolutionary—his presence, his voice, his words are the writing on the wall.

Introduction

By Johanna Fernández

On December 11, 2013, the *New York Times* featured an illustrated article on the discovery of a manuscript penned by hand
in a dank, 19th-century cell by a black prisoner, Austin Reed.
The memoir elicited great interest among contemporary
historians, activists, scholars of African American literature,
and the general public. The Yale professor who is editing the
manuscript celebrated its "lyrical quality" and the singularity
of Reed's message in the American canon. But Reed's text is
also significant because it forms part of a body of searing black
prisoners' narratives on freedom that destabilize, through their
humanism, the demonization reserved for the "black outlaw"
in U.S. history. Reed's writing exemplifies what Cornel West
calls the black prophetic voice in American history—a voice
committed to illuminating the truth about black oppression
and its systemic causes, and to advancing the project of true
justice and freedom.

Because they speak uncomfortable truths, black prophetic
voices of living men and women are vilified or swept under
the rug by those who, in West's words, are "well-adjusted to
injustice." This hard reality has defined the lives of those we
celebrate today, from Harriet Tubman and Frederick Douglass
to Angela Davis and the Reverend Dr. Martin Luther King Jr.

In our lifetime, one American, not unlike Austin Reed,
articulates today's uncomfortable truths. His voice reveals the
centrality of black oppression to the project of American capitalism and empire, the unbridled racism of the U.S. justice
system, the immediate and rippling horrors of war, the unfin-
ished project of American democracy, and the possibilities of a
liberated society not just for black people at home, but for everyone, everywhere. This living black writer enriches the black

prophetic tradition and our social prospects, giving ordinary people a sense of their own power and inspiring those on the margins of society to stand up and fight. From the solitude of a harsh prison cell, not unlike the one in which Austin Reed penned his memoir 150 years ago, this brave and selfless man has dedicated thousands of hours to articulating a rich and resonant message of social redemption.

This man is Mumia Abu-Jamal.

Since his incarceration 33 years ago, Mumia has authored seven unique books and recorded thousands of incisive and eloquent radio commentaries. His critically acclaimed bestseller, *Live From Death Row*, humanized death row from the inside and exposed its racist character. As a revolutionary, his study, literacy, and fostering of connections among people confronting injustice the world over are relentless, even as the powers that be conspire to censor his message and criminalize his speech.

A former Black Panther and imprisoned radio journalist, Mumia Abu-Jamal was framed by the Philadelphia police, railroaded in the courts, and wrongfully convicted and sentenced to death for the 1981 killing of Daniel Faulkner, a white Philadelphia police officer. In the 1990s, Mumia Abu-Jamal came dangerously close to execution, first on August 17, 1995, and again on December 2, 1999. Had it not been for the mass international movement that mobilized in the streets to save his life, we would know less of the quiet power behind the person that the world knows simply as Mumia.

Mumia's thoughtful and humane voice shatters the official narrative of him as monster and unrepentant cop-killer. As politicians and pundits paint the incarcerated as ruthless and worthless, Mumia counters with sober political critiques and a warm message of human connection and caring that call into question the assumptions and apparatus that have imprisoned not just him, but the more than two million other mostly black and brown people in our nation's sprawling prison system.

Today, in this moment of renewed upsurge against racist state violence, his voice is more dangerous than ever.

The most powerful police organization in the world, the Fraternal Order of Police (FOP), is the entity that has steadily sought his execution, marshaling legal actions, lobbying the Department of Corrections and the courts, and undertaking coordinated and aggressive media campaigns that instill public fear. In October 2014, when the FOP failed to prevent Mumia from giving a pre-recorded commencement speech at his alma mater, Goddard College, the Pennsylvania State legislature passed a vindictive gag law, the Revictimization Relief Act. The unconstitutional law threatens to dramatically curtail the free speech of all Pennsylvania prisoners and sue those who help amplify their voices under the pretext that such speech produces "mental anguish" among crime victims and their families. The Abolitionist Law Project and the ACLU have each filed challenges; their plaintiffs include prisoners, university professors, journalists, newspapers, and advocacy groups.

The FOP knows that the widespread discovery of Mumia's case and messages, both written and spoken, by today's generation of young black and brown activists undermines their credibility, existence, and very purpose. The sharp political analysis and valiant history of a former generation of black radicals—a significant number of whom are political prisoners today—could threaten the entire criminal justice system, and the *system itself*. The Black Lives Matter movement that has sprung to life in response to the rampant murder of young black and Latino men and women by police from Oakland to Ferguson to New York City and North Charleston makes the injustices of Mumia's case all the more apparent, and his eventual freedom all the more likely.

—

Writing on the Wall is the first comprehensive selection of

Mumia's short prison commentaries. The volume covers the entire span of time from his arrest in 1981 to the present. On December 8, 1981, while moonlighting as a cabdriver, the Philadelphia radio journalist witnessed through his rearview mirror an altercation between a police officer and a car with two men, one of whom he soon recognized as his brother, Billy Cook. Mumia stopped his car and ran through a parking lot to aid his brother. In the sequence of events that followed, a police officer, Daniel Faulkner, was shot and killed. Mumia was found semi-conscious, slumped nearby with a bullet from Officer Faulkner's gun in his stomach. A gun belonging to Mumia, which he had recently acquired because he had been held up while driving the cab, was allegedly found nearby. At the crime scene, Mumia was brutally beaten by police, held in a police vehicle for 30 minutes, beaten some more, and eventually driven to the entrance of the Jefferson Hospital emergency room, where he was thrown on the sidewalk. Before long he was charged with first-degree murder and railroaded in a capital trial. A discussion of the legal case and its violations can be found in the appendix of this volume.

The earliest of Mumia's writings, from the period immediately following his hospitalization and transfer to a local jail, reflect on social injustice broadly as well as the personal abuse he suffered—his bullet wound and beating to the edge of death by the police, his hospitalization, and his wrongful conviction for the murder of Officer Faulkner.

> I have finally been able to read press accounts of the incident that left me near death, a policeman dead, and me charged with his murder. It is nightmarish that my brother and I should be in this foul predicament, particularly since my main accusers, the police, were my attackers as well. My true crime seems to have been my survival of their assaults, for we were the victims that night.

Delivered at trial by Mumia during allocution, a right to speak that is afforded to defendants after conviction and before sentencing, this statement of July 1982 proclaims his innocence:

> I am innocent of these charges that I have been tried for, despite the connivance of Judge Sabo, Prosecutor McGill and Tony Jackson to deny me my so-called "right" to represent myself, to assistance of my choice, to personally select a jury of my peers, to cross-examine witnesses, and to make both opening and closing arguments. I am innocent despite what you 12 people think, and the truth shall set me free!

Soon after his trial, Mumia begins to write with less frequency about himself, his case and his innocence. It's as if his own unexpected clash with the state has made him a tribune for every youth, adult, family and community of color forced to endure similar abuses as a fact of everyday life. In the early 1990s, supporters published this statement and the seven essays that follow it here in a pamphlet titled *Survival Is Still a Crime*. Written between early 1982 and 1989, these pieces read like quiet explosions. Social justice activists used the pamphlet to help build the movement to free Mumia.

In these initial writings we feel the passion of a younger, militant Black Panther who, steeped in the literature and history of revolutionary struggle, is eager to share his insights with readers. The Panthers argued that, at core, American racism had never been about exclusion or discrimination alone, but rather about the systematic superexploitation and control of black America to advance the interlocking interests of capitalism and empire. Black people had more in common, the Panthers argued, with other oppressed people of the world, such as the Vietnamese, and with oppressed white workers (however misguided by racist ideology) than with the growing ranks of black elected officials who were beginning to manage urban centers.

Mumia's life as a writer, radio journalist and political commentator had begun in the late 1960s, when at age 15 he started writing for the Black Panther Party newspaper in Philadelphia. In 1972, he discovered radio journalism at Goddard College, and by the late 1970s he had become a respected, award-winning voice among Philadelphia's radio broadcasters. He worked for local and national black radio stations, for the city's National Public Radio affiliate, and for the national station's acclaimed signature program *All Things Considered*. In 1981, he became president of the local chapter of the National Association of Black Journalists.

Yet despite having been lauded by *Philadelphia Magazine* as "one to watch" for his talents as a radio journalist, Mumia was fired from a number of local radio stations. Among them were WWDB and WPEN, where he refused to submit to administrative directives to discontinue his on-air challenges to the city's notoriously brutal police department and to the escalating harassment of a local black radical group, the MOVE organization.[1]

MOVE was a Philadelphia-based group of black people committed to a radical vision of cooperative, healthy and environmentally conscious living. Its members took the surname Africa, reasoning that it was "the original homeland of all mankind." In the words of Mumia's biographer, Terry Bisson, its members were "controversial, confrontational, belligerent and profane, calling their detractors 'motherfuckers' and 'niggers,' while pointing out that the real obscenity is the system that allows racism, exploitation, and injustice to flourish." While the comparable white communes of the period retreated to rural areas and were rarely targeted by the state, MOVE had developed anti-establishment politics defined by the violent state repression visited upon black, urban social movements of the 1960s and '70s.

The organization figures prominently in Mumia's writings and in his political worldview for many reasons. Long before his arrest, the plight of MOVE engaged him as a microcosm of state treatment of black people historically. MOVE's honesty and commitment to a combination of personal, spiritual and political uplift—as well as its open denunciation of American capitalism, which preyed on every aspect of human life and the environment—inspired him. Mumia was perhaps the only Philadelphia journalist who covered the organization's ongoing conflict with the police in a way that gave voice to MOVE members' perspectives and grievances. It was this that cost him his job with mainstream radio stations, and later, his own trial proceedings were prejudiced by his coverage, association with and sympathy for MOVE.

Needless to say, MOVE became a priority target for harassment by Philadelphia law enforcement. Mumia writes with indignation after each act of violence committed by the authorities, such as when police trampled a MOVE baby to death, carried out a military-style siege and destruction of a residential MOVE house, or, on May 13, 1985, firebombed a neighborhood to ashes. On that day, the black mayor of Philadelphia, Wilson Goode, in collaboration with the fire and police departments, had a military-grade aerial firebomb dropped on the MOVE house. The bombing killed 11 people—five children and six adults—and burned down 61 homes, destroying the entire African American neighborhood of Powelton Village. Mumia writes:

> People mark time by events held in common, and shared moments of joy and sorrow. Cities, although artificial, non-organic bodies, mark time similarly. Paris is known today as the "City of Light," but the dark shadow of the Nazi Occupation is still within the memory of the living. . . . Yes, cities hold memories, locked in the minds and souls of its inhabitants.

. . . Paris had its Occupation, Beirut its Sabra and Shatila, and Philadelphia its MOVE bombing.

Against this backdrop, Mumia's writings about MOVE and respect for its leader, John Africa, whom he salutes at the end of many of his public presentations, are profound acts of solidarity. In 1986, in the immediate aftermath of both the bombing of the MOVE house in Philadelphia[2] and of his own calvary in the courts, Mumia writes with indignation about one of the major themes in this volume—liberation from oppression through political education and collective struggle from below:

> When will these dismal days of our mind-rending pain, our oppression, our accustomed place on the bottom rung of the human family, end? When will our tomorrows brighten? It will come from ourselves, not from this system. Our tomorrows will become brighter when we scrub the graffiti of lies from our minds, when we open our eyes to the truths that this very system is built not on "freedom, justice and brotherhood" but on slavery, oppression and genocide.

For the first 28 years of his incarceration, Mumia was on death row, isolated for 22 hours a day in a prison cell the size of a small bathroom. During this time he was denied all forms of human contact and twice came within days of being executed. Despite these harrowing conditions, Mumia read voraciously and continued to write prolifically. In fact, the equanimity he gained through the daily ritual of writing probably saved him from the worst consequences of devastating isolation and living with a date to die.

But writing was more than a therapeutic exercise. In prison Mumia disciplined his prose, using his solitary time to develop into a writer of great literary power. Throughout these years he offered analyses of major developments in American society and world politics, with emphasis on the varied contemporary manifestations of racism and inequality; the changing character of work; the growth of class stratification and land dispossession under 20th- and 21st-century capitalism; the causes of war; and the persistence of colonial structures of oppression in Asia, Africa and Latin America in the post-colonial era.

Although most of Mumia's commentaries are political in nature and address the structural causes and historical roots of social problems, his writing is devoid of dogmatic political lines. Nuanced humanism and fierce solidarity pulse through his writing about the vulnerability and resistance of the most disadvantaged, elevating his work from journalism to literature. "Who will sing of the wonder, the terror, the beauty, and the madness of Black life in this new century?" he asks in one of his commentaries. His essays are those songs—"redemption songs," to use Bob Marley's expression.

Writing on the Wall is heir to three historical currents of freedom literature arising from the nation's well of black experience with both oppression and resistance. First, the searing narratives of black prisoners offer a compelling counter-narrative on freedom and disprove by example the ruthless demonization of the black outlaw in the United States.[3] Second, the black radical tradition, which seeks to understand and redress the root causes of social, economic and political inequity. Third, the black prophetic voice in American history, as Cornel West elaborates in the preface to this volume.

For centuries, black voices have responded to the nation's callous indifference to the suffering of oppressed people with calls for rebellion. From the abolitionist petitions written by Prince Hall as the United States was declaring its independence to David Walker's *Appeal*, which called on enslaved black persons to rebel against their white enslavers; from the anti-lynching journalism of Ida B. Wells-Barnett to the calls for self-defense by black journalists writing in the *Crusader* and the

Black Panther, black voices of conscience have risen up against the atrocities of racism and a racially exclusionary democracy organized at its inception to serve the interests of land-owning white men. At every juncture in American history, the struggle for freedom embodied in these black voices has pried open the narrow boundaries of U.S. democracy. It has compelled society to afford its hallowed freedoms not just to those liberated from their enslavers and their descendants, but to those who have been historically positioned outside of both citizenship and full personhood—among them immigrants, women, Native Americans, the impoverished, and, increasingly, Asian Americans and Arab Americans.

Contributing to this great tradition, Mumia posits that we can break free from our oppressive system. But he cautions that justice and equality can be achieved only through the fundamental transformation of society, and that such a transformation can occur only through a democratic culture involving full bottom-up participation of ordinary people and communities.

—

It was in the community of Philadelphia and its people that Mumia found his revolutionary perspectives. In the 1960s and '70s, the criminalization and repression of black protesters in Philadelphia was directed by a police commissioner turned mayor, Frank Rizzo, who made a name for himself as the tough sheriff in town. It was Rizzo who ordered a raid on the Panthers' office during which members were forced to undress and line up on the street clad only in their underwear. It was in this climate that local police, in collaboration with federal agents, compiled an 800-page surveillance file on Mumia between 1968 and 1981.

Mumia's incarceration coincided with the dark conservative era of the Reagan-Bush era, when many veteran activists from the 1960s became demoralized about the possibilities for change or were coopted into mainstream institutions. Ironically, Mumia's death row imprisonment, where concrete reminders of the state's repressive character were a daily reality, preserved and enlarged his revolutionary perspective.

Many of Mumia's commentaries offered humanistic descriptions of the prisoners he observed around him, as well as those on the outside who were dedicating their lives to justice. Among the many he honors are the sole adult survivor of the 1985 MOVE bombing in Philadelphia, Ramona Africa; Black Panthers Fred Hampton and Huey P. Newton; and Attorney William Kunstler. It is also in this period that Mumia's first book, *Live From Death Row*, is published and becomes a critically acclaimed best-seller.

In prison, the writing process was arduous. For the first 18 years of his isolation on death row, Mumia did not have access to a typewriter. With careful attention to penmanship, he wrote his commentaries longhand, in tightly compressed block letters, pressing firmly on two blank sheets separated by carbon paper. Mumia's literary agent, Frances Goldin, often recalls the big lump on Mumia's hand during those days—a quarter-inch callus produced by the ritual exercise of writing with a clenched grip on his pen.

Mumia mailed both copies of each new commentary to volunteers, who then typed his texts. Like a message in a bottle, these commentaries, once transcribed, were then passed on by hand or mailed and reproduced within movement circles. The tireless women who transcribed Mumia's work consistently include the late Susan Burnett (the wife of Ali Bey Hassan of the Black Panther 21) and Sister Marpessa Kupendua. Today, Sister Fatirah Aziz, also known as Litestar01, receives Mumia's commentaries for transcription and distributes them via email and other online outlets. In the early years of his incarceration, activists in the movement to free Mumia, especially MOVE members, hand delivered the commentaries to community newspapers. The *Philadelphia Tribune* and the African American weekly newspaper *Scoop USA*, published in Philadelphia and edited by R. Sonny Driver, were among the first to print Mumia's prison writings.

During the first decade of his incarceration, more than 20 newspapers published his commentaries, including the *Voice of Detroit*; the *Democrat* in Green County, North Carolina; the *San Francisco Bay View*; and the *Atlanta Journal and Constitution*. By the 1990s that number had more than doubled, and with the advent of the Internet, the international Free Mumia movement was among the first to use online methods to raise his profile, educate international audiences on the violations in his case, and distribute his writings to a broad readership.

In the late 1980s Mumia went back to his beloved radio broadcasting. He had first been recognized for his radio journalism in 1981, when he won Columbia University's coveted Edward Howard Armstrong Prize in broadcasting for his report on Pope John Paul's visit to Philadelphia. In 1988, Mumia began broadcasting meditations on the meaning of freedom via a portable telephone delivered twice a week to his death row cell. Since 1992, Noelle Hanrahan has systematically recorded and distributed a majority of these to radio stations around the world through the nonprofit Prison Radio Project. From this period forward, Mumia's commentaries reflect his shift to radio and a consistently shorter format.

Radio was the single most important influence on his writing style: "When you're doing radio and are under the gun of the clock, you have to focus and concretize your message succinctly and evocatively. The goal is always to paint a picture that captures the listener." Recording for radio broadcast also demanded a broadening of his subject matter, so Mumia began to write about the major political events and flashpoints occurring in American society and world politics, as seen in this volume.

—

Mumia Abu-Jamal's prolific body of work is anchored in the understanding that the trafficking and enslavement in North and South America of 10 million Africans financed Western European colonies and the industrial revolution that brought capitalism to maturity. The study of international systems of oppression, and their impact domestically and abroad, frame his perspective. From Mumia's point of view, the historical experience of bondage continues to be manifested in the cruel, violent and repressive role of the state today: systems of oppression operative since the nation accommodated enslavers remain intact, even if recast. Prisons, Mumia writes, are just "steel-and-brick slave ships," and the impunity with which police violence is perpetrated in black communities is just the most current form of lynching. But "the cops are not the problem," writes Mumia:

> They are the symptom of a total systemic disease.
> One that sacrifices the poor, the Mexican, the African
> American and the powerless to the system. It is in this
> context, then, that one must examine the rising inci-
> dence and severity of cop violence. Why do we speak
> of "police brutality"? Why not call it what it is? It is
> *police terrorism*. And the state is not a solution to the
> problem; indeed, it is the problem.

Like other imprisoned dissidents such as Antonio Gramsci, Sacco and Vanzetti, Eugene Debs, Malcolm X and George L. Jackson, Mumia commits to articulating the voices of millions. He presents not just a black counter-narrative to the prevailing formulations of white supremacy, but a redemptive script that strives to achieve a society in which social domination, violence and indignity are both unconscionable and impossible.

Regarding the impact of globalization, he declares that the United States uses "the illusion of 'free trade' to crowbar into local and national economies." His commentaries document the ways in which ordinary working people organize to protect themselves from capitalism's relentless incursions. He also aims to increase public solidarity with social movements around the world. In the spirit of "an injury to one is an injury to all," he addresses crises in Palestine, Egypt, Mexico, Venezuela, Puerto Rico, Iraq, Afghanistan and Canada, and does so with the same sense of urgency he applies to events in Ferguson. To help bring foreign matters into focus here at home, he often makes connections to U.S. political philosophy and doctrine. So, for example, to give a better understanding of programs to help the poor in Venezuela, he discusses them through the lens of Thomas Paine. "What would he think," asks Mumia, "about an America that tried, unsuccessfully, to spark a coup in Venezuela several years ago, because oil companies and money men didn't want that country to spend its national wealth on the nation's poor? Would he find in Señor Presidente Chávez, and his struggle to empower the poor, an enemy or an ally?"

Mumia's voice has offered enduring resistance to the forces of globalized violence. When the photos of orange-uniformed prisoners from the U.S.-controlled Abu Ghraib prison near Baghdad spread around the world, Mumia was among the first critics to note that the dehumanizing treatment of Iraqis at Abu Ghraib had its awful precedents in prisons and police stations across the United States. In 2004 he wrote: "The roots of Guantánamo, of Abu Ghraib, of Bagram Air Force Base, of U.S. secret torture chambers operating all around the world, are deep in American life, and its long war against Black life and liberation."

Ironically, Mumia's transfer in 2012 from death row to the general prison population came with new revelations about the national crisis of imprisonment. He had believed he knew its contours, yet when he was able to see and physically mix with the multitudes of men warehoused in the nation's prisons, he realized that the general population was profoundly different from that of death row. He was especially struck and troubled by the number of elderly prisoners who walk with canes or are in wheelchairs, and by the many others who look like children. "I thought I had read and mastered all there is to know about prisons," he writes. "I've been humbled. . . . Now, I regularly go back and rethink and reread what I thought I knew."

———

Permeating all the decades of his writing from prison is Mumia's profound identification with people in the throes of personal or collective struggle. While watching CNN's Don Lemon interview five young black men about the protests in Ferguson, Missouri, Mumia had to fight to hold back tears when he heard each man identifying himself as Michael Brown —the unarmed black youth gunned down in the street by a Ferguson police officer. Such solidarity rooted in love courses through the selections in *Writing on the Wall*. Solidarity with the downtrodden, the dispossessed, the deported, the imprisoned and the impoverished elevates the writing not only from journalism to literature, but from literature to the prophetic.

In his essay *The Meaning of Ferguson*, Mumia quotes Vladimir Illich Lenin, the Russian revolutionary: "There are decades when nothing happens, there are weeks when decades happen." Mumia then describes how government repression has sown the seeds of a deeper rebellion and a deeper understanding of the relations of power. "The government responded with the tools and weapons of war," writes Mumia. "They attacked them as if Ferguson were Fallujah, in Iraq." In struggle, the people of Ferguson "learned the wages of black protest . . . the limits of their so-called 'leaders,' who called for 'peace' and 'calm' while armed troops trained submachine guns and sniper rifles on unarmed men, women and children." He concludes his ode to the heirs of the black radical tradition with a call to build independent, radical organizations: "Ferguson may prove a wake-up call. A call for youth to build social, radical, revolutionary movements for change."

Although the state has relentlessly persecuted Mumia for over 33 years, painting him as a hardened and hateful killer, his voice is without bitterness. His resilience shows the ability of the human spirit to withstand the worst that this system can do to a person. He enables us to read the writing on the wall—to believe that the days of this system are numbered, and that another world is possible. Like Nelson Mandela, Mumia defies his captors by preserving his integrity and compassion in the face of the hateful repression orchestrated against him. Nowhere is this contrast more apparent than the moment when his death sentence was found unconstitutional. Immediately after his transfer to the general prison population, he wrote a letter to the men and women he was leaving behind on the row:

> I write to tell you all—even those I've never met— that I love you, for we have shared something exceedingly rare. I have shared tears and laughter with you, that the world will neither know nor see. . . . But, Brothers and Sisters of the Row, I write not of death, but of life. . . . Love fiercely. Learn a new thing. . . . Keep your mind alive. Keep your heart alive. Laugh! . . . No matter what the world says of you, see the best in each other and radiate love to each other.

Love and solidarity define Mumia's writings and life behind bars. His voice is defiant and transgressive, yet measured and rational, and always resonating with hope. This book is offered in the spirit of Mumia's uncompromising commitment to love, justice, community and the highest aspirations of humanity.

CHRISTMAS IN A CAGE

January 1982

Shortly before 6 a.m., the speaker in this tiny, barren cell blares a message, said to be from prison superintendent David Owens:

"A Merry Christmas to all inmates of the Philadelphia prison system. It is our hope that this will be the last holiday season you spend with us."

A guard reads Owens's name and the speaker falls silent for a half hour. I wonder at the words, and ponder my first Christmas in the hospital wing of the Detention Center.

Christmas in a cage

I have finally been able to read press accounts of the incident that left me near death, a policeman dead, and me charged with his murder. It is nightmarish that my brother and I should be in this foul predicament, particularly since my main accusers, the police, were my attackers as well. My true crime seems to have been my survival of their assaults, for we were the victims that night.

To add insult to injury, I have learned that the forces of "law and order" have threatened my brother and burned, or permitted the burning of, my brother's street business. Talk about curbside justice! According to some press accounts, cops stood around the fire joking and then celebrated at the station house.

Nowhere have I read an account of how I got shot, how a bullet happened to find its way near my spine, shattering a rib, splitting a kidney and nearly destroying my diaphragm. And people wonder why I have no trust in a "fair trial." Nowhere have I read that a bullet left a hole in my lung, filling it with blood.

Nowhere have I read how police found me lying in a pool of my blood, unable to breathe, and then proceeded to punch, kick and stomp me—not question me. I remember being rammed into a pole or a fireplug with police at both arms. I remember kicks to my head, my face, my chest, my belly, my back and other places. But I have read no press accounts of this, and have heard tell of no witnesses.

Nowhere have I read of how I was handcuffed, thrown into a paddy wagon and beaten, kicked, punched and pummeled. Where are the witnesses to a police captain or inspector entering the wagon and beating me with a police radio, all the while addressing me as a "Black motherfucker"? Where are the witnesses to the beating that left me with a four-inch scar on my forehead? A swollen jaw? Chipped teeth?

Not to end prematurely, who witnessed me pulled from the paddy wagon, dropped three feet to the cold hard earth, beaten some more, dragged into Jefferson Hospital, and then beaten inside the hospital as I fought for breath on one lung?

I awoke after surgery to find my belly ripped from top to bottom, with metallic staples protruding. My penis strapped to a tube, and tubes leading from each nostril to God knows where, was my first recollection. My second was intense pain and pressure in my already ripped kidneys, as a policeman stood at the doorway, a smile on his mustached lips, his name tag removed and his badge covered. Why was he smiling, and why the pain? He was standing on a square plastic bag, the receptacle for my urine.

Am I to trust these men, as they attempt to murder me again, in a public hospital? Not long afterward, I was shaken to consciousness by a kick at the foot of my bed. I opened my eyes to see a cop standing in the doorway, an Uzi submachine gun in his hands. "Innocent until proven guilty"?

High-water pants and cold

Days later, after being transferred to city custody at Giuffre

Medical Center under armed police guard, I was put into room #202 in the basement's detention unit, which is the coldest in the place.

After I was transferred to what's laughingly referred to as the new "hospital wing" of the Detention Center, I found out what "cold" really means. For the first two days, the temperature plummeted so low that inmates wore blankets over their prison jackets.

I had been officially issued a short-sleeved shirt and some tight high-water pants, and I was so cold that for the first night I could not sleep. Other inmates saved me from the cold. One found a prison jacket for me. (I had asked a guard, but he told me I would have to wait until an old inmate rolls, or gets out. So much for "using the system.") Other inmates, and a kind nurse, supplemented my night warmth.

The prison issued one bedsheet and one light wool blanket. When I protested to a social worker, she told me defensively, "I know it's cold, but there's nothing I can do. The warden's been told about the problem." Why am I concerned about the cold? Because the doctor who treated me at Jefferson Hospital explained that the only real threat to my health was pneumonia, because of my punctured lung.

Is it purely coincidental that for the next week I spent some of the coldest nights and days of my life? Is the city, through the prison system, trying to kill me before I go to trial? What do they fear? I told all this to my prison social worker (a Mrs. Barbara Waldbaum), and she pooh-poohed the suggestion.

"No, Mr. Jamal, we want to see you get better."

"Not hardly," I replied.

Miraculously, after my complaints, some semblance of heat found its way into the cells on my side of the wall. Enough to sleep, at least. Is it coincidental, too, that the heat began to go on the night I was visited by Superintendent David Owens?

"It is our hope that this will be the last holiday season you spend with us. . . ." Owens's words ring through my mind again—*is there another, grim meaning to this seemingly innocuous holiday greeting?*

Echoes of Pedro Serrano

There is another side to this controversial case that people are not aware of. My cell is reasonably close to the place where Pedro Serrano was severely beaten and strangled to death. I have talked to eyewitnesses—some of whom I knew in the street. These brothers, at considerable personal peril, have told their stories to police and to prison officials, to city Managing Director W.W. Goode, to the Puerto Rican Alliance, and to me. Some have been threatened by guards for doing so, but they have done so despite the threats.

According to several versions, Serrano, who had already been beaten by guards, was shaking his cell door, making noise to attract attention. Guards, angered at the noise, ordered all inmates into lockup. Most complied. One, a paralyzed, wheel-chair-bound inmate, did not. He drove his chair near a wall and watched in silence.

The guards opened Serrano's cell, dragged him out, and proceeded to punch, kick and stomp him. He cried out in pain and terror, but the other inmates, locked up, were helpless. One guard, well known for his violence, reportedly whipped him with his long key chain, producing thin red welts in Serrano's white flesh.

Before this latest assault on my brother and myself, I had covered a press conference called by the Puerto Rican Alliance and members of the Serrano family. I saw photographs of Pedro Serrano, his face swollen even in death. I saw a body riddled with swellings, bruises and welts. I remember the thick, dark bruises beneath his neck, and I remember calling David Owens for a comment.

"Mumia, Mr. Serrano was not beaten to death, according to all the reports I've received. The Medical Examiner concurs," Owens said authoritatively. "Mr. Serrano was not beaten by any members of my staff," Owens would later proclaim to my radio listeners.

Remember the dark bruise around Serrano's neck? Owens told me he apparently strangled on a leather restraining belt, by exerting pressure until death. Inmate eyewitnesses said a guard wrapped the leather strap around Serrano's neck and pulled him back into the room, where he was again beaten and placed in restraints. Serrano, arrested for burglary, was described by his wife as being in love with life, and surely not suicidal, as prison officials have suggested.

Why have I recounted these intricacies of a case that is now public knowledge? I'll tell you why:

Because my jailers, the men who decide whether I am to leave my cell for food, for phone calls, for pain medication, for a visit with a loved one, are the very same men who are accused of murdering Pedro Serrano.

Remember the DA's claim that police had enough evidence to charge me with murder? How much more evidence do they have on Serrano's accused murderers? Yet every day they come to work, do their do, and return home to their loved ones . . . while others sit in isolation and squalor. Consider the scenario—accused murderers guarding accused murderers! How insane—yet how telling it is of the system's brutality.

Justice for who?

What is the dividing line? That Serrano was a "spic," a "dirty P.R.," and thus his life is subject to the depredations of a system that talks justice yet practices genocide. I am accused of killing a policeman, who was, moreover, white. For that, not even the pretense of justice is necessary. "Beat him, shoot him, frame him, put fear into his family," is the unwritten but very real script.

I have been shackled like a slave, hands and feet, for daring to live. Those who have dared to question the official version have been threatened with dismissal from their jobs, and some with death.

Why do they fear one man so much? Not because they loved his alleged "victim"—but because they fear any questioning of their role as accuser, and occasionally executioner. Who polices the police?

The DA is well known as a character whose only interest is higher political office—obviously he would oppose a special prosecutor, for he wants his office to have the glory of hanging murder on "the radical reporter."

Where was [then-DA] Ed Rendell when Winston C.X. Hood and Cornell Warren were summarily executed, their hands shackled behind them? What credence did he give the witnesses to these murders? Or the outright, cold-blooded killing of 17-year-old William Johnson Green? Or the intentionally broadcast beating of Delbert Africa? Where was his unquenchable thirst for justice then? Need we mention Pedro Serrano?

Make no mistake, Jake! For a nigger or a spic, there is no semblance of justice, and we better stop lying to ourselves.

Who are we to blame? No one but ourselves. For we condone it and allow it to happen. We are still locked in the slavish mentality of our past centuries, for we care more for the oppressor than for ourselves.

How many more martyrs will bleed their last before we wake up, stand up, demand and fight for justice?

And justice, true justice, comes not from the good graces of the Philadelphia Police Department, the District Attorney's office, the court system or your friendly neighborhood lawyer. It comes from God, the giver of your very life, your health, your air and your food.

COURT OF LAW OR HALL OF OPPRESSION?

June 1982

For centuries, people of African descent have entered the courts of their oppressors. For many, and probably most, the courtrooms represented the vestibule to the gas chamber—or life imprisonment. This court today will attempt to follow such a precedent, for this court, and all such "courts" are loath to change precedent—meaning that they wish to do nothing that will depart substantially from what has gone on before.

In the past, Black men paraded before such "tribunals" have come shackled, manacled, chained, imprisoned with slave bracelets. Once there, they are now sure to hear lofty principles such as "presumption of innocence," "innocent until proven guilty," "due process," ad nauseam.

After lofty words, however comes the bitter truth—slavery by decree of "Judge Hoofinmouth," one who is paraded before the people as an impartial innocent, one surely above passions and presumptions of the common man.

In the case of *Commonwealth v. Mumia Abu-Jamal*, however, the judges in this city, and in the state's "supreme" so-called "court," have fallen below the standard. The common man is indeed far above their political chess game with the lives of men.

On several occasions, court-appointed counsel A. Jackson has petitioned for bail, citing classic reasons: my roots in the community; demonstrated commitment to my community; family in the region; the status of my health following my shooting, beating, and attempted murder in Jefferson Hospital; and the testimony of several area elected officials to my reputation for honesty and peacefulness.

Despite a timely application for bail, both here in Common Pleas Court and at the appellate level, both have been denied, without cause.

It is clear, crystal clear, why the Commonwealth fought against bail and why it wasted no time in fighting to revoke bail that was set at $250,000. It was to hamper my efforts to secure the information needed to adequately defend myself—a classic case of punishment before trial, and then trial without the adequate resources to demolish a flimsy case compiled by the Commonwealth.

What is further revealed by the state's actions of the past few months is the intentional falsification of sworn police statements, a new crop of purported "confessions," apparently forgotten until recently. How convenient.

On March 29, 1982, the State Supreme Court ruled on the petition to set or reinstate bail, after holding the motion for nearly three months. The response? "Petition denied." Period. No reasons were given. No opinions were offered.

What happened to the presumption of innocence? The Commonwealth reasoned that a defendant charged with a capital crime, such as first-degree murder, should not be granted bail, as such a defendant may flee the jurisdiction under fear of conviction and execution. By its actions of March 29, the Supreme Court apparently agreed. It is clear that by its actions the court has shown its biased political nature—it ruled not on the merits or demerits of a case but on the personalities of those involved. The deceased was a Philadelphia policeman and the accused is an outspoken activist, a MOVE supporter. . . . Where is the presumption of innocence?

On April 30, 1980, this same Supreme Court found reason to rule differently on a case involving Davico Cabeza. Cabeza, *found guilty* of first-degree murder, applied for bail as an element of post-verdict motions. Common Pleas Court Judge John Geisz granted bail. The State Supreme Court reversed his decision, saying in effect that if post-verdict motions were uncompleted after four months following conviction, the trial judge then has discretion to set bail.

Under the Pennsylvania Rules of Criminal Procedure 4010(A)(1):

> The defendant shall not be released on bail upon a finding of guilty of an offense which is punishable by death or life imprisonment. However, if post-verdict motions are not disposed of within a reasonable period of time thereafter, *the judge may in his discretion allow bail.*

Bail is allowed for some persons convicted of first-degree murder but not for others accused of the same crime? Logically, isn't a person *convicted* of murder more apt to "flee the jurisdiction" than someone accused—someone presumed innocent?

To quote John Africa:

> [Judge], you can sit on a bench and let a person object all day, but you got the authority to overrule that objection, so it don't mean nothin', 'cause when you see indicting examples starting, you can stop 'em. It is the same thing as your freedom of speech—you'll say people can speak freely until the speech begins to threaten your idea of so-called freedom. Then folks ain't free to speak. They're kicked, punched, clubbed, stomped, handcuffed, shot and jailed by the cops and jailed again by the judges. When the so-called trial takes place, you got all kinds of things in your so-called laws you can't explain. This whole procedure is a fraud, a sham, a contradiction to everything true law is about. You can't explain how you can say that a person can't be judged 'til they go to court, when at this moment, these cops are beating, jailin', judgin' poor folks all over the world at will![1]

What should be clear to everyone who reads this is how the courts consistently camouflage their corruption, how they support police against the people, all under the guise of "equal protection under the law."

If you examine the facts of the case, how it has been handled in our courts of "law"—the truth will become clearer and clearer to everyone.

ONA MOVE! LONG LIVE JOHN AFRICA!

3

DIFFERENT SIDES OF THE SYSTEM

June 1982

For several weeks now the pre-trial and trial of the "case" of *Mumia Abu-Jamal v. the Commonwealth of Pennsylvania* has been going on. Ostensibly, the defense attorney court-appointed to the case, Anthony Jackson, is there to defend the interests of the defendant, but his true role seems to have become clearer in recent days.

Despite Jackson's assurances of "allegiance" and "love," his words and statements have shown otherwise. When a defense lawyer acknowledges that he has lost his case, long before its conclusion, what is the sense of pretense of defense? The trial becomes a sham, a predetermined showcase for the oratorical "talents" of the lawyer, a Center City drama without a written script, its actors ad-libbing their expected lines. When the verdict is assured, why have a trial at all?

It has become clear that this "court" has no intention to hear from me: its action, pre-planned, no doubt, to revoke my supposed constitutional right of self-representation, was designed to silence, to gag, to muzzle me, to render me ineffective in the defense of my life.

The decision to revoke came at the "suggestion" of the prosecution, the same office trying to execute me. Hardly an entity that wishes to protect my rights or interests. Initially, such a decision was to be for the express purpose of appeal to the State Supreme Court, but in reality, its purpose was to silence me for the duration of the trial.

If the court-appointed attorney concedes that his defense is ineffective, then he admits he is powerless, nothing more than a cog in the system's wheel. If he cannot or will not defend my life, why doesn't he leave, withdraw, or allow me to defend my life or to appoint someone whose primary interest is my survival, not the court's pleasure? Like a gnat drawn to the flicker of flame, a lawyer is sucked to this case for fame. But as with that gnat, this flame will consume this lawyer whose only real interest is his career, his continued participation in this system, not the freedom of his "client." If a lawyer's interest isn't freedom, why would I want one? If a lawyer simply wishes to "go thru the motions," then why not have John Africa assist in my defense, as *his* interest is *freedom*.

Judges are ex-lawyers, and lawyers are potential judges— and all of them are representatives of the same system. This system will acquit the rich white boy who shoots the president, before millions, on an insanity plea; it will acquit a thief who steals a million; it will acquit a woman who kills her cop husband. But it convicts a nigger for *owning* a gun, convicts a poor person for stealing $50, and convicts a Black man charged with killing a cop!

John Africa is not a slave to this foul, messed-up system— he is not bought and sold. He is not a servant to money, the fuel that keeps this rotten system afloat. Unlike a lawyer, specifically this sellout artist Anthony Jackson, John Africa is committed to true freedom, not weak, phony appearances of defense. John Africa is my counsel. It is *he* whom I trust!

4

LONG LIVE JOHN AFRICA

July 1982

Today's decision comes as no surprise to me. In fact, many will remember that I said this would happen last week, when John Africa predicted and prophesied this jury decision. I want everyone to know it came after a legal, trained lawyer was imposed upon me against my will. A legal, trained lawyer whose interests were clearly not mine—a legal, trained lawyer named Tony Jackson, a man who knew he was inadequate to the task and chose to follow the direction of his black-robed conspirator, Albert Sabo, even if it meant ignoring my directions.

To quote John Africa: "When a lawyer chooses to follow the conditions of the court, he compromises his obligation to his client." What greater arrogance?

It was a legal, trained lawyer who followed Sabo's direction not to introduce the testimony of policeman Gary Wakshul, a cop who, according to his statement of December 9, 1981, arrested me, carried me to his wagon, "accompanied" me to Jefferson Hospital, guarded me, and returned to homicide later that morning to make a statement. According to Wakshul, "We stayed with the male at Jefferson until they were relieved. During this time the negro male made *no comments.*"

According to Wakshul's statement of February 11, 1982, over two months later, Wakshul claims, "Oh, yeah—Jamal said, '*I shot him. I hope the motherfucker dies!*'" Didn't he consider that a *comment?* Why did this trained officer of the law wait for *months* before speaking up about this comment? According to Sabo, Wakshul is on vacation, so despite the fact that his testimony is directly linked to a supposed confession, he would not be called in to testify. How convenient!

It was a legal, trained lawyer who told the jury, "You've

heard *all* the evidence," knowing that wasn't so. The jury heard merely what Sabo allowed. Nothing more. Many jurors were told I would cross-examine witnesses, make opening and closing arguments, and explore evidence. What they saw was a man silenced, gagged by judicial decree, so what they heard was nothing. A man ordered not to fight for his life! Every so-called "right" was deceitfully stolen from me by Sabo—my demand that the defense assistance of my choice, John Africa, be allowed to sit at the defense table was repeatedly denied—and meanwhile, in a City Hall courtroom, four floors directly above, a man charged with murder sits with his lawyer and his father, who just happens to be a Philadelphia policeman. The man (white) was charged with beating a Black man to death, and came to court to have his bail revoked, after being free for several weeks. His bail was revoked after a public outcry in the Black community about the granting of bail at all. Of course, my bail, a ransom of $250,000, was revoked one day after it was issued. For one defendant, everything is granted; for another everything is denied. But isn't justice blind, equal in its application? Does it matter whether a white man is charged with killing a Black man, or a Black man is charged with killing a white man? The truth is clear—for niggers, poor people, Puerto Ricans and what remains of the Indian race: *justice is a sham, a ruse, a joke.* To quote John Africa:

> When you judges hang a person, put a person in a electric chair, gas a person, shoot a person to death for crimes y'all didn't see that person commit, you ain't solving the problem of crime of the so-called criminal or the victim, you've caused a burden for the mother that is now without a son, the wife that is now without a husband, the daughter that is now without a father and society for putting faith in this goddamn procedure, for it is the system that is guilty of the crimes, of all that is criminal; all crimes are commit-

ted within the system, not without, because the influence of that ignorant Black boy you judges gassed to
death, poor white boy judges shot to death, unaware
Puerto Rican boy, girl, adult, you judges electrocuted
to death, came straight from the judges, your bosses,
their crime. . . .[1]

I am innocent of these charges that I have been tried for,
despite the connivance of Judge Sabo, Prosecutor McGill and
Tony Jackson to deny me my so-called "right" to represent myself, to assistance of my choice, to personally select a jury of my
peers, to cross-examine witnesses, and to make both opening
and closing arguments.

I am innocent despite what you 12 people think, and the
truth shall set me free! Long live John Africa! For his assistance
in this fight for my life! It is John Africa who has strengthened
me, aided me and guided me, and who loves me! Could John
Africa have done worse than this worthless sellout and shy-
ster, Tony Jackson? It was John Africa's influence that this court
feared, and his assistance that this court resisted and denied.
And his protection remains despite this court's resistance.

On December 9, 1981, the police attempted to execute me
in the street; this trial is a result of their failure to do so. Just as
police tried to kill my brothers and sisters of the family Africa
on August 8, 1978, they failed, and hence a trial was conducted
to complete the execution. But long live John Africa for our
continued survival!

The system is finished! Babylon is fallen!

LONG LIVE MOVE! LONG LIVE JOHN AFRICA!

5.

900 YEARS FOR SURVIVING
Circa 1983

May 20, 1977, would mark another milestone in MOVE's continued confrontation with this system. It was on that day that MOVE members took to the barricades of their homes and headquarters, uniformed and uniformly armed against any further police encroachment—and the long-festering battle between the MOVE Organization and the armed forces of this system would take on all the trappings of war. Then-mayor Rizzo would order more than 1,000 cops out to Powelton, and once they got there, area residents were personally schooled in the term POLICE STATE.

Rizzo bellowed his murderous intentions from the bold headlines of the reactionary, racist press—STARVE THEM OUT! blared the front page of the so-called "people paper," the Philadelphia Daily News. "I'm gonna lock that place up so tight, not even a fly can get in!," Rizzo boasted with characteristic bombast. Even longtime residents were not immune, as Rizzo invoked police powers to erect street barricades for blocks around, and frisked people going into and coming out of the area. Anyone who wished to enter had to provide ID, apartments were emptied and police took up residence, and where once bright, lively window gardens perched on ledges, the flak-jacketed, helmeted figures of police could now be seen behind rows of dark-brown sandbags. Powelton Village went from North America's first liberated territory to its first site of prolonged contemporary urban war.

It marked a hot flashpoint of resistance against this system, the numerically lesser forces of John Africa against the armed might and military hardware of America's fourth-largest city. Frank Rizzo would gush to a national news reporter at the time, "We're so well armed that we could invade Cuba and win!"

But John Africa's soldiers would not flinch, and on August 8, 1978, the police opened an assault that would drench this system in infamy. The early morning would be shattered by gunfire, and West Philadelphia would be plunged into unforgettable scenes likened to biblical Armageddon, for this would mark the point of rupture—when MOVE would rip free from any semblance of relationship with this system. Firemen would poise powerful deluge guns at a basement window and let loose with thousands of pounds of bone-shattering water pressure; police would operate bulldozers that would rip a hardwood fence apart just like a schoolboy rips a bad report card. Police fired lob after lung-choking lob of tear gas into the house, until the whole area was clouded with the burning, stinking mist. Rounds of semi-automatic rifle fire ripped through the air, and the war had begun in earnest. When the smoke had cleared and the dust settled, 11 firemen and police lay wounded, and one cop lay dead, apparent victims of confused, submachine-gun-wielding cops!

MOVE folk would emerge from the house to a maddened wall of maniacal armed police, and even those with hands raised would be beaten viciously by gangs of cops. The beating of one man, Delbert Africa, was captured on film and replayed around the world, as a form of thrill-seeking sadistic pleasure, no doubt. In a final fit of madness, the physical "House That John Africa Built" would be leveled before nightfall, so anxious was Philadelphia's government to erase any trace of MOVE.

Meanwhile, Rizzo supporters would erect a virtual mansion, an estate of baronial splendor complete with a sparkling, golden doorknob. Such twisted madness!

A farce of a trial into Delbert's beating would be conducted, and a Philadelphia Common Pleas judge, Stanley Kubacki, would put pale, stale, rancid meat on the skeleton of a dying so-called "justice system" by dismissing an imported lily-white jury, only to personally acquit three teary-eyed cops, all of whom admitted beating, pummeling, stomping, rifle-butting and helmet-smashing an unarmed Black man. Later, a jive, traitorous Negress would add her false note to the tune of infamy as she told the court that the Black man was armed, despite police videotapes showing him naked from the waist up and unarmed! The woman, a Channel 6 reporter, would later leave Philadelphia for employment elsewhere.

Months after the controversial, corrupt acquittal, one of the cops involved in the beating would lie suffering, paralyzed on the brink of death, and put there by the rage of another cop—his wife. Carolyn Giest, the wife of Charles Giest, would be convicted of manslaughter, sentenced to seven years probation, and ordered to visit a husband who would be gone within days of the verdict.

Meanwhile, nine MOVE men and women would be sentenced to 30 to 100 years each for murder—in the absence of any murder weapon, any corroborating evidence, any eyewitnesses—on the strength of being simply members of MOVE, John Africa's family! In pronouncing sentence, Judge Edwin Malmed would take his place among a pantheon of pitiful politicians masquerading as judges. Malmed would arrogantly trumpet his twisted vengeance over a Philadelphia radio station, telling listeners he had "no idea" who killed the cop, and further, "They were tried as a family, so I convicted them as a family"!

"*You criminal motherfucker!,*" a MOVE man shouted, "*your own heart's gonna attack you for this attack you makin' on MOVE!*" A year later, Malmed would be quietly hospitalized for the first in a series of massive heart attacks, and months thereafter, cancer would be uncovered, a new devil arising to wrack his ancient body with pain. His intended victims, MOVE members, would grow in strength, loyalty, commitment and number.

That is merely a thumbnail sketch of John Africa's family—the MOVE Organization—spotty, as it must be, for it condenses nearly 10 years of living into brief records of words gathered in several hours. It offers only a glimpse of that remarkably forceful, powerful personality who orchestrated and motivated a group that, in that memorable decade, made an impact greatly disproportionate to its numbers.

In a relatively short period of time, John Africa has succeeded in founding a vigorous, tightly knit, powerful family of revolutionaries; confronted the armed might of one of America's largest cities; personally engaged the U.S. government in a battle of wits and bested them; and opened the door to a vigorous, resistant way of life that has rewarded his followers with glowing health, fierce family loyalty and a free spirit of independence from this rapidly decaying system—but even more incredibly, he's still going strong!

To quote John Africa:

> When you are committed to do what is right, the power of righteousness will never betray you. The MOVE Organization will never give in to this system of sickness, no matter the size of your threats or how often [they are made], for the MOVE Organization's move on this system is working, and people better understand this. Contrary to being impossible for MOVE's strategy—the strategy of John Africa—to work, when you have the truth, it is impossible not to work. So you see, despite what people say—we will win—we must win—we have won.

WE ARE VICTORIOUS! To hell with this system!

LONG LIVE JOHN AFRICA!

6.

THE MOTHER'S DAY MASSACRE

Circa 1985

Mother's Day is traditionally marked by carnations, roses or simply memories of mother. In Philadelphia, the day after became a day marred by carnage, rivulets of blood and a paramilitary massacre. On May 13, 1985, the government of Philadelphia—aided, armed and abetted by agencies of the U.S. federal government—launched its mission of mass destruction, leaving a neighborhood in smoldering ruins, leaving hundreds homeless, and leaving the charred, scattered corpses of men, women and children as silent testament to how America responds to Black resistance.

Philadelphia, once capital of a new nation, home of the Liberty Bell and site of Independence Hall, has become redefined in American and global history. It is the site of the premeditated mass murder, the cold-blooded bombing of MOVE's house, and the resultant mind-blowing massacre of at least 11 people, labeled "radicals." Since this act of state-sanctioned incineration, a whitewash of major proportions and a witch hunt of survivors continues to this very day!

On May 13, 1985, MOVE members took a principled and courageous stand, demanding freedom for their unjustly imprisoned family, and the city that claims to be the "cradle of liberty" responded by an act of absolute overkill that left many in mind of Vietnam. . . .

It doesn't take a Rhodes scholar to figure out that the 1978 arrests, trial and convictions of nine MOVE men and women in connection with the death of a city cop was a setup from the word go. In a trial that had not even the faintest resemblance to justice, the judge who convicted them to a virtual millennium in prison would later boast over the airwaves of a popular talk-radio station that he had not "the slightest idea" who was guilty!

Philadelphia's response to MOVE's righteous demand for freedom has echoed across the earth. During the much touted "summit" meeting between Reagan and Gorbachev, the threatened U.S./U.S.S.R. human rights "showdown" never materialized. Why not? Did the representative of "The American Way" forget? The Soviet news agency TASS offered a more apt reason: "American authorities recently gave the whole world a demonstration of their democracy when they publicly slaughtered more than a dozen black-skinned inhabitants of Philadelphia and bombed a whole city block." This system's propagandists (*Time* magazine) took the Soviet media to task for "omitting" the fact that Philadelphia's mayor is Black, and, added *Time*, "The bombing has provoked much soul-searching in addition to searing criticism and lengthy hearings and investigations."

Did it matter that a "Black mayor" gave the OK that launched the bomb that blew Black bodies of women and babies asunder? Doesn't South Africa show videos of its Black police flogging and flailing Black protesters? Are Black anti-apartheid demonstrators any less maimed, bruised or broken because Black hands wielded the whips? If anything, it was not TASS that omitted pertinent facts surrounding May 13, but *Time* itself (and other U.S. media).

And what of the "searing criticism" *Time* glibly boasts of? Can it produce one example of such criticism in its *own* back files? Apparently the alleged "soul-searching" *Time* wrote of was done in private, 'cus it damn sure hasn't been in print! One telling example of its "searing criticism" put the urban holocaust and firestorm of Osage Avenue into its "proper" perspective.

"Goode insisted," wrote *Time*, "that the fire, one of the worst in Philadelphia history, was simply the result of an accident, not bad judgment." Neither *Time*, *Newsweek* nor any other U.S. newsmagazine elected to publish the critical comments of teenage survivor Birdie Africa, who said that when MOVE men, women and other children tried to flee 6221 Osage, they were repeatedly *driven back inside* a bombed and badly burning building by police automatic rifle fire.

Neither did America's national newsweeklies feel it important to report that the military explosive C-4 (which composed part of the bomb) was a *gift* from an FBI agent to Philadelphia cops. Not one of them reported that the police were "loaned" machine guns and other weaponry by Alcohol, Tobacco and Firearms agents of the Treasury Department of the U.S. federal government.

"Soul-searching"? "Searing criticism"? Bullshit! *Time*'s reference to "lengthy hearings and investigations" is little more than a smokescreen. Has *Time* yet given a definitive account of those hearings? Did *Time* cover the litany of lies that fell from official lips during those hearings? Did *Time* feel it necessary to report that, to date, *no one* has been fired, much less arrested in connection with this deadly disaster?

Finally, did *Time* report that a federal investigation into the MOVE bombing was recently scrapped, because a Philadelphia Justice Department official decided evidence gained during the "lengthy hearings" was unusable—and thrown out? None of these facts proved newsworthy to *Time*, the magazine that dared to chide TASS for "omissions." Meanwhile, U.S. mass media "omissions" continue.

Who knows that MOVE members across Pennsylvania continue to be subjected to a wealth of state-sanctioned harassment and deprivations, from denial of MOVE's raw-food religious diet to MOVE people being thrown into the "hole" for refusing to violate their religion by cutting their hair? An unbiased review of MOVE trials will show, unquestionably, that MOVE members languish in jail today essentially for being members of MOVE.

Case in point: this system's prosecution of MOVE Communications Minister Ramona Africa. Ramona, the only adult known to have survived the blistering May 13 inferno, braved a hail of automatic weapons fire, hundreds of thousands of gallons of water gushing through *her home*, numerous tear-gas grenade attacks, numerous explosive blasts against the walls of *her home*, emerging badly burned after the infernal aerial bombing of *her home*, only to be slapped with a deluge of charges upon her exit, among them simple assault, aggravated assault, recklessly endangering the public, threatening public officials and disorderly conduct.

Remember, not one public official, to date, has been charged with anything, even though they bombed a house full of men, women and children, blasted a city block to oblivion, blew the walls, façade and roof off an occupied home, and *burned* men, women and *babies* alive. In short, the "City of Brotherly Love" committed a premeditated mass murder of MOVE people, and when one had the nerve, the gall, *the temerity to survive*, this city added insult to injury by bringing charges against her. Insanely, this system's latest lunacy is to sue Ramona Africa and Louise James (whose son was murdered in the house) for monetary damages.

In a remarkably detailed 25-page letter to supporters *and* reporters, Ramona described the city government's rationale for the police overkill on Osage Ave. The stated justification for the assault was to serve past bench warrants for minor misdemeanor charges. That paltry reasoning falls flat on its face as Ramona documents how MOVE folks traveled freely across the city, shopping and even visiting other MOVE houses, until *days* before May 13. City claims of having been "afraid of contact" with MOVE, so as not to "inflame a tense situation," seem similarly hollow in light of the beating and arrest of Mo Africa a block from MOVE's house in July 1984, and his subsequent conviction on May 3, 1985—just 10 days before the bombing and razing of Osage Avenue. MOVE men, women and kids walked in city streets and played, ran and exercised in a nearby park until May 11, 1985.

In Ramona's own words, "If the authorities was interested in simply *arrestin'* MOVE people and bringin' us to trial on outstandin' litigation for alleged crimes, there was every opportunity for the authorities to do that as early as 1984, when MOVE people was walking the streets of Philadelphia alone or with maybe one other person, but the authorities were *never* interested in simply bringin' MOVE people to trial; they are *only* interested in stoppin' John Africa, and if killing us is the only way they see to do it, they are willing to kill us."

As to what really happened on May 13, Ramona adds, "It is clear, to all those willing to see, that those cops did *not* come out to 62nd and Osage to simply arrest MOVE people; that could have been done anytime in 1984 if that was all Wilson Goode and those in authority wanted to do. Those cops came out to 62nd and Osage to *kill* MOVE people—men, women and babies—and to put anybody that survived their murderous attack in prison for the rest of their life."

It is past time for people to wake up to this campaign of state terrorism against the MOVE Organization, and to start speaking out against this obscenity of a system! Call for a halt to the religious persecution of MOVE members! Demand the freedom of Ramona Africa, MOVE prisoners, and *all* political prisoners!

ORGANIZE! *INFORM!* ACT AGAINST THIS MONSTROSITY!

LONG LIVE JOHN AFRICA'S REVOLUTION, AND DOWN WITH THIS ROTTEN-ASS SYSTEM!

7

THE POWER OF TRUTH

Circa 1987

From meager, common beginnings comes a man so remarkably uncommon as to defy definition and meager description. Possessing an innate wisdom that is as undeniable as it is startling, the man known as John Africa is a man who has become legendary during his lifetime as a revolutionary of rigorous relentlessness, and a living symbol of smoldering, long-standing resistance to all that this system represents.

To say John Africa is the founder of the MOVE Organization is a true and correct statement, but it does nothing to part the veil over this gifted personality's identity. To insist, as the establishment media does, that he is merely an elementary school dropout and a handyman, is to give value to an empty echo and to ignore the depths of insight to which his unique and dynamic vision has taken us, ignore how deeply his instinctive emotional impact has shaken us, and ignore, too, how his sheer force of will has awakened us. To agree with the media would be to say, by extension, that Jesus was a carpenter, Mohammed was a merchant, and Gautama—the Buddha—was the son of a rich man. All true, but wholly deficient, empty.

One way to see John Africa, MOVE's founder, is through MOVE's eyes, for to look at an artist's creation is to see the artist's clearest reflection, and MOVE is John Africa's creation. MOVE members began coming "aboveground" some 15 years ago, around 1972. They were young people who protested strongly against *everything* in this system, everywhere from shoe stores, zoos and speeches by noted personalities to school board meetings to district police stations. In Mayor Frank Rizzo's tight-fisted town, confrontation was inevitable, and it often came in the form of police vs. MOVE. When it came to demonstrating against opponents, MOVE had no peer, even in a time when protests seemed commonplace throughout America, for no one came close to MOVE's intensity and MOVE's daring, even in picking its targets to demonstrate against.

If a judge or a prison official wronged a MOVE member, a crew of MOVE men, women and kids would board their "MOVE bus" and take it to the offender's front lawn, equipped with bullhorns, ready and willing to demonstrate. Threats to "call the cops" were meaningless, as neither the threats nor the presence of cops would dissuade MOVE. In fact, among MOVE's more common targets of protests were police. West Philadelphians will long remember the hot, steamy, angry summers of the early 1970s, when MOVE members did the unthinkable: when they set up waves of protests in front of one of Black Philadelphia's most notorious police stations—the infamous 16th District at 39th and Lancaster Ave., a site marked in the "Black Bottom's"[1] memory as the place some folks entered handcuffed and exited feet first.

The 16th District had its share of "accidental" hangings of Black male prisoners, as did many districts located in Black neighborhoods. MOVE members set to their task of protesting police just as they protested anyone else—with vigor. Police responded predictably—with savage brutality. Women were not immune. Rhonda Africa would remember being thrown into a glass door of that district by police, her face ripped and bloodied, and both she and Sue Africa would later tell of brutal, vicious beatings that often left pregnant women in the torturous throes of miscarriage.

Still, MOVE's will would not be abated, its determined resistance would not be broken by broken bones, billy-clubbings, battered and bloodied bodies, miscarriages, jail cells or even murder. By mid-1975, MOVE had grown into a collective of Blacks, whites, Puerto Ricans and Asians, living in the polyglot neighborhood of Powelton Village and following the teachings of John Africa. Police would often attempt to break their revolutionary unity, and they would inevitably fail.

March 1975 is a time MOVE remembers, with reason, for rage at this system—it was then that MOVE members, newly sprung from city jails, came home in the wee hours of the morning aboard its massive yellow school bus. Wives and children greeted husbands and fathers with yelps of joy and warm, loving hugs at their reunion. Moments later, police converged at the scene brandishing blackjacks and .38 pistols, yelling for quiet. A neighbor at the time, a wheelchair-bound double amputee, would later tell this reporter that the police whipped MOVE men with a maddened frenzy.

"I saw 'em grab Bob by the hair, and they began to beat the hell outta him. . . . Then Big Jerry stepped in to stop 'em, and they beat him bloody."

Police, often called "peace officers," brought war and chaos to the Powelton Village home and headquarters of the MOVE Organization that night, on the pretext of "restoring order." When the smoke cleared, MOVE members newly freed only hours before would be re-imprisoned, but even more ominous, a MOVE infant—newborn Life Africa—lay dead, crushed lifeless into concrete, killed underfoot in an outrageous police assault.

The neighbor would recall days past in somber, wistful tones: "Janine used to carry dat' boy everywhere; he was a good-lookin' red boy, an' wherever you saw that girl Janine, you saw dat baby."

Police would claim innocence, saying they were sure no baby was killed, suggesting no baby ever lived, reasoning that there was no birth certificate, nor a death certificate, so what were people so upset about? Area newspapers carried these apparently pious police reports, suggesting, by inference at least, that MOVE folks were lying, as a cheap grab for publicity.

But police didn't have the last word. I interviewed the grief-stricken mother, and the pain wrenching her guts was all too real and all too common in confrontations between the police and residents of "The Bottom"—hot, angry, grieving tears were always on the faces of Black mothers, while on the fat, pale faces of the oppressors, the police, were expressions of smug self-righteousness and racist arrogance. But John Africa would have the last word.

Several days after the police raid, when both police and the allegedly "impartial" press had inferred that MOVE were liars, media grabbers or worse, MOVE would host an unusual meeting in their Powelton Village home and headquarters, attended by area politicians, photographers and Black press persons. The guests were feted on chicken and rice dinners, cooked "delicious," as Powelton's City Councilman Lucien Blackwell later recalled. After this sumptuous supper, the guests were taken to another room, bare except for a cardbox sitting in the center of the floor.

What was in the box would NEVER be forgotten by any of those present. Up from the floor shone the naked form of a reddish-brown-complexioned, brown-haired baby boy, little Life Africa, his body surrounded by bits of fruit and bits of roots, dead to this world.

8

CHRISTMAS IN A CAGE II

December 1986

In each year's wintry season comes the façade of festival in the West, allegedly to celebrate the birth of Jesus of Nazareth some 2,000 years ago. Who, among the faceless millions who sing the cheer and charity, remembers that their songs are sung in praise of a prisoner—indeed, in every sense of the word, a *Death Row prisoner*, destined to face state execution by crucifixion? What means cheer and charity to those facing more modern methods of state execution? To those encaged in Babylon's dungeons, what could it mean?

To many, it is a time of utter hypocrisy.

To those many millions mired in poverty, its meaning is cruel. To those who live literally in the streets of America, it is a time of bitter cold, no relief, no respite, and much too often a fate as frozen corpses huddled in windswept alleys. No, for far too many, far from being "the season to be jolly," 'tis a season of need, and an hour of aching loneliness.

I sit among the hopeless and the living dead, among the many who populate your prisons and your dungeons of death, and I see neither cheer nor charity, but rather falseness, fakeness and empty flash in your holidays. The only things not empty are the tills of the mega-merchants, for Christmas is celebrated not in remembrance of a Christ, but to fill the coffers of commerce. For, in this season, the poor truly get poorer, and the rich are further enriched.

For over 300 years, since our forefathers trudged upon these shores enchained and enslaved, we were forced to forget and to reject our tongues, our tribes, our very gods, under pain of death. Forbidden, and branded criminal, was the mere mention of any word in Wolof, in Fons, in Mandinke, languages of our fathers. Forbidden, and branded criminal, were natural and normal links of clan and tribe and family, as slavers mixed slaves amongst different clans, to enforce this foul and fiendish prohibition. The drum was also deemed taboo, and to play it was called a crime.

From the lips of a people, the names of ancient gods like N'gai, Obatala and Allah were ripped away. In their place, the teachings of Christ, a tale of eternal life and joy, of heaven and hell, of piety, of obedience to master and patient servility from the slave. God, the slavemasters taught their wretched chattel, commands that slaves obey masters, and resistance—rebellion against authority—is sinful.

That twisted lesson endures in Black psyches to this very day. For, though it were righteous and glorious for Europeans in the New World to resist and rebel against the tyranny of King George, there were few crimes among Africans enslaved in the colonies worse than resistance and rebellion against American tyranny. So, by history and by indoctrination, those two messages have been drummed into Black minds by teachers and by preachers, by mothers and by sisters: that to obey this system's way is right, and to resist against this system's way is wrong.

History is rife with that hypocritical message. Blacks who taught subservience, à la Booker T. Washington, were lauded by press and public alike as "responsible" leaders. Pan-Africanist Marcus Mosiah Garvey was accused of "rabble-rousing" for daring to suggest Blacks look to Africa for economic, social and spiritual strength. The charismatic Rev. Nat Turner, who dared rebel against that most un-Christian of American institutions, human slavery, was damned as a fanatic. Martin Luther King Jr. received accolades for his nonviolent ministry, but Malcolm X received assassination for his ministry of militancy. When Rev. King began to emerge as a vocal opponent of America's genocidal war on Vietnam, his lifeclock was stopped. In a young nation born in bloody resistance to England's crown, resistance is still the ultimate offense by Africans.

Today, a mayor who claims faith in Christianity entered U.S. history books as a Black man who ordered the bombardment and obliteration of a home where Black rebels lived. One thing can be said: here was a neo-slave who imitated his malevolent masters well! Can the saga of the rebel, the Nazarene, the Christ who confronted the Roman Empire, truly have any meaning to such a one?

A generation after Blacks died, rebelled, struggled and demonstrated for Black folks' empowerment, some Black persons were elected to positions of power. But once elected, these Black political novices raced to mimic their political mentors. All manner of political maneuvers were given the green light, and Black politicos studied at the same shrines as their mentors did—Machiavelli's. Their watchword was imitation, not innovation. And as Black politicians' numbers grew exponentially, the lot of the masses of Blacks, looking for change, grew in grimness. Black poverty grew, and as some bourgeois Blacks widened the gap between their lot and the less fortunate, the many remain mired in the quicksand of the status quo. As everywhere in America, politicians promised brighter tomorrows, but days got depressingly dismal. Unemployment soared, and politicians promised. How did things change, people wondered, and more each moment, folks realized that instead of changing for the better, things got progressively worse. Today is worse than yesterday.

Once more, just as many of our ancestors took the names, the language and the religion of our slavemasters, so we also adopted the political process of our oppressors. As with similar adoptions, we took too much form, too little substance.

Philadelphia's Blacks reacted with joyous pride at the prospect of electing a Black mayor. It had been attempted several times over a dozen years, but to no avail, until the election of self-professed non-politician Wilson Goode. Because of the pivotal role he played in the bombing and mass murder of MOVE men, women and babies on May 13, 1985, however, the once-joyous pride has been dampened considerably. He has truly made history, but it is a legacy of loss for which he'll be long remembered: the blasting of Black life into oblivion.

The global Black community has been saddled with the sad spectacle of the appointment of an Afro American, Edward Perkins, to the post of U.S. Ambassador to the Afrikaaner government in South Africa. He brings the policies and prejudices of one of the most racist of U.S. presidents in recent years to the American Embassy in Pretoria. The accomodationist and apologist politics of the United States are to be mouthed by a Black man. To the millions of Blacks living under the oppressive hell of the apartheid, fascist system in South Africa, the change of complexion of the messenger, while keeping essentially unchanged the message of acquiescence and massive American trade to the Botha regime, is an insulting slur on African intelligence. Would the United States have had the arrogance to appoint a Jewish ambassador to present his credentials to the Nazi Reich of 1933? Would a Jew have dared to go?

In this dispensation, we have seen Blacks appointed prison officials over increasingly blacker prison populations. Shades of the overseers and straw-bosses of yesteryear? Black police describe themselves in shades of blue, not black. Black politicians dress like, think like, talk like and act like their white political predecessors, with the reality of the Black masses markedly different from that of their false political standards.

When will these hypocrisies—of Black politicians serving white political interests—end?

When will these hypocrisies—of empty holiday farces based more on commercialism than on deep religious commitment—end?

When will these hypocrisies—of racist politics fronted by Black faces—end?

When will these dismal days of our mind-rending pain, our oppression, our accustomed place on the bottom rung of the human family, end?

When will our tomorrows brighten?

It will come from ourselves, not from this system. Our tomorrows will become brighter when we scrub the graffiti of lies from our minds, when we open our eyes to the truths that this very system is built not on "freedom, justice and brotherhood" but on slavery, oppression and genocide.

One century ago, one of the brightest legal minds in America, Chief Justice Taney of the U.S. Supreme Court, wrote:

> The question is simply this: can a Negro, whose ancestors were imported into this country and sold as slaves, become a member of the political community formed and brought into existence by the Constitution of the United States, and as such become entitled to all rights, and privileges, and immunities, guaranteed by that instrument to the citizen? . . . The plea applies to that class of persons only whose ancestors were Negroes of the African race, and imported into this country, and sold and held as slaves. The only matter in issue before the Court, therefore, is whether the descendants of such slaves, when they shall be emancipated, or who are born of parents who had become free before their birth, are citizens of a state, in the sense in which the word "citizen" is used in the Constitution of the United States. . . . *We think they are not, and that they are not included, and were not intended to be included, under the word "citizen" in the Constitution, and can, therefore, claim none of the rights and privileges which that instrument provides for and secures to citizens of the United States.* [emphasis added]

> —Chief Justice Taney
> Opinion of the U.S. Supreme Court,
> *Dred Scott v. Sanford* (1857)

In the century after those damning words of the U.S. Supreme Court, the words have changed, but a grim reality remains. Taney's spiritual heir reigns again as Supreme Court Chief Justice in the person of William Rehnquist, who won his high government post despite sworn charges that he harassed and intimidated Black and Hispanic voters in the 1960s in Arizona, and used illegal and improper anti-voter literacy tests.

Still, what "constitutional rights" did the Mohawk Nation, the Sioux, the Sac and Fox, the so-called "Indians," have in the stolen land of their ancestors?

What "constitutional rights" did the Japanese "Americans" have, back in the 1940s, when they were rounded up and locked in concentration camps?

What "constitutional rights" do the descendants of Africans have today in the land of their ancestors' anguish?

We *do* have the God-given right to rebel against an existence of lies! We have the God-given right to live the Way of Truth. We have the God-given right to resist a way that strangles us. We have the God-given right to reject this system of falseness!

We have the God-given responsibility to wake up from this American nightmare, and to make our tomorrows based on Natural Laws, not the way of the outlaw.

We have the God-given right to define for ourselves who we are, what our beliefs are, how we will walk, talk, sing—*be*. We have the God-given right to embrace the truest freedom, and reject the captor forever!

THE PHILADELPHIA NEGRO
REVISITED

Circa 1989

Several decades ago, the brilliant, yet beleaguered African American scholar Dr. W.E.B. Du Bois penned a remarkable treatise on that curious creature, the Philadelphia Negro. I revisit that theme, albeit from quite another perspective, with all due respect to that illustrious intellectual and radical sage, proof sufficient that a Philadelphia Negro is indeed still alive, if not at all particularly well. In these times, circa 1990, we have good reason to shout, "Is there a doctor in the house?" and seek not a surgeon or a general practitioner, but a Dr. Du Bois anew, for the Philadelphia Negro is a sick nigga indeed.

People mark time by events held in common, and shared moments of joy and sorrow. Cities, although artificial, nonorganic bodies, mark time similarly. Paris is known today as the "City of Light," but the dark shadow of the Nazi Occupation is still within the memory of the living. Parisians over middle age remember their city's submission to Hitler's Panzer divisions, and its subsequent liberation and renewal by the Allies. Yes, cities hold memories, locked in the minds and souls of their inhabitants. Philadelphians also mark time by shared moments, such as an exciting citywide election or an unforgettable music concert down at the Civic Center. Or a bomb—fluttering downward beneath the whipping, chopping blades of a state police helicopter, bursting in a white-hot blaze of hatred, fury, murderous madness, agonized dismemberment and death.

As much as the white media whines that May 13, 1985, be "forgotten," or "put behind us," it remains unmoved, a malevolent shadow that pierces the very vitals of the "City of

Brotherly Love" and unleashes a foul bile of raw hypocrisy. Paris had its Occupation, Beirut its Sabra and Shatila, and Philadelphia its MOVE bombing. Each event left its indelible stain, and Philadelphia is permanently marked. The city's government has since spent millions in a vain public relations campaign, featuring figures such as the stentorian Patti Labelle and a host of hoofers dancing through Philadelphia's various landmarks, imploring the curious and cautious to come to Philadelphia, and "Get To Know Us"—as catchy a commercial as was ever taped.

But not even Patti Labelle's golden voice or Bill Cosby's ever-smiling mug can mute the screams that accompanied the deadly, hungry flames that ate the heart out of Osage Avenue [site of the MOVE bombing] that May day, nor can a star's smile obscure the ugliness that erupted on that Mother's Day eve. Premeditated mass murder, it seems, is more than a public relations problem; it is a human one.

Philadelphia, try as it might, cannot escape May 13. Nor can Black Philadelphia.

Ever since the 1960s, Blacks spoke of Black communities in a separate sense, recognizing the obvious, that Black communities were, and in fact are, separate. The rise of Black politicians and a small petty bourgeoisie who aspire to possess white symbols of status and power, has not changed that reality one iota. Blacks have lived in quite distinctly Black neighborhoods, in a separate reality, enjoying its distinct music styles, its dress styles, its *own style*, for generations now.

There is, of course, considerable cross-pollination between the ethnic and racial communities. But some events appeal more to one community than to the other. A few events of a popular nature come to mind.

Several years ago, the Pope of the Roman Catholic Church rode through city streets. South Philadelphia, its huge Italian enclave, thronged both sides of Broad Street to welcome a non-Italian pontiff. Blacks were few in number.

Several years ago, the professional hockey team the Flyers won the Stanley Cup, and much of the city's young white populace erupted in a spasm of sportsmania, pouring into the streets, "mooning" passersby, drinking, fighting, enjoying a team's triumph. With less than a handful of Blacks in the entire National Hockey League (and *none* among the Flyers), many Blacks observed this night of beer-drenched bacchanalia with a mixture of detachment and wonder.

And how might whites have observed that orgy of hatred on Osage Avenue? This writer doesn't profess to know. I doubt it was with detachment (although perhaps in some cases), but wonderment may have been in the mix, à la "How in the hell did this happen?"

Blacks played a pivotal role in the events on Osage. Blacks ran to Black politicians to "save" them from Black radicals. Blacks in positions at the summit of political power commanded, okayed and oversaw the unleashing of one of the most destructive forces in U.S. history: *white racist paramilitary state power.* That a Black mayor who boasts of being the son of a sharecropper can order the firepower, the ordnance, the bombardments that were brought to bear on that one single household of Black revolutionaries, should give one some inkling of the nature of the Philadelphia Negro.

What might any among the legions of white, heavily armed cops have thought to himself, after receiving the "green light" from "upstairs"? ("Jeeezus H. Kee-Rist!! I can't believe I'm bein' ordered by a nigger to open up, full-steam ahead, on a buncha MOVE niggers!! Mamma mia—I think I've died and went straight to heaven! Ha, Ha, Ha! There is a Santy Claus!!")

Imagine that, in addition to the Head-Negro-In-Charge, Mayor W. Wilson Goode, a cabinet member, Goode's Managing Director (and former Army general) Leo Brooks, was stationed at the scene. Brooks, second in command only to the Mayor, is Black.

Now many will point out pickily that neither Goode

nor Brooks was a true native son, as both migrated from Southern cities years ago. But in fact, this is true of most Black Philadelphians, for a considerable number of Blacks now in their 50s and 60s moved north from Dixie long ago in search of new opportunities. Most of Philadelphia's Black community are, in fact, the first generation born north of the Mason-Dixon line.

But Goode is still an archetypal Philadelphia Negro, because this curious phenomenon infects Blacks over a wide range of geography. Like AIDS, it has spanned the globe.

The political stoogism symptom of the Philadelphia Negro malady is seen even beyond U.S. borders. For political stoogism, manifested by an inordinate political ambition to serve white economic interests, even by the bloodshed of fellow Blacks, can be seen in the shameless opportunism of Zulu Chief Gatsha Buthelezi, all the way over in South Africa. Buthelezi is a Philadelphia Negro.

Another symptom of the Philadelphia Negro Syndrome (P.N.S.) is an insane hatred of, or extreme displeasure with, Black life, especially Black infant life. Another infectee of the dreaded P.N.S. is also on the African continent, and is known as the former "Emperor" of the Central African Empire (now Central African Republic)—Jean-Bedel Bokassa, charged with killing children who refused to purchase school uniforms.

H.N.I.C. W. Wilson Goode displays both these symptoms of P.N.S., as shown by May 13. For seated at the throne of city power (the first "Black" person so elected), he okayed the Osage Avenue onslaught while sitting in his living room, watching TV, several miles away. In one fell swoop, he reigned over a Black bloodbath to serve white political interests and sanctioned the incineration of Black men, women and babies, as well as animals. Bokassa and Buthelezi would be proud of their brother in Africide.

But to millions of Blacks who prefer the militant manliness of a Biko to a Buthelezi, to the millions who'd druther the vision of a Nkrumah to the Napoleonic Bokassa, the grubby political servility of a Goode will pale behind the pall of Philadelphia Negro Syndrome.

It is time for that disease to pass into antiquity, never to rise again. No vaccine, no hypodermic needle is necessary! Only an honest assessment of the state of "Afro-America" and, indeed, the global Black world, and a gritty commitment of determined resistance to all oppression will suffice.

We have chafed, and starved, and burned, and bled under the grinding heel of oppression for far too long. Does it matter the color of the man wearing the boots? Or does a Black foot in the boot make the pressure somehow easier to bear?

For generations, the Duvaliers reigned in arrogance over the oldest free Black community in the Western Hemisphere, Haiti. After strong and determined resistance, the Duvaliers were forced into exile. Though still not free, the Haitian people are en route to true *liberté* for the first time in nearly half a century, if they continue to agitate and resist.

Prior to Goode's mayoral election, when he was still managing director, MOVE members approached him and explained how innocent MOVE men and women were languishing in state jails. Goode expressed concern, and pledged he would do "all in his power" to correct the situation were he elected mayor. Blacks swarmed to the polls, giving Goode overwhelming support and electing Philadelphia's first Black chief executive. Once seated, Goode turned a deaf ear to MOVE. Once in a position to act, he committed overkill, murdering some of the very people who had approached him while he was Managing Director.

What a creature, this Philadelphia Negro! What a foul disorder, this Philadelphia Negro Syndrome. During his tenure, the state prisons were swelled to bulging with Black men from Philadelphia. City prisons, judged unconstitutionally overcrowded, were bursting at the seams, and Goode swore he would oppose the release of any prisoners. The homeless slept and huddled in the cement and marble caverns of City Hall while Goode argued about the height of William Penn's hat. Joblessness grew epidemic while city contracts were passed to friendly corporate supporters of the regime, who supported his initial win. Center City went into a construction boom, while North Philadelphia—the oldest, poorest, Blackest section of the city (and, incidentally, the biggest pocket of Goode voters)—slid deeper into the economic abyss. Philadelphia cops, comparable only to Houston's in their racist, brutal and vicious manner, continued their campaign of *state terror*, emboldened by the "excesses" of Osage.

With Goode in charge, Black and interracial families were hounded out (and burned out) of their homes by white racist mobs. The deadly agent *crack* seized whole neighborhoods, replacing the laid-back joint with the numbing paralysis of crystalline cocaine. Judges sold "justice" and cops committed crimes, while the H.N.I.C. sat in City Hall, projecting the illusion that Blacks were "in power." Who will tell this proud and quite mad Philadelphia Negro that the emperor has no clothes?

The name "Goode" has become synonymous with a liar, a logical progression from his public performances following May 13. From his May 14 press conference, featuring an icy-faced braggart boasting, "I'd do it again, and again, and again!," to his post-commission teleconference, complete with crocodile tears—"I deeply regret the loss of life" (Where were those raw onions?)—Goode displayed a chameleonism that Master Machiavelli would have had to applaud. ("Bravo, Signor Goode! Buon politico! Molto bene!")

But still the Philadelphia Negro sits among us, like the cold and clownish clergymen who dared to come to the smoldering ashes of Osage Avenue to throw "holy" water on that holocaust and bless this political perfidy. "Goode is a Christian," they explained, as a reason for their religious support. (And Herod Agrippa was a Jew, but so what?)

When will the global Black community be free of these parasitic political beings? When and only when Africans everywhere demand that all so-called leaders serve their interests, their needs, not first, but always! Blacks are under a global boot, because it is in the interests of European and American political systems to keep Blacks under social, economic, military, physical, educational, intellectual, yeah, even spiritual control. It would be an impossible task were it not for the sellouts among so-called Black leaders, who smilingly accept pieces of silver for their racial treachery. Judas, it seems, has always been available at bargain basement rates.

But perhaps some are awakening to the illusions offered by these traitors in three-piece suits: recently, Philadelphia's first Black Mayor arrived at Harvard University Law School to deliver a lecture on "freedom of expression"(!). Goode was met by a group of demonstrators with charcoal smeared on their faces, who shouted, "Murderer! Murderer!" Several signs rose, reading, among other things, "Nazi of the Year for Murdering Babies."

Goode immediately left the room.

That's an encouraging start. Now, how do we keep him and his kind from returning?

BIRTH OF A REBEL

May 1, 1989

What brought Ramona Johnson, a shy, introverted but strong-willed woman, to Courtroom 253 of Philadelphia's decaying City Hall? A law student at Temple University, she seemed drawn to the legal drama unfolding around nine men and women of the MOVE Organization. The trial, *Commonwealth v. Africa*, was an aftermath to the spectacular police assault of August 8, 1978, a siege of the MOVE home and headquarters that took on all the trimmings of urban war. Few were untouched by the widely televised raid, and many were split into angry, polarized camps. Ramona did support work for the Tenant Action Group and was jailed once, briefly, while demonstrating on behalf of then–State Senator T. Milton Street, for housing rights for the poor. She began showing up regularly at MOVE trials and became a legal runner on their behalf, getting cases and doing research for the imprisoned Africas.

At the MOVE 9 trial, as a matter of principle and religious belief, the Africas elected to represent themselves. This decision evoked public comments of derision in the press, many citing the old axiom "He who represents himself has a fool for a client."

The Africas defended themselves acutely and aggressively, making a number of points in their defense as they examined and cross-examined witnesses, while nine court-appointed lawyers sat idly, and for the most part silently, by.

There was no jury, so a squadron of regional press sat in the box. On the bench sat Edwin S. Malmed, an old, white, grandfatherly-looking jurist who was approaching retirement.

By trial's end, that image, like the illusion of American "justice" itself, would be shattered.

Central to the state's objective, convicting MOVE, was the issue of representation. The media clamor grew in protests of the unorthodox style of self-representation reflected by the Africas, and in midtrial, Judge Malmed made his move. The Africas—Merle, Delbert, Debbie, Mike, Janine, Phil, Janet, Chuckie and Eddie—were, by his order, removed from representation, over their strenuous objections. It appeared the Africas were defending themselves too well.

Nearly a century before the United States came into being, back in 1682, the Pennsylvania "Charter of Liberties" of William Penn provided, in Article VI, that "in Courts all persons of all persuasions may freely appear in their own manner, and there personally plead their own cause themselves. . . . " In 1789, the new nation's First Congress enacted a law, signed by President Washington, protecting the right of self-representation. In the 1975 Faretta case, the U.S. Supreme Court affirmed that right in a state criminal trial and held that the state may not force a lawyer upon a defendant who wanted to defend himself.

In 1980, in the Africa case, nearly 300 years of common law, as well as Pennsylvania and U.S. precedent, was trashed when Malmed forced lawyers upon the unwilling nine defendants. The dramatic communal defense sputtered to a chaotic halt as nine lawyers each tried to outshine the other. Lost in the Latin-strewn shuffle of legalese were nine lives, the defendants'. Denied the fundamental right to present their own defense, they spent much of the trial in protest absentia, and were convicted of all charges despite significant evidence of their innocence.

Shortly after the trial, the judge would publicly admit he had "no idea" who slew the cop on August 8, 1978, but such a critical question didn't stop him from sending all nine men and women to jail with sentences of 100 years each.

Ramona Jackson sat throughout the long, hard-fought trial, and what she saw bore little resemblance to what she had been taught in law school. The trial both enraged and enlightened her, as she saw the "law" of the system perverted for political ends, and she learned of the Teachings of John Africa, MOVE Law, which denounced this system's law as the way of the outlaw. She was radicalized by repression, and emerged from the painful trial determined to resist the system that could casually consign nine of her innocent people to a century in jail, and with such determination came solid commitment to a cause.

You know her as Ramona Africa, survivor of May 13, 1985. But that is another story to tell. From Death Row, this is Mumia Abu-Jamal.

COMMUNITY SERVICE
FOR CONTRA COLONEL

July 8, 1989

*All men recognize the right to revolution: that is, the right
to refuse allegiance to, and to resist, the government when
its tyranny or its inefficiency are great and unendurable.*
—H.D. Thoreau, *An Essay on Civil
Disobedience*

The recent "sentencing" of former Lt. Col. Oliver North sure
shows crime pays. In a show trial as ridiculous as it was political, the right-wing lieutenant colonel, weathering a withering
paper blizzard of charges amounting to high crimes and mis-
demeanors, has emerged none the worse for wear, thank you.

Except for a few unpleasantly satiric cartoon caricatures
depicting him as a snitch and a stool pigeon, North faced little
more than a few bad words following his undercover orgy of
state subversion, lying to Congress, destruction of evidence
and "misappropriation" of millions of state monies in further-
ance of his fascist scheme to arm the brutal mercenaries of
the Nicaraguan Contra forces. Nor would the snowy-haired,
parchment-faced Judge Gesell punish the lieutenant colonel in
any substantive way.

For lying, stealing millions, violating the Boland
Amendment forbidding arm sales to the Contras, and destroying evidence, North got hit with a fine, a few hundred hours of
community service and no jail.

Funny, I didn't hear no outcry from the "law and order" set.

Now North, raising big bucks in speeches across America's
vast hinterland, gets to "pay his debt to society" via VISA (or

MasterCard). What is significant about the case *U.S. v. North* was not the farce of a trial, nor the judicial "love-tap" of a sentence. No—what was most significant was the silence.

With reports emerging that the Contra arming scheme was paid for by billions in narco-dollars, why did the U.S. government, and its prosecutors, remain silent on the cocaine connection?

Despite credible accounts of Contra supply planes touching down in Honduras with weapons and taking off for U.S. bases loaded up with cocaine, this angle—seemingly compelling in an age when the government proclaims its anti-drug character—went untouched in the North case. Why?

Now, in the crowning touch of irony, a man suspected of participating in, and indeed masterminding, one of the biggest drug transactions in U.S. history, was sentenced to "community service" in D.C., presumably to work with Black youth whose minds have been atomized by the recent avalanche of cocaine and crack into the United States.

Doncha' just love American "justice"?

When right-wing representatives raise the outcry for tougher and longer sentences, they mean, of course, not for white middle-class citizens with property, but for the Black, the Hispanic, the poor. What the court said, in deafening terms, was that the jails, prisons and dungeons of America are not for the rich, the white, the wealthy and the well connected. (Perhaps jail would "harden" their "misconceptions" about U.S. justice!)

A man charged with stealing millions gets a pittance of a fine, which amounts to a tax, and no jail.

When a man steals a hundred bucks, it's go—don't stop—straight to jail.

The North case clearly shows that double standards of "justice" remain deeply embedded in the system. Such corruption has been present before the very Republic was founded.

It will remain, until folks organize and rebel against it.

C'MON IN, THE WATER'S FINE

July 24, 1989

We're not fooled about yall's claim of pollution being safe so long as it is held at a safe level. We ain't fooled of your claim of purifying water with chemicals that came from science and not from God, for the existence of water under God's law is pure, to add the pollution of industry is to make it impure, and to add more so-called purifying chemicals, industry, to so-called clean the water up is to only add more industry to what has already been fouled up and make it more foul, for unless anybody in this system can claim to know the formula God intended for pure water, unless you are using the very same formula God uses, you're using something different, God's water is pure, but the water yall produce ain't.

—John Africa, *The Judge's Letter*

As Labor Day weekend 1989 loomed near, a small group of merchants gather at shoreside in southern New Jersey to ponder the sad state of the incoming Atlantic, its waves bearing syringes, hypodermic needles and bundles of garbage. Here, human waste rides the waves.

Knowing that state inspectors planned bacteriological tests later in the day, the informal group has hit upon a solution.

Chlorine!

With haste born of greed they storm the beach with bags of hockey-puck-size tablets of chlorine, 100 pounds total, and toss them into the salty, polluted sea.

Why the chlorine pills?

To spike the tests, so that state inspectors will give the all-clear, and so the summer throng will come, and buy, and not find fun elsewhere in the sun. In short, their motives are profit.

I thought of John Africa's words about the purity of water when I heard about the merchants' vain attempt to clean the sea with 100 pounds of chemicals. Greed. And arrogance.

Rivers awash in filth and disease, and seas choking in human waste, are to be found not only in Jersey, nor only in the United States.

Polluted waters are global menaces, direct results of a "civilized" way of life that threaten to disrupt the very balance of nature. Nor is this problem merely one of the waste of capitalist societies.

In Hungary, the Danube River is more grayish than the fabled blue. In a remarkable three-part series on pollution in the Eastern Bloc nations back in November 1987, the *Christian Science Monitor* quoted Lenka Mareckova, of the Czech human rights group Charter 77, on pollution in her country: "When trees are dying, when the water is dirty, when the air is dangerous for little children, that's worse than prison."

Around the chief Japanese island, Honshu, red tides of aquatic death swirl, tribute to growing offshore dumping of mountains of garbage from Asia's economic powerhouse on the Pacific rim.

Pollution is a global problem.

Like the foolish and greedy merchants tossing 100 pounds of chlorine into the mighty, massive sea, the world's governments are opting for the quick fix—a Band-Aid, a stopgap measure to hold off the tide of filth until another generation, another administration, is left to solve this herculean problem.

But time may be what the "civilizations" of Earth have too little of. Somewhere, the cycle of creating pollution must cease and new strategies of survival must be tested, leading to a road not traveled.

The common road, traveled by capitalist and socialist societies, has left our common Mother, Earth, regurgitating on our filth.

We must acknowledge that yesterday's way is the wrong way—and resolve to chart a new road where neither profit nor production is king, and where the unique blessings of this blue-green ball do not fade to gray.

RONALD REAGAN FIDDLED WHILE THE PEOPLE FROZE

August 11, 1989

> *Any ordinary city is in fact two cities, one the city of the poor, the other of the rich, each at war with the other; and in either division there are smaller ones—you would make a great mistake if you treated them as single states.*
> —Plato, *The Republic*

As Plato aptly observed, the history of "civilization" is riven with conflict, driven by class division, torn by the needs of the poor vs. the wants of the rich.

As America's ruling class goes gaga over the French Revolution's bicentennial and sheds crocodile tears for oppressed prisoner Jean Valjean, the character in Victor Hugo's book (and the Broadway play) *Les Misérables*, the hungry, homeless throng in the United States grows into a bitter sea of misery, estimated at more than 4 million people.

New, growing evidence suggests this sad spectacle is a direct result of Sir Ronald Reagan's eight-year war against the poor.

Reagan's appointment of Black New York lawyer Samuel Pierce as head of the Department of Housing and Urban Development (HUD) elicited some cheers—and some hisses, for Pierce was no stranger to those in the U.S. ruling circle. Back during the incendiary 1960s, rabidly racist FBI Director J. Edgar Hoover tried to posit Pierce as a conservative counterpoint more worthy of Black people's attention than the increasingly radicalized Rev. M.L. King Jr., but to no avail. Years later, he served ruling-class interests to helm the scuttling of HUD. Rich, white GOP right-wingers could beat up on the poor with a "Black club," so to speak.

"Silent Sam" Pierce sat amidst social disaster in stoic silence, whilst federal hovels were denied the needy.

Eight years later, the nation saw housing funds cut 81 percent, elderly and handicapped programs cut by 50 percent, and community development funds sliced 47 percent. Reagan's Department of "Housing" and "Urban Development" housed fewer folks, and its policies of neglect led to the development of urban Bantustans. Now, HUD is embroiled in scandal to the tune of over $2.5 billion.

While public housing rotted for want of repairs and homeless people were evicted into city streets, consultants, lobbyists, lawyers and ex–government appointees supped at the public trough and laughed all the way to the bank. Reagan's former Interior Secretary, racist jokester James Watt, pulled down a cool $300,000 for lobbying on behalf of Maryland projects. Former Ford administration HUD Secretary (and Bush U.S. trade envoy) Carla Hills was paid by a Florida "developer" to shake the HUD money tree for two housing developments in Dade and Broward counties, with partial success. Ex–Massachusetts Senator Edward Brooke received $185K in consultant fees on state projects.

Programs designed to assist the poor were awarded to middle- and upper-class folks, as the poor got poorer and the ill-housed got homeless.

It is interesting to note that Victor Hugo's central character in his post-revolutionary epic, Jean Valjean, is tossed into the Bastille for daring to steal a morsel of bread to stave off starvation for his family. But even the wretched Valjean, before imprisonment, has a place for his family to live. Such is "progress" that today, in Bush's "kinder, gentler" America, the poor—women and children among them—huddle on steam grates, in makeshift cardboard coverings, in America's wealthy cities with no place to live.

Sir Ronald can be thanked for this state of affairs, and a system of cold, capitalist greed can be thanked for perpetuating these conditions of squalor.

In Valjean's France, Marie Antoinette lost her pretty head for her reported retort to the poor's plea for bread, "Let them eat cake!"

In Bush's America, for the poor, there is no bread, no cake, no homes and no hope.

Valjean's generation took to the barricades to speak Revolution, and toppled a king and a corrupt class of the idle rich.

What is this generation to do?

BLUES FOR HUEY

August 28, 1989

The blaring trumpet of African exile, Hugh Masakela, screams out of the speaker at the door of a storefront on North Philly's Columbia Avenue, soaring, plummeting, slicing a sharp, clear cut through the thick, muggy, midsummer midday mist, playing "Blues for Huey." The author sits hypnotized by the horn, stiffened into a stupor by the Masakela sound, brassy, acute, clean, powerful, full of the melancholy tones of tears, pain and soggy lust crafted in dusty Soweto shebeens, laced with the new-found militancy of Black U.S. youth, Africa and Afro-America, reunited in Masakela's righteous horn, reignited into one fire.

"Blues for Huey" blared from Philadelphia's Panther office.

The awesome instrumental came, unbidden, into my consciousness when news burst that Huey P. Newton, the once–Minister of Defense of the Black Panther Party, was found shot to death in an Oakland street. It hit like a Masakela solo—in the gut—in the heart.

It's amazing Huey was almost 50—it's almost more amazing that Huey's tragedy, and ours, could be met with the innocent query by millions of Black teens and preteens: "Huey who?"

I had to reach back some 20 summers to summon up "Blues for Huey," that bittersweet set that may or may not have been in homage to Newton. Some songs mark an era, and this energetic tune does that for me.

Always a small fry in the Panther organization, never a bigwig, I only met the Defense Minister once, when he came to Philadelphia and I was assigned to bodyguard duties. I doubted he knew my name, but I loved him. Huey, self-taught, brilliant, taciturn, strong-willed, molded the righteous indignation and rage of an oppressed people into a nationwide, militant, revolutionary nationalist organization. Huey's courageous spirit touched the downtrodden, Black America's so-called lumpen proletariat classes, and energized them into a balled fist of angry resistance, prompting FBI Director J. Edgar Hoover's observation that the party posed "the most serious threat" to America's internal security. Huey woke up the historically ignored strata of Black life and put them in the service of the people, via Free Breakfast Programs, Free Clothing Programs and organized units of community self-defense.

To the U.S. ruling class, this stirring of Black life into liberation activism proved too much—enter the dogs of deception. The government unleashed the FBI, whose function, in Hoover's words, was to "frustrate every effort . . . to consolidate . . . forces or to recruit new or youthful members" by the party, which, at its apex, had chapters in 45 U.S. cities.

Government efforts at disruption were swift and deadly. Setups with regional police became routine, sparked by America's historical phobia about "niggers with guns," and in the aftermath, some 38 Panthers were shot down by racist cops. Party ranks were riddled with FBI-paid agent-provocateurs and informants. Paranoia swelled as cop raids grew in frequency and intensity, beggaring the party by bails and legal fees.

By the mid-1970s, the party, split by government disruption and internal strife, suffered a sharp membership decline and faded from the world stage. Huey, a Supreme Commander without a command, a visionary with no outlet for his vision, a revolutionary bereft of a revolutionary party, retrogressed into a fascination with the street hustlers of his Oakland youth; the pimps, the players, the "illegitimate capitalists," as he called it, called him. It was, to be sure, a fatal attraction.

Huey was, it must be said, no godling, no saint. He was, however, intensely human, curious, acutely brilliant, a lover of

all the world's children, an implacable foe of all the world's op-
pressors. He rapped philosophy with the late Chinese premier
Chou En-lai; he met Mao; he supped with North Korea's Kim
Il-Sung; he was a guest of Castro.

Huey Percy Newton, by his will and great heart, marked
his age with militance, making a noble contribution to the
Black Liberation struggle. That he could die at the hands of
a crack fiend is a sobering testament to how low he, and we,
have fallen. The best memoriam to such a one is to purge our
communities of the poison that plagued, and finally plugged, a
truly remarkable man, and to use the highlights of his memory
to spark a renewal in revolutionary consciousness.

15

OPPOSING ANTI-ARAB RACISM

February 7, 1991

As war fever spreads across the United States like a raging wildfire, the toxin of anti-Arab racism follows like a plague.

An Arab motorist, wanted for a simple traffic citation, finds his dark features plastered across countless wanted posters, the libelous and deadly label "terrorist" emblazoned thereon. Arab merchants, U.S. citizens for generations, find slurs spray-painted upon businesses, and in some isolated yet ominous cases, the smoking remnants of firebombs amidst middle-American storefronts.

An Arab American traveler finds himself subjected to a chilling, intimidating interrogation, until the revelation comes that the traveler, Jameel Farrah, is none other than the talented comic actor of *M.A.S.H.* fame Jamie Farr.

American disc jockeys ape American everyday attitudes toward the newly minted enemy: "towel-head," "dune monkey," and the creatively cruel Reagan-era epithet now taking on new currency—"sand nigger." Words of hate demean and dehumanize an entire people.

Americans of Arab descent are awash in a flood of fear. Suddenly, in the land many came to over a century ago, they find not the land of the free or the home of the brave, but the land of terror, the home of fear.

Arabs have flocked to U.S. shores for well over a century, in flight from religious or cultural intolerance at home, or simply for a better, more stable life. Renowned poet Kahlil Gibran left his beloved Lebanon to live and write in Boston. While a youth, the morose but extraordinarily gifted writer joined a coterie of like-minded Arab word crafters in a nascent Arab American community in Boston. Gibran later wrote classics treasured for their soaring prose, such as *The Prophet* and *A Tear and a Smile*. His contemporary Mikhail Naimy wrote a mystic tome called *The Book of Mirdad*, then returned to Lebanon.

Despite his extraordinary gifts to the literary world, were Gibran alive today, he too would suffer the slurs slung at Arabs daily—"camel jockey" and the like. The good ole American racism.

It is a deadly virus that Americans of all ethnicities should and must denounce and eradicate. All wars evoke the ugly atavistic urge to dehumanize the adversary. There are faded newsreels that refer bitingly to "Jap bastards," "slant-eyes" and the like. Indeed, America's hallowed Declaration of Independence makes explicit reference to "merciless Indian Savages."

Readers from the Vietnam era should have no difficulty in recalling the violence-laden term "gook."

In short, all these words reflect racist hatred at the "other," and license the dehumanization of an entire people. Millions of Americans are of Arab lineage, and even during wartime they should not be tainted with the brush of hatred. It is ironic that several months ago, politicians were lip-synching songs of sorrow over the unjust property confiscations and internments of thousands of loyal Japanese Americans during World War II (while paying a pittance to the survivors of this injustice).

In the past weeks of the Iraq-U.S. war, however, that serpentine spirit of racist slander has arisen in America with a wicked vengeance, aimed at U.S. Arabs.

The potential for extraordinary evil launched against them is real.

All people must combat that spirit, or the anti-American epithet the "great Satan" may become a sobering truth.

16

RODNEY KING

March 10, 1991

As the psychic ripples from the Gulf "War" recede from the shores of memory, other visions arrest the nation's attention.

From the country's Southwest came the gripping imagery of a continuing urban war, the videotaped vicious street beating of an African American motorist as he lay prone, dazed, utterly unresisting, in a Los Angeles gutter.

Witnesses counted at least 50 bone-snapping blows by police billy clubs, plus assorted kickings and zappings by an electric stun gun.

The motorist's crime?

Running a stoplight (allegedly), and daring to flee a uniformed crew of malcontents. The initial police reports, predictably, charged Rodney King with resisting arrest, but the existence of videotape of the arrest relegated such charges to irrelevance. For there, in living color, stood the obvious— a Black man, suspected of an offense, is publicly beaten in a spasm of insensate racist rage, for no reason other than the lamentable fact that it has long been American custom to do so, when the doers are armed with the power of the state.

In that blinding, naked moment, the fears of generations of Black men leapt to the fore, for by such customs our common reality is marked.

For who knew, among his vicious pursuers, who this young man was? Who among them cared?

He could've been a white-collar professional, like insurance man Arthur McDuffie, whose murder by cops in Miami evoked paroxysms of rebellion; he could've been a cop, driving in plainclothes; he could've been the son of California Congressman Ron Dellums. In short, he could've been any

Black man, of any social stratum, and the beating would've been just as brutal, just as harrowing, and just as disbelieved, had not a camera captured this cacophony of cruelty.

To his armed, uniformed assailants, the driver was just a "nigger," and hence fair game.

He might've been a returned warrior from Desert Storm, or a blood relative of Martin Luther King Jr., but would it have mattered?

Hardly.

Prepare for the official obfuscation, i.e., the old "bad apple" theory, to be unleashed upon the public.

"There's always a few bad apples in every bunch," the cops will say, adding, "Don't blame the bunch!"

One wonders—where, pray tell, are the "good apples" who treat people with human decency? Arthur McDuffie, Eleanor Bumpurs,[1] MOVE, and on and on and on?

To now cry "bad apples" is to insult Black intelligence.

It is not "bad apples," but a bad system, that relegates Black life to the psychic underworld of terror.

For what did Black youth cross the seas of Saudi sand? For what did their fathers wage war in Vietnam?

For what did their grandfathers fight a fascist Hitler? To be beaten in the streets like dogs?

That is today's ugly reality.

What reality will our sons face?

17

NEVER AGAIN

August 12, 1992

When millions of Jews, gypsies and other assorted *Unter-menschen* (German for "subhumans") were herded into Europe's concentration camps for slaughter, the Western world, man's so-called "civilization," stood by in almost blithe indifference, until the Hitlerian task of making Europe *judenrein* ("cleansed of Jews") was nearly two-thirds completed.

The resulting Holocaust of much of the world's Jewry left a world in shock at its depth of evil and spawned the growth of the world's human rights movement, moving Jew and Gentile alike to saying in heartfelt unison, "Never again."

It is 1992, and 50 years have passed since the ovens of Bergen-Belsen smothered scores of Jews.

In the region of Bosnia, Eastern Europe, concentration camps are once again filled with thousands of suffering humans, their gaunt, starving, skeletal forms macabre mirror images of the living dead of Dachau and Treblinka.

In Bosnia, tales of mass murders, gang rapes, systematic starvation emerge, part of a depraved political program by Serbian militias to have the area "ethnically cleansed." In an ironic twist of history the victims are now not Jews but Muslims, ethnic brethren of the Serbs who dog them, descendants of the ancient Ottoman Empire that subdued the Balkans in 1453, bringing it under Islamic dominance.

There is a familiar ring in the terms *judenrein* and "ethnic cleansing," the same racist tendency separated by languages and half a century in time. After the Muslims of Bosnia are eliminated, will we once again hear the pledge "Never again"?

When the Bosnian-Serbian region was incorporated into the now-defunct state of Yugoslavia, inter-ethnic and regional conflicts were sublimated in favor of the larger entity, the state, or crushed under the iron fist of Marshal Tito, an anti-Nazi partisan who took power under the Communist Party and established the nation-state in 1945.

In 1980, Tito died, and in 1991, the Soviet Union died. Nominally within the Soviet orbit, Yugoslavia was largely independent, trading with the United States and Britain for years while COMECON crumbled.

Today, Yugoslavia is no more, and centuries of religious, class and "ethnic" hatreds fuel the Balkan sprint into barbarity.

Concentration camps, "ethnic cleansing" and liquidation campaigns all reveal how little humans have changed in a half century.

The German-born American philosopher Hannah Arendt, a spectator at the infamous Nazi war crimes trial, said she was struck by "the banality of evil."

Five decades later, the same fiendish passions from the bubbling cauldron of hatreds boiling in the human breast reveal how truly banal such hate remains.

For even in the darkest hours of 20th-century humanity, "never" never means never.

18

LEGAL OUTLAWS: BOBBY'S BATTLE FOR JUSTICE

October 12, 1992

The name Bobby Brightwell was not a new one. In my mind's eye he stood in clearest memory: short, stocky, 230 pounds sitting easily on a well-muscled, superbly conditioned frame; an elfish perpetual grin that gave birth to belly laughs from a face turned reddish brown by midsummer. Memory proved a poor match for the description given of the Bobby Brightwell seen just days ago on a witness stand in a Cumberland County courthouse; pale, listless, sickly, shrunken to a mere 150 pounds, his body bent and atrophied.

"He looked like an old man," said one spectator. What could cause such a dramatic deterioration in just three years? Brightwell, barely 40, was not just a witness but the defendant in his own prison assault trial, stemming from incidents that occurred in April 1992 at Rockview Prison in central Pennsylvania.

The story Bobby told from the witness stand was a harrowing revelation of official barbarity, a reflection of what happens daily in the state-constructed shadows called prisons across the United States. Brightwell had a prison history of being a "complainer"—one who files institutional complaints against staff members who violate their own rules—and hence had earned the enmity of prison staffers.

On April 10, 1992, shortly before noon, he was returning from the prison exercise yard while handcuffed, escorted by four armed (baton-wielding) guards. He was repeatedly searched, and after the fourth such search, quite rightly inquired as to why the repeated searches. He was ordered to face the wall, and as he did so was punched in the back of the head and the neck, called "nigger" and warned, "Mind your goddamn business!" A lieutenant grabbed a baton and, using its tip like a dagger, jabbed Brightwell forcefully and repeatedly in the belly, knocking the wind out of the handcuffed captive. Upon his return to his cell, the sergeant intentionally slammed the metal cell gate into him. When he could make it to the toilet, Brightwell vomited, and later urinated and defecated blood. Shortly thereafter, he was taken to the prison's psychiatric observation unit, a strip cell (or "DW"[1]) with nothing, no toilet (a hole in the floor), no sheets, nothing except a mattress drenched in urine.

It wasn't until April 13 (three days later) that he saw a doctor, who briefly prescribed a liquid diet, but even now Bobby has difficulty keeping his food down. On April 21, 1992, on the order of prison deputies, Bobby was ordered moved from DW and returned to the RHU[2] (the site of the initial assault), despite his pleas and clearly justified fears of retaliation. Such pleas fell on deaf ears, and his brief return amounted to being literally thrown into a cell with a non-functional light and being beaten again by approximately 10 guards, who knocked his glasses off with punches, pulled his arms, choked him and pummeled him so that, as he told the court, "I felt punches and pain everywhere."

Knocked to the steel bench, he had his legs pulled savagely apart and sadistically twisted, prompting him to yell in a mad fit of pain, "Why don't you just break 'em off?" He lay twisted, cuffed and shackled to a leather restraint for over five hours in a cell from hell, denied medical treatment, in a pool of vomit, in pain and terror, before being returned to the strip cell, DW.

In early September 1992, on trial under charges of assault by a life prisoner, a Common Pleas jury found him not guilty, acquitting him of all charges.

A trial observer said that when the verdict was returned,

Brightwell didn't even smile. His mind was probably taken up with a picture of his tormentors, the well-paid civil servants, the guards who stole all but his very life, who have never been charged with anything.

19.

GANGSTERS IN BLUE

July 20, 1994

A ruthless band of criminals strikes a series of homes, robbing inhabitants of money and other valuables, threatening certain violence to those who dare to tell.

A greedy group of thugs forces young people to hit the streets to sell drugs for them, and will beat and even shoot them if they don't produce profits fast enough.

A brutal bunch of armed rapists attacks and sexually assaults a group of defenseless women.

These and other events happened in New York and in Philadelphia recently, proof positive of an ugly crime wave in those and several other cities, perpetrated by gangsters in blue—members of the police department.

The recently released Mollen Commission Report, which deals with several aspects of corruption, crime and cop violence in the New York Police Department, tells of cops shaking down drug dealers, beating them and shooting them.

For instance, in one reference, the report noted that "Officer Alfonso Compres not only allegedly robbed a drug courier, but shot him in the stomach to steal his drugs." (Not, the author might add, as evidence, but for resale or even for his own use.) Some cops, the report adds, "are violent simply for the sake of violence."

As an example, the commission document cited a case from Brooklyn North Precinct in which cops threw a bucket of ammonia at a person being detained in a holding pen; another cop, known as "the Mechanic" (because he "tuned people up"), routinely beat folks up, visiting indiscriminate violence upon all—young or old, male or female.

One cop testifying before the commission, when asked by

a commissioner whether such violence prompted complaints from aggrieved citizens, replied, "Who are they gonna complain to—the police? We are the police!"

And the killing of those they claim to "serve and protect" goes on. The deadly toll: 412 people killed by cops in 1976; 333 in 1984; 385 in 1990.

They obviously haven't "served" or "protected" the thousands they've murdered over the years—so who do they "serve and protect"?

They "serve and protect" the system—not the people.

To the people, they are predators who take the health, the property, the freedom and the lives of the very people who, through their tax dollars, pay their bloated salaries.

They are blue-uniformed vampires who live on the blood and misery of the many.

They are the best criminals of all.

VOTING FOR YOUR OWN REPRESSION

October 1994

The recent passage of the 1994 Clinton crime bill marks the official dawn of the U.S. police state.

This law, the most draconian in the nation's history, calls for spending over 30 billion bucks for more prisons, more cops and more death penalties. More tools of state repression—more un-freedom.

Those who voted for this "Death Bill" have done more to foster crime than anything else. For years it has been said that prisons are but the universities of crime. Under the new law, all prisoners will have an opportunity to learn—crime—because Pell Grants, which provided the possibility for a few thousand prisoners a year to gain higher education, have been cut to zero.

Thus, of the 1.3 million prisoners in America, whether serving six months or 66 years, not a single one will receive a single cent to learn a single useful fact to enrich the society he or she will return to one day.

In essence, this system has legislated ignorance.

This crime bill is a declaration of war on Black men. The sections of the law on gangs and cocaine tell the tale. People designated gang members under the new law can have 10 years tacked on to their original sentence . . . even if the offense is unrelated to gang membership!

The Crime Bill has criminalized affiliation.

Those persons convicted of crack cocaine offenses face severe penalties up to 100 times more punitive than those convicted of powder cocaine offenses.

Is it mere coincidence that poor folk use crack and rich folk snort powder? I think not.

Researchers for the Washington, D.C.–based Sentencing Project as well as the Chicago-based Committee to End the Marion Lockdown have calculated the rate of Black incarceration at 1,534 per 100,000, as compared to a white imprisonment rate of 197 per 100,000. This crime bill criminalizes Black life.

The weak-kneed political forces that supported this Referendum on Repression, from the so-called Congressional Black Caucus to "new" Democrats to "moderate" Republicans, have authored an authoritarian act that is itself criminal.

It will not only not solve a crime: it is a crime.

WELFARE REFORM
OR WAR ON WOMEN?

January 30, 1995

Across the nation, from state capitals to the nation's capital, the cry resounds: "Welfare reform!" Politicians, going for the lowest common denominators—envy and fear—are on the warpath against those in this society who possess the least political power and influence: welfare mothers. From North to South, from East to West, politicians foam at the mouth at those who exist in the pit of poverty.

Envy?

Yes, for social and psycho-historians have demonstrated that anti-female campaigns have occurred and recurred throughout Euro American history, based on little more than male envy of the feminine powers of birth, nurturance and sexual attraction. As Dr. Joseph H. Berke notes in *The Tyranny of Malice*:

> Theories about the womb and the role of women changed radically with the writings of St. Augustine and other Christian theologians, who affirmed that female maladies, in particular hysteria, were caused by an "alliance with unholy powers" (typically "seduction by the devil"); hysterical women were thus equated with witches.[1]

Dr. Berke explains that things really went cuckoo when Charlemagne, Emperor of the Holy Roman Empire, issued a decree against "witchcraft" that called for the death penalty; the decree signifies an abhorrence and hostility toward women's powers—their bodies, their functions, their products and their pleasures—that culminated in 1487 with the publication of *Malleus Maleficarum*, also known as *The Witches' Hammer*. The impact of this work was immediate and long-lasting. It became an international bestseller and an established authority by which untold numbers of women were tortured and executed *ad majorem Dei gloriam* [Latin for "to the greater glory of God"—ed.] over the next couple of centuries.

"Witchcraft" meant any action that excited lust, any action that extinguished lust, and generally, anything anyone in authority said it was.

Nor was this merely a European delusion, as evidenced by the Salem witchcraft trials and executions in "New" England. Male envy and hostility didn't die in Salem, but live now, under camouflage, in politicians who are plumbing those sentiments anew, exploiting those who are the poorest in this land of plenty, damning them for their poverty, cursing them for their fecundity, in the name of "fiscal responsibility."

These same politicians, who often receive more per diem than do welfare families monthly, spit on the poor, while suckling military industries spend billions in minutes on technologies for killing.

Those who create life are pissed on; those who create death are praised.

THE STATE OF PENNSYLVANIA HAS EVERY INTENTION OF KILLING ME

August 11, 1995

Justice is just an emotional feeling.
—Judge Albert F. Sabo, PCRA Hearing,
Commonwealth v. Abu-Jamal

In the late morning of August 7, 1995, Senior Judge Sabo surprised many in the courtroom by issuing an extended stay of execution, citing "pending appeals" in my case. The decision seemed expected by the prosecutor, but stunned members of the defense team, whose client had 10 days 'til death and who expected nothing from the crusty, acerbic jurist.

Observers believe this was the first stay issued in the judge's career.

Questions abound—among them, "What does it mean?" To simplify, a stay is a judicial stop sign, and in this case, stopped a death warrant. It should be clear, however, that the writer remains on Death Row, under a death sentence—only the date has been changed.

The state of Pennsylvania still has every intention of killing me—just not right now. Thus the stay is a limited victory, not just for the Jamals and the Africas, but for thousands and tens of thousands of people from every corner of the globe—to these many, our most profound and heartfelt thanks for your militant and spirited protests.

Long live John Africa!

Although many radicals and progressives expressed joy at news of the stay, other political analysts saw it as a clever move by a clever judge who did what higher courts would've done, and in doing so attempted to blunt the edge of a growing, militant anti–death penalty movement in Philadelphia and beyond, thereby stymieing a series of planned demonstrations.

Whatever the reasoning, let us utilize this precious time to build a stronger and broader movement, not to "stay" one execution, but to halt them all. Down with the racist U.S. death penalty!

In an age when South Africa, once the pariah of the international community, has abolished all executions as an affront to the inherent right to life, our task cannot be to merely stay (or slow down) one man's execution. No! It must be to echo the world—the European Community, Australia, South Africa et al.—in total abolition of this racist vestige of the lynching tree, all forms of state murder.

It will take the power of the people—you—us all—to bring it about.

We can do it.

If you are truly committed, we will do it.

I know I am doing my part—will you help me?

This stay is but the first step, although in the right direction, in our long walk to freedom.

No matter where you live, there is a support group near you. Contact: Concerned Families and Friends (International) (267) 760-7344, ICFFMAJ@aol.com . We are growing—thanx to you!

THE PASSING OF KUNSTLER: PEOPLE'S LAWYER

November 20, 1995

This is what you shall do: Love the earth and the sun and the animals, despise riches, give alms to every one that asks, stand up for the stupid and crazy, devote your income and labor to others, hate tyrants, argue not concerning God, have patience and indulgence toward the people, take off your hat to nothing known or unknown.

—Walt Whitman

A look at the extraordinary life of William Moses Kunstler is like looking at a roll call of radical American history during the 20th century. On a calendar that marks almost eight decades of life, Kunstler's legal career is a shimmering watermark of highlights.

Cases that seemed impossible yielded to the frog-voiced counselor—a warrior whose weapons were words. He battled in serious cases going back to the 1960s, like the late Congressman Adam Clayton Powell's case against McCormick; to the recent case of Qubilah Shabazz, the daughter of the late Black human rights leader Malcolm X; to the flag-burning case *Texas v. Johnson*, in which the U.S. Supremes declared anti-burning laws unconstitutional. In all of them, Bill Kunstler rumbled for principle, for the fight, and against a government he saw as more concerned with power than freedom.

His words resonated far beyond the sterile ambience of courtrooms. He was more than mere attorney—he was activist, writer, and yes—actor! He wrote 13 books, mostly of poetry. He was a friend and counselor to some of the most militant and passionate people in the Black Liberation movement, from Malcolm, whom he deeply admired, to the Attica brothers, whose state massacre he fought to prevent. He represented Black Panther martyr Fred Hampton, Black Liberation Army soldier Assata Shakur, the Harlem 6, and Adam Abdul-Hakim (better known as Larry Davis).

He didn't bite his tongue.

How many lawyers have worked in courtrooms of judges who were little more than fascists? How many have dared to say so—publicly? Bill Kunstler did. Many know of his courageous denunciation of a racist jurist as a "disgrace to the bench." He got "disciplined" for speaking the truth.

The word "Kunstler" has become synonymous with "fighter," "winner" and "people's lawyer."

In an age where the rich get richer and the poor get prison, Kunstler, with his characteristic humor, made it a point of honor to shun great wealth, and became a man rich in the well-earned respect of many across the nation as a man who loved people, and hated all forms of injustice.

Mobbed by a crush of admirers as he left an anti–death penalty speech before New York's Marxist school, Kunstler handed out his business cards—"Here's a get-out-of-jail-free card," he told them.

An entire generation of radical lawyers owes its existence to this man, who did his thing with style, with wit and with humor.

In one of his biggest cases, the Chicago 7 trial (with Leonard Weinglass Esq., as co-counsel) someone mailed Kunstler a well-known yet illegal herbal substance. Bill immediately alerted the judge, Julius Hoffman, who barked, "What are you telling me for? Do something with it yourself!"

Bill's reply: "I assure you, Your Honor, that I will personally burn it tonight."

To remember a man is one thing; to remember him with

laughter, with human warmth, with the glow of memory, marks that man as extraordinary.

Such a one was Bill Kunstler—and as such he would've wanted to be remembered.

FUGITIVE FROM JUSTICE, VERONICA JONES

October 4, 1996

On Tuesday, October 1, 1996, a woman named Veronica Jones walked into a courtroom, and a few hours later walked into history. In a throaty, deep voice she announced to a packed courtroom, "I lied" in *Commonwealth of Pennsylvania v. Jamal* in 1982, when she denied seeing two men jogging away from a Center City killing. Police detectives, she testified, visited her in jail, where she was being held on armed robbery charges, and told her not only to change her statement, but to finger this writer. She went halfway.

"They told me I'd hafta do ten years away from my children if I said what I saw," she explained, weeping. "I couldn't leave my babies!

"That's a part of my life I tried to erase," she said.

After her 1982 testimony, serious weapons charges (two loaded pistols were allegedly seized by police from the waistband of her pants), robbery charges and related offenses resulted in—probation!

Moments after her recantation, prosecutors promptly produced two New Jersey cops who arrested the young woman on an outstanding bench warrant stemming from a 1994 bad check charge (for less than $250) in New Jersey—and hustled the startled witness off the stand and into a jail cell.

Imagine that—a woman leaves her home state, crosses the bridge to give sworn testimony in a court of "law," and gets busted there as a "fugitive from justice"! Is this proof that there ain't no justice in American courtrooms?

The courts are their courts—places where, as Judge Sabo

so aptly put it, "Justice is just an emotional feeling." And because justice is foreign to U.S. courts, a woman can be hauled off to jail for speaking a powerful truth, the fact that detectives tried to intimidate her into lying on the stand.

For over 20 months Ms. Jones lived openly in New Jersey, and state officials let a warrant sit in a file gathering dust. Only when she appeared in court in the *Commonwealth of Pennsylvania v. Jamal* case did detectives "find" her, in another state!

This poor, single mother, now on the brink of grandmotherhood, summoned up the courage to speak the truth, and the state attacked her savagely. As she was being led away, tears lining her dark face, stunned by the unprecedented, premeditated prosecutorial ambush, she managed to say, "You think that's going to make me change my story? It's not!"

In teary-eyed defiance, she was marched off to jail to await a hearing in southern New Jersey.

Hours later, adding insult to injury, Philadelphia police announced it was arresting Ms. Jones again, this time on a bench warrant for a prostitution charge from 1982.

That's right—14 years ago.

New Jersey waits over 600 days and Philadelphia waits over 14 years to serve warrants, and city prosecutors have the gall to say that my defense lawyers could've found her any time, when cops from two states couldn't find her to serve bench warrants? Amazing.

In a blatant act of judicial vindictiveness and prosecutorial petulance, a witness is punished and humiliated for coming to court and speaking the truth. In such a case, the law is naught but a tool of state repression, and the statute of limitations nothing but a forgotten memory.

Just like "justice."

WHEN A CHILD IS NOT A CHILD

November 19, 1999

When is a child not a child?

When he is a Black child, apparently.

The spectacle of Nathaniel Abraham sitting in a courtroom, his life in the hands of 12 strangers, is a stunning indictment of the American "justice" system, where youth is no mitigator. A troubled youth, to be sure, he was less an individual than an opportunity. An opportunity for some political animal to make his mark, not on a young, tender life, but on someone's future career. In a remarkable compromise verdict, the jury in the case acquitted the boy of weapons charges while simultaneously convicting him of second-degree murder, a charge that may result in his banishment to the netherworld of America's prison-industrial complex for the very rest of his life.

America, which preaches to the world of its vaunted "human rights," is also the world's leader in incarceration rates. It is creating and sustaining one of the most repressive prison systems in the Western world, and increasingly becoming much more repressive for juveniles. But more and more, a juvenile is just another commodity, a body to be caged, for longer periods of time. Not a person in need, not a youth to be rescued, not a life to be transformed. Nathaniel Abraham was such a one. When he was charged in the accidental shooting of a Detroit neighbor, the state mobilized its anti-life forces to capitalize on the case and to secure careers. After decades of fierce and unprincipled demonization by the elite media, the lives of Black, Hispanic and poor youth, once they are exposed to the "tender mercies" of the system, are in direst jeopardy. It is in this spirit that a boy like Nathaniel became more than a boy; he was, and is, projected as a dark symbol of social pathology, with little or no hope of his renewal.

If there is some constant in the psyche of the young, it is that they are in a constant state of growth and development. Their essential nature is that they change; that is perhaps what they do best. But Nathaniel Abraham, a little boy of 11 at the time of the shooting, and a little boy of 13 at the time of his trial, will not be allowed to really change, for legally he is an adult, and any change is irrelevant.

At the very least, young Nathaniel will be held in Michigan confinement until he is 21 years of age—10 years. At most, he will be caged forever, frozen like a small museum exhibit in a block of time, no matter how long he lives nor what he may achieve, no matter who he later becomes as a man: he will be a symbol, a relic that denies his essential reality as a living, growing being.

It is an irony of American history that where once grown Black men were seen as boys, now boys, of no matter how tender an age, are seen and treated as men. The constant feature in this social and historical process is the projection upon the eternal "other" of values of worthlessness and powerlessness—a relic of our dark and tragic past that we drag along into the future. The astute writer James Baldwin once noted:

> It comes as a great shock around the age of 5, 6 or 7 to discover that the flag to which you have pledged allegiance, along with everybody else, has not pledged allegiance to you.[1]

Young Nathaniel Abraham, if denied the natural right to be seen and treated as a child, unwittingly serves as another form of social symbol: he is the canary in a cage, and as he is carried deeper and deeper into the bowels of the earth, he warns us of an impending catastrophe.

MORE THAN POLICE BRUTALITY

February 4, 2000

Every day, a cop places a hand on the Bible, swears to tell the truth, and lies with utter abandon, in a courtroom in every city in America. The judge doesn't blink, the prosecutor doesn't stutter, and the so-called "justice system" swallows another body into the labyrinth.

There's even a word for it—"testi-lying."

What has occurred in Los Angeles in recent months has shone only a sliver of light on a department-wide, and indeed nationwide, practice. Why does it occur? For the simplest reason ever.

It works!

A recent *Los Angeles Times* piece covers a wide range of overt injustices in daily practice:

> The big question is: Do the police regularly lie? . . . Some police administrators and legal commentators believe that police often tell . . . small lies, mostly to justify unlawful searches [involving] claims that officers saw a defendant drop drugs on the ground when an officer actually turned them up in a search of the defendant, or . . . because he merely saw the drugs lying near the defendant and inferred that they belonged to him.[1]

As the scandal arising from the LAPD Rampart Division spreads, people are finally beginning to question the words of "sworn officers." Theoretically, the sight of a uniformed, decorated cop on the stand, hand raised to be sworn in, is proof positive to most jurors that the truth is about to be uttered.

Theory, however, is rarely practice.

This was revealed in the infamous Serpico police corruption hearings in 1970s-era New York, the later Mollen Commission hearings on corruption two decades later, the Christopher Commission hearings in L.A., and now the widening Rampart Division scandals—and what of the 39th District in Philadelphia?

Decade after decade, scandal after scandal, commission after commission, and what has changed? In city after city, in case after case, cops take the stand and say whatever is necessary to insure convictions. Judges, prosecutors and juries alike see and understand what they are seeing, but it matters little. In a culture based on demonization, anything goes, and thus begins the process of the prison-industrial complex.

In L.A. alone, cases have come out involving cop violence, rampant criminality, perjury and murder. Cops there have pulled drug heists and have then turned around, gone to court, sworn on their Bible and lied like shameless whores. Is this new?

Not by a long shot, and the DAs, the judges, the public defenders, the mayor, city council and other public officials know about it, yet they turn their head and close their eyes.

The cops are not the problem; they are the symptom of a total systemic disease. One that sacrifices the poor, the Mexican, the African American and the powerless to the system. It is in this context, then, that one must examine the rising incidence and severity of cop violence. Why do we speak of "police brutality"? Why not call it what it is?

It is *police terrorism.*

And the state is not a solution to the problem; indeed, it is the problem.

The poor, the Black, the Chicano are subjected to this campaign of terror, to keep them contained in the ghettoes of the community. But we view the violence of that state far differently from retail violence, as activist Larvester Gaither points out:

In recent years, reports of police brutality have become routine. Yet most of the corporate-owned media has focused on hate groups such as the Ku Klux Klan or the Aryan Nation. This has largely obscured police brutality and racism within the criminal justice system. By situating anti-black vigilantism and state-sanctioned violence in the same framework, we can better devise strategies that allow us to move one step closer to, without moving two steps backward from, the solution.[2]

We will hear, no doubt, of a new (and improved) police commission to study the latest reign of police criminality, and it will be equally successful as those of the past. It is important for us to understand the role of the cops, as they serve not the people, but the rulers. Indeed, they admit as much. Think of the last time that there was a shooting of a so-called "citizen" by the cops. What do they say?

"We were just doing our jobs!"

Act like you know.

THE DEATH MACHINE

March 2, 2000

Everything in the world has a rhythm to it, a wave frequency, so to speak, that shows its ebb and flow.

The same could be said of the American Death Machine, that scattered and fractured political tool of extinction that is so distinctly American, yet so continues to fascinate and disturb the country's European cousins in France, Italy, Germany and the U.K.

Why is this so? It is so because no European state presently practices the death penalty, and most have formally abolished it. From that perspective, gained after several generations without the gallows, the American appetite for death seems perfectly ghoulish to them.

They cannot now fathom the specter of George "Dubya" Bush, a governor who has sent more people to the gallows than any recent governor in U.S. and certainly Texas history. With his enigmatic smirk and shattered syntax, "Dubya" may well be termed Guvna Death for his embrace of the American regime of extermination.

Texas has become emblematic of America's dark passion for death. Yet, as ever, Texas has become a larger-than-life quasi-caricature of the American death culture, with a system that dispatches the poor, the African American and the Mexican to the next world after trials in which lawyers have drooled in slumber while seated at the defense table. Only in the Lone Star State could a co-called Supreme Court justice defend such a procedure, claiming that "the Constitution may guarantee a man a lawyer, but there is no guarantee that the lawyer be awake." It is these kinds of "defenses" that have land-ed the poor on the steps of the gallows, the lineal descendant of the lynching tree.

These judicial opinions, like many similar ones across the United States, are for domestic consumption, for political consumption, and are not meant to be shared with a global audience. In the vacuumed silence of their absence from international review, one can make all manner of empty claims about the "rule of law," the hallowed "right to counsel" or any other alleged constitutional "right." In truth, what kind of right can there be without the fundamental right to life?

For poor people facing the armed might of the state, to speak of rights is but to converse in a language that one side cannot speak or decipher. While the bourgeois and middle-class Blacks lament the flying of a Confederate flag in a Southern state, a long campaign of legal carnage takes place among the urban poor, under the American flag, in courtrooms from coast to coast, daily.

Their fear lies not in the archaic symbolism of a dead Confederacy, but in the very real slaps and assaults on Black life and dignity, whether in the streets, in the stores, in police stations or in the courts of the land. We have all been conditioned to look askance at the white hood and robe, while we are taught to look respectfully at the very same actor who wears a black robe. Before the field of red, white and blue, and beneath the Seal of the State.

Through her courts, and under her legal pronouncements, the country's legal structure implements a kind of new-age slavery, which exploits not the labor but the very lives of Black men and women. It is this social factor that gives resonance to the concept of the prison-industrial complex.

This nation would not exist were it not for the slave coffle, the Winchester, the noose, and the ghetto of social exclusion. The American Death System functions now as a modern reflection of the violent and nightmarish horrors that attended the birth of the nation. It is part and parcel of a machinery of fear, of pain and of repression that lies in the seed of American nationhood.

Foreigners who yet marvel at this current wave of U.S. bloodlust need only study true American history.

WHAT AMADOU DIALLO
REALLY MEANS

March 13, 2000

The doorway execution of Amadou Diallo, and the subsequent acquittal of the four killer cops by a distant jury in Albany, New York, in late February 2000 is contributing to a firestorm of controversy and community outrage in New York and other parts of the country. Perhaps the most interesting responses have been the political ones, which seem to suggest that the tragedy could somehow have been averted if only the city had been led by a Democrat. While it is undeniable that the repressive regime of Torquemada Giuliani has contributed to the aura of police aggression against the people, that is not a distinctive feature of Republicanism, but rather of statism, for the two faces of the state wear Republican and/or Democratic garb.

The interests of the state are power, and conservation of the status quo, no matter how unjust that status quo happens to be. When one considers the behavior of the police under the Democratic Dinkins administration, one finds the same kind of brutality, of racist anti-Black police terror, as, indeed, the infamous police riot in front of New York's City Hall demonstrated, where the target of cop ire was the mayor himself!

There, memory recalls, hundreds if not thousands of cops likened their "commander-in-chief" (the Black mayor) to a washroom attendant! No mayor can claim an administration where there was a true dearth of police violence against the poor and the powerless, and against the Black and Latino communities.

The dangers presented by the Diallo killing are twofold: 1) It is a harbinger of greater violence against unarmed Black and non-white life by the cops; 2) It will be used to mobilize Democratic political campaigns for mayor, the Senate or the presidency.

The first, of course, is self-explanatory, but as to the second, the danger lies in the illusion that perhaps Black life will somehow be safer in the city with Democrats in political control.

The depth of that illusion is illustrated by the tepid and weak comments that are uttered by many major white candidates for political office on the Democratic side.

The Democratic senatorial candidate Hillary Clinton, in the aftermath of the Diallo killers' acquittal, issued a statement to the effect that "police officers should work to understand the community, and the community should understand the risks faced by police officers." This in the afterglow of a whitewash quasi-prosecution and acquittal of four cops who glocked Diallo to death in his doorway for committing the capital crime of "standing while black"—SWB. This in studied political reflection of a case where cops fired 41 shots at an unarmed man! Do you really think that this is a promise of safety if and when she gets elected? If this is what she says when she wants and presumably needs Black and Puerto Rican votes, what will be said after the election? This, then, is the voice of the "New Democrat." One that sounds suspiciously like the Dixie Democrats, the voice that protects the status quo, changing nothing and promising to change even less.

The legendary R&B group the Temptations used to sing, in "Ball of Confusion," about politicians who say, "Vote for me, and I'll set you free!" "New" politicians don't even promise freedom. They promise tolerance. As if the poor are beings of pestilence, who are to be "tolerated." They can't even promise "freedom" in this, the Prisonhouse of Nations, where 2 million souls groan in the American Gulag. Indeed, they cannot begin to promise this, for they have been pivotal in the very construction and consolidation of the prison-industrial complex.

They are not the solution, for their only claim to fame is to bring in some Black management for this Menagerie of Pain. A few high appointees. Some cabinet members. A new diversity over the same system of repression. It's time for us to look further for our political solutions. We need to think in terms of new political configurations that speak to our deeper social, racial, ethnic and class identities. For, clearly, this has not worked and does not promise to work. The objective of all politics is power. No major political party in America can even begin to promise Black folks in America the power to stand on their own doorstep, or ride their own car, or walk the streets of the urban center, without the very real threat of being "accidentally" blasted into eternity. A politics that cannot, or will not, control the agents of that polity (that is, the police) is unworthy of our support.

THE DAMNING OF DISSENT

April 27, 2000

All across the nation, hundreds of people, and ultimately thousands of people, are involved in protests against state or corporate policies and activities, and therefore they are acting on their alleged First Amendment rights "guaranteed" by the U.S. Constitution. The Constitution contains a provision stating, in essence, that "Congress shall make no law abridging the freedom of speech," and further attesting to the rights of the people to assemble for the purpose of seeking "redress of grievances" against the government.

Every schoolchild can quote these sections, so interwoven are they into the American framework and traditions of the so-called "law." Yet for hundreds of people, the very act of assembly, of free speech, of protesting against state and corporate policies, means arrest, jailing and in some cases convictions and sentencing, all for acts said to be "protected" by the First Amendment to the U.S. Constitution.

If someone can be punished by the state for the mere exercise of a so-called constitutional right, then there ain't no such thing as a right. If one is punished in the name of a right, then one is wronged for doing that which is right!

From the Seattle demonstrations to the Mumia demonstrations, and so on to the D.C./anti-WTO/IMF demonstrations, protesters are punished for their beliefs—by a state that disagrees with the content of their message. Where is the "right"? That famous baby-rapist and U.S. President Thomas Jefferson once wrote: "I have a right to nothing when another has the right to take it away." Spoken like a true slave owner, eh? Yet there is truth in his words, for they illustrate the limits imposed by governments against "rights" that they oppose.

The U.S. Supreme Court, in the famous Buckley case, equated money with speech, in finding that a law that limited political ads limited free speech. Thus the wealthy, and those with financial resources, can buy speech, over every network, every TV station and radio station, and all the media available.

For the poor, however, and those without resources, speech is an expensive commodity. For them, for trade unionists, for activists, and anyone even remotely in opposition to the corporate state, speech may be many things, but "free" it ain't.

For many protesters, the right of redress and assembly is more than a "legal inconvenience," for they were not just arrested, mug shot, convicted and sentenced; they were beaten, brutalized and in fact terrorized by the state for their nonviolent practice. What can the words written in the U.S. Constitution, no matter how glorious their promise, mean to them? What can a court victory mean? What can any of it mean to men and women in Chicago, Minneapolis, San Francisco and D.C., who were beaten by agents of the state for their protests?

What people learn from these experiences is that the courts are not their courts, and that the agents of the state do not serve their interest. They learn that the words written in Philadelphia in the 1770s, no matter how gilded, no matter how deified, no matter how hallowed in the traditional national memory, are only words.

I think it was Judge Learned Hand who, when a litigant complained about an injustice in his proceedings, lectured from the bench; "Young man, this is a court of law, not of justice!"

Like something out of a cheap grade-B movie, the people who dared to protest against the state's death machine were ordered to surrender their passports, and the government was thenceforth to be instructed of any of their movements, anywhere in the country. Free speech? Freedom of protest? Free assembly?

For well over two centuries after the founding of the United States, the Constitution promised to protect the rights of all in the nation; that didn't pertain to African Americans. And for a century after the U.S. Constitution was amended to include Blacks (the 13th and 14th Amendments), the courts spat on the Amendments, ignoring, restricting and misreading them to insure white supremacy and the repression of a Black rural labor force.

The clock has changed, the scenes have changed, and the restrictive spirit of an ancient time now restricts the First Amendment to a dead letter.

THE LIFE AND FREEDOM OF
SHAKA SANKOFA (GARY GRAHAM)

May 5, 2000

At the tender age of 17, a youth named Gary Graham was faced with a terrifying reality. The state of Texas and the Harris county district attorney picked him as another expendable Black life form: a Black youth to feed to the death machine. In a case of murder, where neither fingerprints nor ballistics nor any credible evidence points to any notion of his guilt, Gary Graham faces a legal murder.

Over half his life spent in hellish and harsh Texas death cells, Gary Graham has grown into the man now known as Shaka Sankofa, a young man who is deeply conscious of his individual and collective self and of his place in history.

If there is a crime for which Bloody Texas seeks his death, it is this: it is a crime in a racist nation for a Black youth to be conscious and thinking in political and collective terms. For Shaka Sankofa, innocence is not enough. The state and federal judiciary have, it is true, provided oceans of process, but not an iota of justice. His life, and the lives of thousands of young men and women like him, were expendable at birth, not just at trial. Why should it be otherwise before the lily-white and wealthy appeals courts?

The Sankofa case presents a challenge to all of us, not just those of us who steadfastly oppose the death penalty, but those of us who say we believe in fundamental fairness and basic human rights. Under the terms of international human rights pacts (to which the United States is a party) the execution of a person who is a juvenile when the alleged crime occurred is a violation of international law. But the American Empire sneers at international law.

It is necessary to mobilize unsparing protests and stiff resistance to the death machine to bring about what should be our obvious goal: the life and freedom of Shaka Sankofa.

Editor's note: Sankofa was executed by lethal injection at 8:49 p.m. on Thursday, June 22, 2000, in Huntsville, Texas. He was 36.

TEXAS: THE DEATH STATE

May 2000

> *Amendment VI. In all criminal prosecutions, the accused shall enjoy the right to a speedy and public trial, by an impartial jury of the state and district wherein the crime shall have been committed, which district shall have been previously ascertained by law, and to be informed of the nature and cause of the accusation; to be confronted with the witnesses against him; to have compulsory process for obtaining witnesses in his favor, and to have the Assistance of Counsel for his defense.*
> —from the Bill of Rights, U.S.
> Constitution (1791)

As the issue of the death penalty in the United States stirs and quickens the storms of controversy, the Lone Star State of Texas, in its hunger for death, causes even some proponents of capital punishment unquiet moments of pause. If the American South is the nation's Death Belt, then Texas is the buckle of that belt. With 215 executions since the U.S. Supreme Court allowed the resumption of capital punishment in 1976, the Lone Star State leads the nation in executions.

Texas may also lead the nation in another way: the highest number of cases where lawyers slept during death penalty trials! While perhaps no one knows the exact figure (it being not important enough to note or record), Texas has no shortage of cases where court-appointed lawyers were assigned to serious death cases in which they spent most of their time not investigating the case, not cross-examining witnesses or preparing the case for litigation, but sleeping. Sleeping!

Consider the case of Joe Cannon, court-appointed counsel for the defense in Harris County, Texas. Cannon, known as a "courthouse legend" in the county, slept soundly at many of the trials to which he was assigned. Cannon's "clients" were those who were most apt to be executed by the state, and according to one scholar's count, a dozen of them went to Death Row in a decade. David R. Dow, a University of Houston law professor who handled an appeal from a conviction where Cannon was counsel, took a look at the trial record and was flabbergasted.

"It was like there was nobody in the room for [his client]," Prof. Dow recalled. Dow, in an interview, spoke of reading the transcript and finding that it "goes on for pages and pages, and there's not a whisper from anyone representing him."[1]

Small wonder.

This is the system that Texas Governor George W. Bush defends as one in which he is "absolutely confident." Despite the corporationist press's sweet slant on the issue, there are a growing number of folks who are vigorously opposed to the death machine, and the candidacy of Bush for U.S. president.

When Bush made a May 13, 2000, appearance at the historically Black college (now a university) Prairie View A&M, he met messages of resistance from a number of groups, among them N'COBRA (National Coalition of Blacks for Reparations in America), the National Black United Front, the Nation of Islam's Muhammad Mosque #45 and supporters of Texas Death Row captive Shaka Sankofa (né Gary Graham), who were protesting for either a pardon or clemency.

Administrators at Prairie View, according to some published reports, were not pleased with the protests. The university, established shortly after the Civil War in 1878, is a prestigious place, and its administrators were justly proud of its 300+ graduates. Yet activists from various movements were also justly concerned that the grads, embarking on a career of privilege, not forget the 70,000 African Americans held captive in the Texas Department of Corrections, under draconian conditions. Some grads joined the protesters in shouting "Bush go home!" and booing the governor.

Such protests are a good beginning, but must be the seeds of movements to come. Free Shaka!

32

THE REAL
"CONSTITUTIONAL CRISIS"

November 21, 2000

Politics is the art of preventing people from taking part in affairs which properly concern them.

—Paul Valéry, French poet

As the swarm of lawyers descends on Florida (not to be out-done by the pack of journalists accompanying them), the language of legalese sends observers into fits of fury, as terms like "statutory construction," "stare decisis" [abiding by legal precedent —ed.], and "public policy" merge into the muddle over "chads" (dimpled or pregnant?), voters' intent, and butterfly ballots.

The legal battles waged in the Sunshine State are remarkable as much for what they ignore as for what they entail. They involve, of course, the counting, as well as the method of counting, ballots involved in the election. What they ignore is the remarkable revelations presented by a panel convened by the heads of the NAACP (National Association for the Advancement of Colored People), the Lawyers' Committee for Civil Rights Under Law, and People for the American Way on November 11, 2000, the Saturday after the elections.

Held like a formal hearing, with a stenographer acting as a court reporter, the panelists (among them NAACP CEO Kweisi Mfume, LCCRUL Executive Director Barbara Arnwine, and PFAW President Ralph Neas) questioned and examined a number of witnesses, all of whom had some involvement in the Florida elections.

What the witnesses testified to, less than a week after the

polls closed, was nothing less than astounding. Adora Nweze, president of the NAACP State Conference in Florida, told of fighting for over 90 minutes with election officials at her polling place for the right to vote. She was told that an absentee ballot was sent to her (which she never received) and thus she was ineligible to vote. She told the panel, "We wanted you to come, even though we may not know the law, we knew it certainly was not right."

One wonders, if this happened to a savvy civil rights leader in Florida, what of someone who wasn't so savvy?

Several students from FAMU, the historically Black university in Florida, told of registering online at election.com, only to find out that they weren't registered when they tried to vote.

A voting rights canvasser who organized car rides to the polls told of hundreds of elderly who were told they weren't registered. Indeed, this canvasser, a young woman named Fumiko Robinson, told of her own mother being denied the right to vote, based on an apparent error in the official's log books, which wrongly recorded the spelling of her first name and middle initial. Fumiko's mom, a Japanese American, was only able to vote because her husband, an African American, returned to the polls and fought for her right to vote.

Stacy Powers, a journalist and radio producer, told of going to half a dozen polling places where she saw systematic harassment and the denial of voters who were Black. She told of a news source who provided her with a list of 940 voters who filed absentee ballots (before the election) that were improperly rejected. When one considers the more recent winning margin claimed by the Bush camp—930 votes—the improper rejection of the 940 absentee ballots seems somewhat ominous. Powers, asked how many Black voters were disenfranchised in the Hillsborough County, the fifth most populous county in the state, replied, "Thousands."

A Haitian American women's activist, Marliene Bastien,

cited "dozens" of cases where Haitians were denied help. She told of a call from a man who said, "I spent so many years waiting to become an American citizen, to get the right to vote, and now I can't vote!" He was, she said, "crying on the phone."

Yet how many of these voices have you heard represented in the courts, on the news, in the corporate press? Silenced by their suppression at the polling place, they are silenced yet again when their very real concerns are ignored in a national debate that speaks gingerly of "mistakes" yet makes no mention of fraud, intimidation and blatant violations not merely of the Voters Rights Act but of the 15th Amendment to the Constitution.

Silence in the face of such crimes is a criminal indictment of the entire system, which remains deeply opposed to black political power.

33

MANY TRAILS OF TEARS

January 15, 2001

An anthropologist comes up to an Indian, and asks him
what did the Indians call America before the whites came,
and the Indian replies, "Ours."
—Vine Deloria, Native activist

When the phrase "Trail of Tears" is used, many people think of the horrendous death march of the Cherokee peoples from what is now called Georgia to reservations in the Western territories. Thousands died during the forced march from cold, from sickness, from heartbreak at the idea of leaving their ancestral lands, to satisfy the land greed of the white settlers.

However, many such trails of tears have occurred across the land we now call America, most of which are ignored and forgotten in the national amnesia that we call history.

Of course, even in that infamous Trail of Tears of the Cherokee dispossessed, there was a trail within a trail, for the Cherokee, one of the so-called Five Civilized Tribes, imitated white people in some ways, including the possession of black slaves. On that trail, along with Cherokee were hundreds, perhaps thousands, of Blacks held in captivity. There is uncertainty over how many, because few people felt it important enough to keep count.

From the tropical swamps and lowlands of what is now called Florida another indigenous people, the Seminoles, were forced along a deadly trail. Florida was the intersection of at least three spheres of global conflict: the interests of Spain, the British, and the Americans (the French were involved relatively briefly). Caught in the middle were Indian and African peoples.

For Seminoles (who broke away from their Creek kin),

Florida was home, as it was the home of the Timuquan, Muskhogean, and Apalachee people before them. It was here, in the early 1500s, that the Spanish sought the hidden Fountain of Youth. It was here that perhaps the oldest European city [in America] was begun, St. Augustine, around 1565. And it was here that land greed spelled the beginning of the end for free Seminole life on their ancestral lands. For whether it was the Spanish, the French, the English or the Americans, the expansion of white settlement means the contraction of red lands, and in several hundred years, their removal.

When Spanish authorities were in possession of the territory, their relative weakness in terms of population, army and immigration forced them to make the territory attractive to those who would defend her imperial interests. The Spanish Crown therefore ordered that any Black person who escaped from slavery in the Anglo "north" (of Georgia or the Carolinas) would be free in Florida if they swore to bear arms and defend it. Thousands did. The famous Stono Rebellion, where hundreds of Black captives armed with makeshift weapons marched toward St. Augustine, drumming as they went, gives some idea of Florida's appeal. It also gives some idea of why Georgia and the Carolinas (and the United States) wanted to take Florida from Spain: to extend slavery. This factor also sheds light on why the Seminoles were always the object of U.S. derision and hostility. The Seminoles, themselves a breakaway branch of the Creek Confederacy (the name is said to mean runaway or breakaway), treated their African runaways as friends and fought hard to resist American attempts to recapture and re-enslave Blacks, who became members of the Nation. Americans were critical of what U.S. General Thomas S. Jessup called "the influence of the Negroes" upon the Seminole council.

After at least three devastating wars, trickery, deceit and cheating, the Seminoles were marched off to Oklahoma. There, they were given inferior lands; none of the promised equipment, clothing, blankets or food was provided. They were overcharged and left on land that had been promised to the Creeks.

While some army records suggest that more than 4,000 Seminoles died during the deadly trek west, no figure accurately recorded those who died after arrival in Oklahoma. What mattered to the Americans was that they were gone.

They were further devastated by the Civil War, as they were once again put in between the fights of others, and they were punished after the war by still more land theft.

The history of the relationship between the settlers and the Native peoples of the Americas is one of naked injustice, greed, violence and death. It is but one feature of a rarely told and little-known facet of American history.

34

MESSAGE TO THE FIRST WORLD CONGRESS AGAINST THE DEATH PENALTY, STRASBOURG, FRANCE

June 22, 2001

Bonjour mes amis du mouvement pour l'abolition de la peine de mort dans la République française. I thank y'all, and particularly our hard-working sister Julia Wright, who has been a light and strong arm of freedom movements for several generations. *Merci, ma sœur!* Friends, supporters, comrades: your vigorous and various struggles against the death penalty are a light unto the world, and a welcome voice for many of us who dwell in what has become the prisonhouse of nations. America's voracious appetite for death is growing.

The recent selection of George W. Bush to the American presidency bodes ill for men, women and juveniles on Death Rows all across the nation—state and federal. Bush the younger was elevated to the office by the Supreme Court in an unprecedented act, following a hotly disputed election. His term as governor of Texas is among the bloodiest in history. While he was governor of the Lone Star State, the death chambers were drenched in blood. Texas led the other American states in legal lynchings, and that gruesome fact became an important qualification for higher political office. Governor Bush became President Death.

To the United States (called a "hyperpower" by some French critics), international law is just a tool to be used against nations it doesn't like, and something to be ignored when it comes to the United States itself. Several international treaties forbid the execution of people who are 18 years or under at the time of their offense. The legalized lynching of

Shaka Sankofa (born Gary Graham), who was 18 at the time of his arrest, proves that, to the American Empire, international law is a dead letter. And to such a "hyperpower," international law can be violated and passed over with impunity. They are so powerful, so feared, that their very violation of the law is seen as legal.

Recently, the U.S. press has reported a series of cases in which juveniles, some as young as 12 or 13 years old, have been tried as adults. Those children have been sentenced to adult prisons for literally the rest of their lives. Others, who were 16, 17 or 18 years of age, are waiting for death at the hands of the state, as we speak. How can the world's leader in prison population parade as the paragon of human rights? How can women be the fastest-growing segment of [internees in] the prison industry, and the nation that cages them be the arbiter of international law? To an empire, its will alone is law. No other law exists.

Many nation-states have beginnings in struggles against foreign elites, against repressive feudal elites, and as a by-product of economic activity. America has her roots in slavery. When the Constitution was written, representatives from the Northern and Southern states formed what they called "the Great Compromise," a not-so-great agreement that rewarded the South with more and more representation and power in Congress as the region acquired more and more African slaves.

Now, a civil war and centuries later, the shadow of those deeply anti-democratic beginnings falls over U.S. domestic policy. For is it but coincidence that prisons are reserved for the poor (especially Black urbanites), or that Death Row is a predominantly African American reservation?

During the Nixon administration years (circa 1969 to 1974), the nation embarked on a so-called "law and order" binge that continues to this day. It is the modern-day trigger to the prison-industrial complex, and one of Nixon's top aides, Chief of Staff H.R. Haldeman, revealed the thinking behind the jargon when he wrote in his diary about discussions with his boss:

> [President Nixon] emphasized that you have to face the fact that the whole problem is really the Blacks. The key is to devise a system that recognizes this while not appearing to.[1]

Every major government so-called anti-crime initiative, from the evisceration of ancient habeas corpus rights by the Clinton administration to the stark militarization of American police—as best shown in the brutal, vicious police bombing of the MOVE commune in Philadelphia on May 13, 1985—flows from that tortured, racist logic that Nixon whispered to his top aide. They have created a system that is racist to its core, "while not appearing" to be. When people are charged with capital crimes, they face a jury that has been purged of virtually all Black representation, by design. In what are now known as the McMahon Tapes, a chief homicide prosecutor in Philadelphia's District Attorney's office, while training junior prosecutors in how to select a jury, made the following remarks, captured on video:

> The case law says that the object of getting a jury is to get . . . I wrote it down. I looked at the cases. I had to look this up, because I didn't know this was the purpose of a jury. "Voir dire is to get a competent, fair, and impartial jury." Well, that's ridiculous. You're not trying to get that.

The prosecutor (named McMahon) left no room in the minds of those whom he was training what the objectives of jury selection really were: "The only way you're going to do your best is to get jurors that are as unfair and more likely to convict than anybody else in that room."

That's how the District Attorney's office in Philadelphia picks juries, according to their own words. Is there any question that such a system is one that echoes Nixon's old adage to achieve racist ends "while not appearing to"? Indeed the District Attorney, on the same tape, referred to Black Philadelphians and their neighborhoods as "garbage" and taught his juniors how to remove Blacks from the jury for racist reasons, "while not appearing to." Is there any wonder that Philadelphia has one of the largest, Blackest Death Rows in America, exceeding some Southern states?

There can therefore not be a World Congress that seeks to abolish the death penalty without an acute examination of the Philadelphia experience—for here is the epicenter. There can therefore not be a World Congress to abolish the death penalty without an acknowledgement that the racist instrument of white supremacy devalues Black life, whether that of an accused or that of a potential juror, while elevating white life. There can be no real movement here unless there is the recognition that law, whether international or domestic, is an illusion designed to perpetuate a polite status quo that for decades has been based upon the premise that "the whole problem is really the Blacks," and that the system must recognize this "while not appearing to." It is this very status quo that is the lifeblood of the vampirish American death machine. And it must be shattered if abolition can ever become reality.

Thanks!

Ona MOVE! Long Live John Africa!

35

THE REAL MEANING OF GENOA

August 1, 2001

When one mentions the very name of Genoa these days, the historical significance of its Columbian roots mixes with its new-found renown as the site of the G-8 meeting and the state killing of a young anti-globalist demonstrator, Carlo Giuliani. It is now a historical marker of another kind—one of the state's brutality. The images from the tear gas–streaked streets of the ancient Italian city mark a transformation in the growing anti-globalist movement. It marks a new low in the violent savagery of police, who will go to any lengths to protect those they are sworn to really protect: the rich, the wealthy and the established.

Much less is known or reported about the vicious, unprovoked attacks on young people who were working out of the Independent Media Center in Genoa. Squads of hooded Genoa cops unjustly raided, beat, brutalized and terrorized independent journalists covering the massive protests. Some bystanders reported hearing screams emitting from the building for hours. Others on the scene reported that activists were taken to a room at a nearby police station, shown a picture of the late Italian Fascist dictator Benito Mussolini, and ordered to shout, *"Viva Il Duce!"* ("Il Duce" was a term of respect accorded Mussolini during Italy's Fascist, World War II period, similar to the Nazi honorific "Der Führer" for Hitler; "Viva" means "Long live.")

This is a scene that reflects the hidden, fascist heart of Genoa. Where were the millionaire star reporters who love to gather in ritzy five-star hotels to lament what happens to their brother journalists in the Third World, or Bosnia? When have you heard a peep out of the corporate punditocracy about the assaults on poor, independent or radical journalists who were at the front lines in Genoa?

When young activists were peacefully assembled to write, to interview, to report, to prepare and to broadcast what they witnessed at the Wealthfest (G-8 Summit), their persons were attacked, their freedoms were shattered, and their terrorization at the hands of a repressive state was all but ignored. Their shocking treatment at the hands of neo-fascist, hooded cops for capital was simply not news.

"So sorry," the genteel corporate press sniffs. "We don't see a story here."

And, in truth, there is no story, simply because it is not in the interests of their bosses to do such a story. That way, they can continue to engage in useless prattle about "freedom of the press," or the "right to peaceful assembly," or even the "right to dissent" and the like. For, aren't the G-7 (plus Russia) "industrial democracies"? They cannot afford to report what happened in Genoa, for it tells us too much about what really happens in democracies. The terror, the torture, the brutality, that lies at the heart of all "industrial democracies."

"Viva Il Duce!" indeed, for great dictatorships have ever been great bedfellows of capital. The Nazi state worked with a cruel efficiency that used Jews, the Romani and other *Untermenschen* (German for subhumans) as slave labor that earned healthy profits for the wealthy, ruling industrial class.

Genoa, which sent forth the greed of Columbus to pilfer and colonize and enslave, unleashes her corporate army upon those who now look unkindly upon the neo-colonialization and exploitation hidden under the rubric of a New World (Economic) Order.

The anti-globalist movement, so young, so precious, spawned just a few moments ago in Seattle, must now come of age.

That is the gift of Genoa.

36

LAND

August 8, 2001

There are millions of people who look at the situation in the area called the Middle East. They look at the situation and throw up their hands, as if helpless to do anything about it. Some say, "It's a religious feud!" Others lament, "They've been fighting for thousands of years! It's been so long, there's nothing we can do!"

This is the argument for non-interference, one promoted by the curious American reliance on the Bible as a kind of primeval history textbook. This widespread American presumption is far more than an argument for non-interference; it is an argument to perpetuate the status quo.

What is most surprising about this public (mis)perception is the fact that, with the possible exception of Britain, the United States is perhaps most responsible for the establishment of Israel, and certainly for its continued maintenance. The State of Israel is one of the youngest nations in the world, dating back to 1948. At least a third of all living Americans (and perhaps almost a half) were alive the day the State declared its independence from its British territorial and colonial roots. The fact that millions of Americans think of thousands of years, instead of decades, is a true testament to the functioning both of American schools and of corporate media.

The Israeli-Palestinian conflict stems not from religious enmity, but from profound political and territorial differences. When Anglos came to the United States from Britain (that is, before there was a United States), they surely regarded the indigenous peoples as "heathens," but that was not the source of their conflict. The whites wanted the land that these "heathens" were living on. Indeed, when Indians by the thousands converted to Christianity, and thus, as "Brothers in Christ" and co-religionists, were no longer "heathen," they were still ruthlessly uprooted from the land of their fathers and sent into a form of internal exile on sparse, non-productive so-called "reservations." The Cherokees were militarily ejected from what is now called Georgia over 150 years ago in what they came to call the Trail of Tears, when thousands died from cold, hunger, or a broken heart.

The impetus for the raging conflict there in the Middle East is land.

Some will ask, well, why the hatred? Why the deep enmity? The answer, again, can be seen by examining America's history with the indigenous, aboriginal people who were here before Europeans sought it as a so-called "New World." When Christopher Columbus (Cristoforo Colombo, Cristóbal Colón) made landfall in what we now call the West Indies, he described the inhabitants as "gentle" and "friendly," and in similar terms. In less than a hundred years, accounts were sent to Europe of "savages" and "heathens" and "barbarians."

Israeli writer Israel Shamir recently recounted the results of a poll conducted by an Israeli newspaper about their feelings regarding the Palestinians:

> The Russian-language newspaper *Direct Speech*, published in Jerusalem, asked hundreds of Russian Jews about their feelings toward the Palestinians. Typical answers were: "I would kill all Arabs," "All Arabs should be eliminated," "Arabs must be expelled," and "An Arab is an Arab. They all have to be eliminated."
>
> I am not sure a street poll of Berlin in 1938 would produce more damning results, as the Nazi idea of the Final Solution did not emerge until 1941.[1]

The fact that some of the speakers had to be fairly recent immigrants from Russia (as the country didn't allow much immigration until 20 years ago or so) is most alarming, yet it reflects a spirit not unknown to millions of Americans. If you doubt this, let's have our own test.

Fill in the blank: "The only good Indian is a _____ Indian."

If you are American (no matter your ethnic origin) you know the answer that pops into your mind. It ain't pretty.

The bulldozers, the snipers, the F-14s, the tanks, the Uzis, all of the might of the Israeli state is arrayed to achieve what they may not call, but each know to be, Lebensraum. Living space.

The Arabs, even if they and their ancestors have lived there under the Ottoman Empire for a thousand years, are seen to be what Cherokees were seen as by the white settlers in 1880 Georgia: expendable.

This is the source of the conflict, the hatred, the derision.

And America, which funds one side while ignoring the other, can never be a fair arbiter at any table of mediation. For it sees one side as a younger version of itself: and it sees the other as Indians—Others.

Guess who they will always favor?

When they say "Peace," they mean "Silence!" The silence of a Trail of Tears.

37·

IMPERIAL PIQUE IN DURBAN

August 30, 2001

As organizers, activists and scholars gather in Durban, South Africa, for the UN-sponsored World Conference Against Racism, the United States sends the global gathering an imperial raspberry by not allowing the nation's highest-ranking African American to attend. Colin Powell, the first Black U.S. Secretary of State (in essence, U.S. Foreign Minister), won't be there, because the international conference refused to abide by a U.S. pre-conference demand to jettison anti-Zionist language from conference documents. (One wonders, is Powell the Israeli Foreign Minister–designate?)

Some U.S.-based nongovernmental organizations (NGOs) and national civil rights groups expressed shock and dismay that General Powell wouldn't attend the first such conference in decades. That shock and dismay reflects political naïveté. For Powell is not, and has never been, the foreign minister of Afro-America. He is the representative of the executive branch of the United States government. And, as he's done all of his professional, military life, the General will follow the orders he's given, even if he is in disagreement with them. After decades of obedience to higher orders to kill in Vietnam, or the Balkans, or Iraq, obeying the order to dismiss a UN conference, even one on racism, is relatively easy.

If one examines the long and deep national aspirations of Black Americans, across almost two centuries, for national independence from the central, white supremacist state, perhaps two figures emerge who performed, in admirable fashion, the functions of de facto foreign ministers of a nationalistic Afro-America: Malcolm X (after his split with the Nation of Islam) and Eldridge Cleaver (before his split with the Black

112 ·

Panther Party). Malcolm X's historic tours of Africa are still the stuff of legend, and his reception by North African and West African States was on the order of ceremonies welcoming a head of state.

When the late Eldridge Cleaver headed the Intercommunal Section (International Section) of the Black Panther Party in Algiers, the voice of militant Afro-America, of revolutionary resistance to U.S. imperialism, was echoed globally through the Party's popular paper, *The Black Panther*, and through Eldridge's unremittingly militant messages and pronouncements on matters impacting the global scene.

Neither man could be mistaken for an emissary of the imperialist United States. They opposed it with every fiber of their being. Both men came to their historic roles not by service to their masters, but by long, hard service to organizations that represented various nationalistic strains in the Afro American community.

Both men came from the nation's gutter, its prisons (à la Tupac), and spoke with an eloquence and passion not learned in the perfumed parlors of higher learning and academia.

They spoke from the heart, what they knew in their hearts, from lives lived on America's margins.

Imagine a UN World Conference Against Racism that had the presence of either a Malcolm X or an Eldridge Cleaver, speaking truth to power, and resistance to the Empire!

Who would care about any government emissary?

How many great movements in human history have been launched by governments? How many have been stifled and scuttled by governments? The great movements of our times arise not from the governments, but independent of them, and often in stark opposition to them.

Members of the Abolition movement were seen as the "crazies" of their day, and Lincoln made jokes about shooting them!

The Women's Suffrage movement was widely ridiculed in

its day as a bunch of "crazy wimmen" who didn't know their place—home.

The Civil Rights, Anti-War and Black Liberation movements were all the targets of government repression, spying and violence. They were movements of the people—not governments. And that's why they had meaning, and enduring power, in the hearts of people.

The UN Conference will be a success not because of what any government does, but because of globalist organizing by organizers and activists who see the particular similarities, and discrete differences, between peoples living under various repressive systems, in various parts of the world. Without support in the hearts of the people, no such conference can ever succeed. With it, it cannot fail.

Furthermore, no empire, no matter the color of its emissaries, can thwart the desires of the majorities of the peoples of the world.

Were it not for Cuba, the apartheid regime would still be in power in Jo'Burg, South Africa. Mandela would be in Robben Isle. And the U.S. would still be saying "constructive engagement" was the way to deal with the racist regime. Popular, grassroots movements, coupled with Cuban military prowess in Southern Africa, changed that horrendous equation. We would do well to remember our history!

9-11 . . . WHY?

September 17, 2001

The woman's voice on the phone was as plaintive as a tear, as she implored the non-responsive talk show host to please tell her, "Why do they hate us so much?" Why? Her voice, while not commonly projected in the current media, resonates in the consciousness of millions of Americans, who look at the carnage of the World Trade Center, shiver at the violent audacity of it, and wonder "Why?"

This is a particularly American response, one made in a culture that has no yesterdays, only a tomorrow of creature comforts, no-fat ice cream and luxury cars. History, to millions of Americans, is John Wayne, or the vaunted Founding Fathers, who have no blemishes or flaws. Much of the outer world and its inhabitants are of no import, as they are subjects of the Empire, and thus expendable.

Their histories, deeply intertwined with the United States, are of no serious consequence. Hence the question "Why?"

This almost willful ignorance on the part of millions of Americans allows them to look at the bombing of the U.S.S. *Cole* and at the veering jetliners of September 11, and ask "Why?"

If you, the reader, don't want to hear an answer to this rhetorical question, feel free to turn the page, for the writer's response will not please you.

The airplane bombing of the World Trade Center towers and of the Pentagon didn't begin on September 11, 2001. Nor are they, as some politicians glibly suggest, "a war against civilization." But it ain't the job of politicians to inform you.

It is the job of the media, but their central concern is to sell you, and therefore they don't want to upset you. Their primary responsibility is not to their readers but to the owners, or the stockholders. And it is in the interests of the military-industrial complex that millions remain uninformed and misinformed.

The suicide flights over New York, Washington and Pennsylvania had their beginnings in the mountainous terrain of Afghanistan, in the 10-year guerrilla war against the former Soviet Union. That war was supported and facilitated by the U.S. CIA, which pumped billions into the anti-Soviet insurgency. The result? Algerian sociologist Mahfoud Bennoune told an American journalist in Algiers, "Your government participated in creating a monster." The sociologist added, "Now it has turned against you and the world—16,000 Arabs were trained in Afghanistan, made into a veritable killing machine."[1] A U.S. diplomat in Pakistan echoed these sentiments when he said, "This is an insane instance of the chickens coming home to roost. You can't plug billions of dollars into an anti-Communist *jihad*, accept participation from all over the world and ignore the consequences. But we did. Our objectives weren't peace and grooviness in Afghanistan. Our objective was killing Communists and getting the Russians out."[2] How did the Afghans pay for the weapons, in such a poor, war-ravaged country? How many know that Afghanistan is the world's greatest producer of heroin?

Short on hard dough, the Afghan *mujaheddin* traded heroin for arms with their CIA suppliers, and the "Golden Crescent" heroin ring was born.

When the Soviets were whipped and the war ended, the insurgents looked around and saw not Soviet, but U.S. dominance in the region. They saw the military presence of the United States in the Islamic holy places in Saudi Arabia, its backing of anti-democratic client states, its ravaging of Iraq and its one-sided support of Israel at the expense of the beleaguered Palestinians—and as they examined the United States, they saw the imperial similarities to the Soviets.

Afghanistan, one of the poorest, most rugged places on

earth, has a population with a male life expectancy of 46 (45 for females!). It has a literacy rate of about 29 percent. It looks at the swollen opulence of the Americans, the global reach of the American Empire, and bristles.

This nationalist, cultural, religious and class distance fuels a deep and abiding hatred of American dominance.

Humiliation, of which the Islamic world has had a great deal since the fall of the Ottoman Empire in 1922, and the colonial era of the early-to-middle 20th century, is a powerful force. It brought a humbled Germany to the brink of world conquest after World War I. It is not to be taken lightly.

Afghanistan may prove another turning point in world history, which is why we all should learn about it.

39

WHEN NEWS ISN'T NEWS

June 12, 2002

Nothing is more amazing than the ability of the U.S. media to deep-six one story while gang-banging another, ad infinitum.

In this post-modern age, when hundreds of media outlets have been squished together through mergers and acquisitions, and all of the heads of U.S. mass media can meet together in a modest two-bedroom apartment, news has become the mouthpiece of the mighty, and an appendage to the people who wield corporate power.

This maddening merger-mania has spawned the recent spate of one-issue, star/personality/sleaze-driven "stories" which have so inundated the media that they can each be encapsulated in one name: O.J., Monica, Chandra and the like.

The problem with this "all-O.J./Monica/Chandra/etc.-all-the-time" TV is that much of the world remains woefully uninformed about events that have occurred that may have a good deal more meaning than these sleazefests.

Barely a paragraph broke through the corporate media morass about a jury verdict in the police framing and bombing case involving two Earth First! activists, stemming from the early 1990s.

The federal jury, after extended deliberations, found federal and local cops liable, and awarded over $4 million dollars in damages to the estate of the late Judi Bari and a severely injured survivor of the bombing, Darryl Cherney.

When a bomb exploded in a Subaru holding Bari and Cherney, the FBI and Oakland police pointed the finger at the two environmentalists—essentially charging that they bombed themselves—as they lay in critical condition as the result of the blast. Twelve years later, a U.S. jury found government officials liable for false arrest, illegal search, slander and conspiracy. Some of the feds involved in the case were veterans of the infamous COINTELPRO program and were involved in the framing of Geronimo ji-Jaga (Pratt) and other former Black Panthers.

In a time when the FBI and other police agencies are being given loads of new monies as well as vast new powers over the people, isn't it important for people to know what they've done just 10 or 12 years ago? Isn't this arguably more important to the life of the nation than Britney's new love, or Hillary's new hairdo? Isn't this more important to the average American, especially in light of 9/11, when some evidence emerges that some government agencies had prior knowledge of the events of 9/11?

Two American citizens sat in their car on a nice summer day in 1990 and were almost blown to bits. Judy Bari, to her dying day, argued not only her innocence, but the guilt of the government agents, who miraculously appeared on the scene within moments. A jury has vindicated her, in part. But who tried to kill them? The lumber companies? The FBI? Why wasn't this story on every front page in America?

40

WAR ON THE WATERFRONT

September 11, 2002

In times of war, even one so nebulous as the "War on Terrorism," there are wars within wars. Wars not merely fought abroad, but little, internal wars of interests battling for dominance.

With the elevation of George W. Bush to the nation's highest office by the Supreme Court, business interests know they have "their guy" in the White House, and they are now trying to change the rules of the game, using government muscle and federal power to threaten labor into compliance with their bosses' interests. This can be seen clearest in the struggle between the Pacific Maritime Association (PMA, the waterfront employers) and the International Longshore and Warehouse Union (ILWU, the unionized workers).

The PMA allowed the labor contract to expire on July 1 and has issued harsh demands to the unions that would seriously undermine long-standing and hard-fought labor rights. The PMA wants to introduce new technology into the shipping industry, which the ILWU has agreed to—but the PMA wants to use these technologies to circumvent the time-honored union hiring hall, a move that cuts into pivotal union power.

The union hiring hall didn't always exist; it came into being as a result of long, hard, deadly struggles organized not by union leaders, but by everyday rank-and-file ILWU members, who pushed the Great Maritime Strike of 1934 into labor history.

Historian Howard Zinn writes:

Longshoremen on the West Coast, in a rank-and-file insurrection . . . held a convention, demanded the abolition of the shape-up (a kind of early-morning slave market where work gangs were chosen for the day), and went out on strike. Two thousand miles of coastline were quickly tied up. The teamsters cooperated, refusing to truck cargo to the piers, and maritime workers joined the strike. When the police moved in to open the piers, the strikers resisted en masse, and two were killed by police gunfire. A mass funeral procession for the strikers brought together tens of thousands of supporters. And then a general strike was called in San Francisco, with 130,000 workers out, the city immobilized.[1]

While union organizers recall it was six strikers killed by cops, the point remains that the hiring hall wasn't a gift bestowed by the bosses, but a right won by blood and death. The PMA wants to computerize it away, to move it to distant points like Utah, Arizona and even overseas!

Another tool of the wealthy owners has been the corporate press, which has falsely portrayed the longshoremen as if they were pro baseball players making over $100,000 a year, when, in fact, their average wage is closer to half that. While the ILWU quite rightly takes pride in the fact that it has fought for decent wages for its members—over 70 percent of whom are African American or Latino in the San Francisco–Oakland ports—the PMA's tactic is designed to stir up labor envy in the midst of a falling and faltering economy.

Into this simmering labor conflict now comes "Unconstitutional Tom" Ridge, the stone-faced Homeland Security Czar, and guess on whose side? Czar Ridge placed a less-than-veiled threatening call to Jim Spinosa, ILWU president. The message? A breakdown in talks (not to mention a strike!) threatens "national security." Why is it that when a worker, or even thousands of workers, face job loss, that isn't a "national security" threat? Why isn't job security "national security"? How is it in the "interests" of a nation to abolish a hard-fought right that labor won through terrible battle?

Despite the whines of the wealthy and the bleats of the corporate press, the ILWU has every right to hold firm in the face of this state-managerial assault on their glorious traditions.

The radical writer Randolph Bourne once observed, "War is the health of the state."[2] By this he meant that governments accrue tremendous powers during war, and rarely, if ever, return power to the people.

The ILWU should fight, and fight hard, in its noble tradition, against this new-age "shape-up" scheme pushed at it by management and threatened by the Bush regime. The ILWU, with the aid and assistance of sister unions, can once again teach a historic lesson, that "Labor security is national security."

41

THE CUBAN 5
AND "HOMELAND SECURITY"

December 19, 2002

Right now, the American Empire is girding its loins for a war, based at least in part on the alleged "threat" posed by a Third World adversary—Iraq. Few seriously view the Ba'ath state as a threat, but that's the rationale advanced to the American people.

What if there were a nation, one that was relatively close and was not only an avowed enemy, but had staged traceable acts of war against your people, resulting in considerable loss of life and human suffering?

Well, the Cubans don't need to look far. Their "avowed enemy" is the Colossus to the North—the United States, which has not only threatened to do harm, but has done so, for virtually half a century.

The United States has admitted trying to kill the Cuban head of state, Dr. Fidel Castro, at least 11 times. It has invaded the nation, it has sown its soil with poisons, it has spread contagion among its livestock. (Again, this is what the U.S. *has admitted to doing*.)

Recently, five Cuban nationalists were imprisoned in Miami and charged with spying for Havana. In fact, the five were actively exposing and working to stop terrorist acts launched by Cuban exiles in Miami against their homeland. When they saw plots against their nation, they monitored them and reported back to their people what was happening. The Cuban government promptly passed on the reports to the U.S. government, in a bid to stop the terrorism that has cost more

124 • The Cuban 5 and "Homeland Security"

than 3,000 Cuban lives from the 1959 Revolution to 1999. The United States responded to their reports by rounding up the five, charging them, and treating them as spies.

They have been convicted of charges relating to their monitoring activity, and have been sentenced to terms of 15 years to life for defending their nation from terroristic attacks!

The United States insists that it has the right to stage a preemptive strike against a nation that has not attacked it (Iraq), and yet insists it is wrong to defend one's homeland from further terroristic attack. That is illogical.

So, for over 33 months now, five Cubans have languished in U.S. jails, separated like wheat from the chaff, all around the nation. They are more than the rallying cry "'The Cuban 5"; they are real human beings: Gerardo Hernández, Fernando González, Ramón Labañino, Antonio Guerrero and René González. They committed no acts against the United States, nor did they monitor any American secrets. They entered the Miami exile community, observed the planning of acts of terrorism against their own country, and reported it. That is their "crime." Despite never participating in any terrorist acts, and indeed, preventing more than 170 terrorist acts against Cuba, they have been consigned to U.S. gulags. One wonders, is there really a War on Terrorism? For, if there is, how can it be furthered by the imprisonment of those who fought to stop terrorism?

As for those in the Miami Mafia—the *rabiblancos*, as they are called (rabid anti-Castro Cubans)—they have actively engaged in terror against the Cuban populace, but they have nothing to fear from the Americans, for the U.S. government indirectly supports and indeed funds their efforts.

People are organizing around the nation to demand Freedom for the Cuban 5. Please contact them and help give life to this effort. By doing so, you will be opposing terrorism for real, and supporting an anti-terrorist group of people who only want to defend their nation from foreign-backed aggression.

Free the Five!

42

ANALYSIS OF EMPIRE

January 1, 2003

To sit in darkness here
Hatching vain empires.
　　　　—John Milton (1608–1674) *Paradise Lost*

There is something quite quaint, and faintly disturbing, in hearing Americans speak of their nation as a "democracy." America, given its richness, its diversity and its complexity, is many things, but a democracy it ain't. This is especially obvious if one considers the true imperial nature of the modern American nation-state. This is not a rabid call of the wild radical, baying at the pitted moon. For perhaps the first time in almost a century, leading voices of the elite and the corporate press admit as much. In the pages of the *Wall Street Journal* one finds scattered references to the imperial nature of the U.S. Empire, even if there is no overt recognition of it in the platforms of the political parties, or the alleged history taught in grade schools these days. But if history teaches us anything, it is that nations may describe themselves one way, and be another. When I hear nativist propagandists speak of the United States as the "Birthplace of Freedom" or some such, I feel compelled to ask, how can the "birthplace of freedom" be built on slavery—the very antithesis of freedom—the heart of *unfreedom*? (Why not call it "the birthplace of White freedom"—or is that too revealing of those who weren't free?)

Of such fictions histories are born.

It is in this light that we must view the newly announced Bush Doctrine, as recorded in the recently published document National Security Strategy of the United States of America. It calls for and justifies (or tries to justify) preemptive strikes all around the globe, against anybody, anywhere, who even thinks about posing either a threat to or parity with the Empire. To make a long story short, the document calls for the canning of the Cold War strategies of "containment" and "deterrence." Using its supremacy in the technology of death, the United States reserves to itself the right to preemptively attack and even overthrow any nation-state in the world it deems threatening, attempting to acquire WMDs (you know, weapons like the U.S. already has), harboring terrorists, or failing to sufficiently suck up to the Big Dog on the street (U.S.A.).

The UN is but a minor annoyance (as has been shown in the Iraq war example). Neither is the European Union much of a deterrent to U.S. hubris, for while it may possess an inordinate amount of wealth and economic strength, it is, at present, no match for the martial power of the American Empire—and it knows it.

As long ago as 1991, when the late French President François Mitterrand and former German Chancellor Helmut Kohl announced their plans for a joint Franco-German "Euro-corps"—an official military arm of the EU—Bush the Elder issued a thinly veiled message to his European "allies": "Our premise is that the American role in the defense and the affairs of Europe will not be made superfluous by European union. If our premise is wrong, if my friends, your ultimate aim is to provide individually for your own defense, the time to tell us is today."[1] The "Euro-corps" idea was quietly shelved, and the Cold War relic of NATO has been edged into its place—under continued U.S. strategic and command dominance, of course. Indeed, even NATO has its limits, as scholar Michael Ignatieff noted in a recent *New York Review of Books* article:

> Britain's prime minister can shuttle usefully between Islamabad and New Delhi, but the influence that determines outcomes in the region comes from Washington. This is a painful reality for Europeans,

who like the Japanese believed the myth that economic power could be the equivalent of military might. Events since September 11 have rubbed in the lesson that global power is still measured by military capacity. Having rallied to the American Cause after September 11, the NATO liaison officers who arrived at CENTcom in Florida had to endure the humiliation of being denied all access to the Command Center where the war against Osama bin Laden was actually being run. *The Americans trust their allies so little—the same was true during the Kosovo operation—that they exclude everyone but the British from all but the most menial police work.*[2]

An empire neither has, nor needs, allies. It is sufficient to itself. It has subject powers. It has vassals. It does not have, nor tolerate, equals. The Bush Doctrine is replete with threats for the rest of the world, to keep it that way.

Forever.

43

WHO'S "WILDING" WHO?

January 8, 2003

For over a decade, five Black and Brown boys, caught in the crosshairs of the cops and the press, suffered in virtual silence in the prisons and hellholes of New York.

Although they have recently been exonerated, it is useful to review what happened to them and how it happened, particularly if we are to learn whether it may have happened to others, and may be happening still today.

Integral to this process is the role of the press, a role that is often underestimated, or at least understated, in any real recounting of the now infamous Central Park jogger case in midtown New York.

How did the local media fuel the furor that captured the dark imagination of the city in the spring of 1989?

When one recalls the covers of the New York dailies and recaptures the visceral spirit of the time, the official, media-sanctioned rage and hatred directed at the five—and by extension their families and their communities—is palpable:

CENTRAL PARK JOGGER: WOLF PACK'S PREY, blared the cover of the *New York Daily News*. In a subtitle: "Female Jogger near death after savage attack by roving gang."

A SAVAGE DISEASE CALLED NEW YORK was the message streaming across the expanse of two pages of the *New York Post*. There, two of the newspaper's prominent columnists wrote separate pieces under the same thickened banner headline. The *Post*'s celebrated Pete Hamill would pen an opinion piece that seemed to be a declaration of war against the poor of the city, and served to reduce the five boys from youngsters theoretically armed with the heralded "presumption of innocence" to the dark mob who were living exemplars of pathology:

They were coming downtown from a world of crack, welfare, guns, knives, indifference and ignorance. They were coming from a land of no fathers. . . . They were coming from the anarchic province of the poor. And *driven by a collective fury*, brimming with the rippling energies of youth, their minds teeming with the violent images of the streets and the movies, they had only one goal: to smash, hurt, rob, stomp, rape. The enemies were rich. *The enemies were white.*[1]

The incendiary *Post* would give its readers a lesson in interpreting this new urban underground, by tossing the word "wilding" into the lexicon, meaning "packs of bloodthirsty teens from the tenements, bursting with boredom and rage, roaming the streets getting kicks from an evening of ultra-violence."

Gotham's Mayor Edward I. Koch would pronounce the young suspects "monsters."

In this maddening maelstrom of rank fear, along with printed and verbal violence (via radio and TV), the youths were blown up into dark, threatening icons of perpetual menace, and removed from the realm of boys. They were animalized, monsterized, demonized into nonhumans, and as such, every official, semiofficial and worthy hand of influence was turned against them. They were, in the deadening universe of legalism, in the province of the law, utterly, terrifyingly alone. Indeed, those who, one would think, would be most responsive to their humanity and most resistant to the swelling chorus of chaos coming from the media, Black journalists, for career reasons, or for fear of alienation from the herd, offered little variance from the majority narrative. One journalist for the now-defunct *Newsday*, Sheryl McCarthy, recently recounted her surprise at a salient fact that she didn't notice when covering the case: "I was really surprised, in reading recent accounts, to learn that the defendants were only fourteen, fifteen, and sixteen at the time."[2]

An African American journalist, who covered the story for her paper, *never really noticed* the actual ages of the accused. She never noticed.

And neither did anyone else.

Hamill's phobic rant on the poor of the city did not reflect the backgrounds of the boys or their families. Most had hardworking mothers and fathers, and went to good or decent city schools. Yusef Salaam, for example, went to Catholic school and was well-regarded by his classmates, who called him "very easygoing."

But stereotypes made them vulnerable, more alien and more distant than the writers who were crafting their treks to the gulags.

They were presumed to be guilty, and it is interesting that all of the problems with the so-called "confessions" that have emerged were present before they were formally indicted 13 years ago. And no Supreme Court (trial court in New York), no Appellate Court, no justice of the Court of Appeals found any of it problematic. These weren't "citizens," or even "juveniles"—they were "monsters," and the law is no protector of monsters.

They had every institution of white, corporate power arrayed against them: a savage, venal press; the cynical police; and a complacent judiciary, who were (to quote Hamill) "driven by a collective fury." These boys, and too many boys like them, never had, nor have, a chance. They were but the forerunners of the war against the poor and the young that has come to typify the American prison-industrial complex.

Over 40 years before their legal lynching in New York's Supreme Court, the U.S. Supreme Court wrote in the 1948 case *Haley v. Ohio*:

> A 15-year-old lad, questioned through the dead of night by relays of police, is a ready victim of the inquisition. . . . We cannot believe that a lad of tender

years is a match for the police in such a contest.

He needs counsel and support if he is not to become the victim first of fear, then of panic.

He needs someone on whom to lean lest the overpowering presence of the law, as he knows it, crush him.[3]

(Amazingly, the *Haley* case dealt with a 15-year-old Black boy who falsely confessed—to murder.)

It is also ironic that the very case that so stigmatized the families and communities of those five youths revealed that there was an inherent, deep, undeniable imbalance in the allocations of power in the United States. For the man who confessed to the crime, who raped the jogger, also raped a nonwhite woman, nearby, in that same park, scant hours before.

And we do not know, or really care to know, her name.

The fury unleashed on these dark boys was occasioned by the toxin of race: the race of the accused, the race of the victim, and the bone knowledge that a barrier had been breached. They were "wildin'," in the eyes of the white press, not because they were allegedly rapists—but because they were Black and Brown rapists of a white woman.

Who was wildin' who?

44·

GOVERNOR RYAN'S SONG
January 11, 2003

Governor George Ryan of Illinois, in the final passing days of
his first and only term, saved the best for last.

He sent shock waves across the nation when he issued four
pardons to men sitting on the Condemned Units of the state's
prison system, opening the doors of the dungeon for four men,
one who had sat in the shadow of the gallows for nearly two decades. Speaking in a soft, Midwestern accent, his words were as
damning as the death sentences that his orders negated: "The
system is broken."

With these orders, he ushered four men, Stanley Howard,
Madison Hobley, Aaron Patterson and Leroy Orange, from the
darkest corners of the land into the light. Quoting a tale of that
famed Illinoisan, Lincoln, he recalled the job of the nation's
chief executive, who, reviewing execution orders for those who
were convicted of violating the military code during the Civil
War, asked one of his generals why one young man had no
letters in his file from anyone who wished his life spared. The
general, shrugging his shoulders matter-of-factly, said, "He's
got no friends." Lincoln, lifting his pen, remarked, "He's got
one friend," and pardoned the man, delivering him from the
clutches of the hangman.

Ryan said those four denizens of Death Row—each having
been subjected to police torture, falsified confessions, prosecutorial misconduct, and judicial blindness to these vile transgres-
sions—had one friend, and decided to cut the Gordian knot by
issuing full pardons to the four, proving himself a friend to men
who had few real friends in the dark, deserted abode of death.
Before day's end, three of the four walked away from the closed

• *133*

cell of state repression into the fresh air of a windy Chicago, and freedom.

By so doing, Ryan has dealt a serious, crippling blow to the state system of death, and the inability of the system's dignitaries and officials to cure the serious problems of the death penalty was shown in sharp and stark relief.

It is fitting that Ryan, a one-term, embattled politico and a non-lawyer ("I'm a pharmacist," he repeatedly explained), would be the one to solve these deep and troubling problems. It is equally fitting that the problems of the Illinois death system came to light not through efforts by the members of the Bar, but through the meanderings of journalism students, whose investigations led to the ultimate conclusion voiced by Ryan some years later: "The system is broken."

Hours after his unprecedented announcement of the pardon package, Ryan's office would announce another earth-shattering event: the full commutation of the sentence of every man on Death Row in the Prairie State. By the end of the week, 167 folks would no longer be on Death Row.

Elected as a conservative Republican who "never gave a moment's thought" to the rightness or morality of the death penalty, Ryan would be the last politician one would expect would strike down the seventh-largest Death Row in the United States.

With a hoarse voice, his nervousness evident by his fidgety presentation, the one-term governor struck a mighty blow against the Death System in America. Exercising a breadth of vision that is truly remarkable in an American sitting (albeit departing) politician, Ryan spoke not just of the problems facing those condemned to death, but of the problems in the processes, prosecutions and judgments affecting those condemned to "life." His words were a rare gubernatorial recognition of the deficits in the entire system: "The system has proven itself to be wildly inaccurate, unjust, unable to separate the innocent from the guilty . . . and racist."

His commutation of more than 150 death sentences un-questionably stays the cold hand of death, but it does not ad-dress the injustices that led many to Death Row, or keep them confined on "Life Row," for those problems, those deep cracks in the system, remain. It is tragically true that, as Ryan charg-es, "the system is broken." The bitter truth is that his efforts, while undeniably noble and unquestionably historic, do not fix the mess.

To his credit, Ryan assembled a blue-ribbon panel to ex-amine the state's death system, and the commission, after three years, came to a political, yet systematic, conclusion: "The system is broken." The commission, composed of prosecu-tors, judges, defense lawyers and scholars, issued some 85 rec-ommendations to "fix" the system, including the recording of confessions from beginning to end, the end of "jailhouse con-fessions" (which are notoriously unreliable, yet influential to unknowing jurors), and a host of others. The legislature opted to ignore the recommendations, just as the state's highest judi-ciary chose to ignore many of the most blatant injustices, and Ryan, the "non-lawyer," felt compelled to act.

If the system is broken, how can the system fix the system?

Ryan's very extraordinary act seems to suggest that it can-not. For while those four men are free of unjust convictions, were they the only four innocents on the state's large Death Row, or larger Life Row? That seems unlikely.

In another sense, as the underlying system remains tightly embedded in place, what of those to come? How many years will other innocents suffer in the suffocating holds of steel-and-brick slave ships (prisons) before another scandal threatens the stability of the system?

Like the notorious cycle of police corruption cases that plagues U.S. cities like New York, Philadelphia, Los Angeles and—yes—Chicago, the problem isn't fixed, but passed on to later administrations.

It seems an abolition movement must take this not as a

final victory, but as a first step of a systematic battle for real change.

We may all agree that the system is broken. But that mere agreement does not insure that that which is broken will indeed be fixed.

45

BLACK FARMERS, STILL FIGHTING

January 14, 2003

Millions of people who proudly call themselves "African Americans" have relatives who lived and worked on farms in the U.S. South, either as sharecroppers (workers who farmed for others, for a "share" of the crop or the proceeds), or as farmers whose ancestors fought and scraped for a patch of land to call their own.

Black farmers, who have been battling for decades against their treatment at the hands of the Agriculture Department of the U.S. government, have reason to feel that the vaunted Civil Rights movement has passed them by. Nothing so clearly highlights the class-conscious nature of the U.S. Civil Rights movement as its objective to place Blacks in the professions or in jobs in major industry, and its unwillingness to improve the plight of those who chose to try their hand at the tilling of the soil.

Now, Black farmers, angry at the meager fruits of 20 years of class-action litigation, are staging what is becoming their own civil rights action: protests around the offices of the U.S. Agriculture Department, speak-outs and public information campaigns designed to educate and inform the people about the situation facing those who stayed to till the soil, feed the people and build a fruitful family business.

The Black farmers in America are in trouble.

Decades of discriminatory treatment at the hands of the local and regional offices of the U.S. Department of Agriculture, empty promises by politicians and courts, and repeated betrayals by those who are sworn to "protect" their interests has left them holding the bag—and the bag is virtually empty.

Back in June, 2002, then–U.S. Congresswoman Cynthia

McKinney (D-Ga.) spoke out openly and clearly about the problems facing them.

In a June 26, 2002, "News Brief" item on her congressional website, McKinney assailed both the Bush administration and the courts for their inability or unwillingness to reasonably resolve the issues facing the farmers. The release of the legal ruling by a three-judge panel of the U.S. District of Columbia Court of Appeals gives legal credence to our ongoing outrage and disappointment over the racist and wrongful actions of the USDA, the Department of Justice and the private lawyers who represented Black farmers in the Black Farmers' Class Action Lawsuit, a.k.a. *Pigford v. Veneman*, which was supposed to right the wrongs of years of the USDA's self-admitted discrimination against Black farmers in the Farm Agency's farm lending programs.[1]

R. Abdul Mu'min Muhammad, a syndicated columnist and spokesman for the Nation of Islam farms, has written that the situation can be broken down into two main perspectives centered on the choice of relief. One group of farmers elected to use the courts for a class-action suit. The other group wanted to use the USDA's administrative process, because it was believed this would result in larger individual awards.

What they have learned, however, is that to win a lawsuit is one thing. To force positive change is another. The farmers did indeed win a court action, and it was deemed, according to Muhammad, "the largest civil rights lawsuit in the history of the country." Yet none of the perpetrators has been terminated. Therefore, having won in a court, the farmers are being forced to contend, in their future dealings, with the very personnel they complained about in the USDA.

Gary Grant, president of the National Black Farmers and Agriculturalists Association, blasted the consent decree ordered by the U.S. courts, saying, "The decree was never workable, causing more than 20,000 Black farmers not to be compensated adequately for the years of discrimination and the loss of millions of acres of land and billions of dollars in income because of the illegal, blatant racist tactics of local FMHA [Farmers Home Administration] and USDA officials."

The stalwart McKinney, torpedoed by the conservative wing of the Democratic Party, is no longer a member of Congress, but her words remain, and should be a spur to action for those of us who perceive the real worth and potential of farmlands toiled by Black hands for Black health and wealth. Biting no tongue, she spoke directly to the problem: "I am outraged at the conduct of the U.S. Department of Agriculture and the United States Department of Justice Civil Division. The decision filed by Judge Tatel confirms legally what I have said for the past three years: these agencies have never had the intention to correct the horrendous discrimination against Black farmers."

As ghettoes continue to swell throughout America's urban areas, the potential of Black farms cannot be underestimated as an important natural resource that can positively impact the daily lives and well-being of millions. Often, those in the inner city must pay the most money for the least fresh and least nutritious of life-giving foods. An intelligent program of economic assessment and regional planning, which routes the produce from those farms to the neighborhoods where the goods may be best utilized, can heal two breaches—urban malnutrition and economic self-sustenance—at the same time.

To solve the Black farmer problem may mean, ultimately, to solve our own.

46.

TO BE YOUNG, GIFTED AND . . . NINA SIMONE

May 7, 2003

Our sweetest songs are those that tell of saddest thought.
—Percy Bysshe Shelley (1792–1822),
To a Skylark

When the historical record of the 20th century is finally written, a special chapter will have to be penned about the remarkable and talented singer who was called Nina Simone (1933–2003).

In any true history, words, no matter how skillfully crafted or masterfully molded, will fail to capture the brilliance of the woman. Some recording must be appendixed, so that the student will be blessed to hear her thrilling contralto, dark, full, rich as earth in the promise of spring.

Also required will be a collection of her lyrics, so that no one may miss the words that she dared set to music and bring to life, with a fury, a passion, sheer artistic courage that continues to dazzle years, decades even, after their creation.

She was an Artist with a capital A in every sense of the word, but she was far more than that term now suggests. She was as proud, imperial, majestic and deliciously arrogant as say, the late jazz great Miles Davis was, in his prime.

The writer remembers her appearing in the late 1970s in an outdoor midday concert at the Bell Tower at Temple University. She looked out at the crowd with nervous irritation, not fear driven by the uncertainty of her performance, but a barely suppressed anger that there were only hundreds of people gathered to hear her, not thousands.

She sang songs with bite and grit and pride and longing .

. . and rage. Deep, down, boneset rage, at how cheaply life was lived for Africans in America. Her "Mississippi Goddamn" was an anthem that stirred not merely the Civil Rights movement but also the Black Liberation movement: "You don't have to live next to me, just give me my equality!" she demanded. Her songs could also be tender, loving odes to the multi-flavored beauty and spirits of Black women, as in her signature "Four Women," which spoke of the various moods and hues of her sisters. Decades before Erykah Badu would wear the head wrap, Simone did so, and walked as regally as the Nubian princess that she became.

Although she was born in the Jim Crow South, the apartheid way of quiet acceptance was never hers, and she spoke out boldly, in her art and in her interviews, against the injustices suffered by her people. When the Nixon era began, she bade her homeland adieu and, like a generation of other brilliant Black Americans (such as the writer Richard Wright) who could not abide the nastiness, meanness and racial indignities of the time, she migrated to live with dignity in France.

Some reviewers pronounced her career essentially over when she left the United States during the 1970s, never to rise again. But great artists, like great music, have a habit of resurrection.

In the early 1990s, an American film emerged that was a borrowing from the French. Bridget Fonda portrayed an alienated, drug-addicted youngster who got caught up in a failed drugstore robbery-turned-killing. She was spirited into a shadowy spy agency where she worked for the government. The character, when she was alone, invariably played Nina Simone records in the background to reflect her moodiness. The film was titled *Point of No Return* (a U.S. remake of *La Femme Nikita*). A generation of young filmgoers was thus exposed to the wonder and power of Simone's magnificent instrument.

Where are the Simones of this generation? They are there . . . in the shadows, perhaps, but they are there. They are perhaps afraid of giving as much as their recently departed ancestor. For they know that she sacrificed a good deal to sing the songs that moved her great heart. Such a prospect is no doubt scary.

Yet, one wonders, who among the madding throng will be remembered, not to mentioned revered, 30 years from now? How much of what is produced now furrows its way into the heart, or rings the deep bell of recognition in the soul? Who will sing of the wonder, the terror, the beauty and the madness of Black life in this new century?

47.

SONS OF MALCOLM

May 10, 2003

It has been almost 40 years since the assassination of Malcolm X, and the influence of the Black nationalist leader continues to grow, particularly among generations that were not alive when he was in the thick of his advocacy. While some of this is no doubt due to the powerful film done on his life by the Black filmmaker Spike Lee, it is also true that the writings of Malcolm X continue to be read, as does his popular autobiography, co-authored by the late Alex Haley.

One particularly remarkable example of the continuing influence of Malcolm X may be seen in the recent case of a young man, John Walker Lindh, who came to be known derisively as "Johnny Taliban." Lindh, who converted to Islam and went to live and fight among the Taliban government in Afghanistan, traced his Islamization to his reading of the Alex Haley work.

Among the so-called hip-hop generation too, the imagery of Malcolm, as shown by the reproduction of photos of the slain leader adorning some rap albums, or imitations of famous poses adopted by some rappers as covers for their albums, can be seen.

Students of the Black Panther Party should know that the organization perceived itself, in its earliest days, as a realization of the deeply held dreams of the late Muslim leader.

Black Panther Party founder Huey P. Newton would later write:

> Although Malcolm's program for the Organization of Afro American Unity was never put into operation, he has made it clear that Blacks ought to arm.

Malcolm's influence was ever present. We continue
to believe that the Black Panther Party exists in the
spirit of Malcolm . . . ever-present.[1]

Today, as Malcolm's life is performed on screen (by the
brilliant Denzel Washington) and the U.S. Postal Service has
even issued a stamp in his honor, much of Malcolm's experience as a dissident is lost in time's transition. The government
that now speaks his name with praise once saw him as its greatest threat. Everywhere Malcolm spoke, there too were the
spooks from the FBI, writing down notes or taping his speeches. Although they labeled him a "hatemonger," it was clear that
it was the government that used its awesome powers to act on
their hatred against Black Americans, and particularly those
Black leaders and spokespersons who opposed the repressive
status quo. Consider the tone of his FBI file of March 13, 1963,
which records his speech in Charlotte, North Carolina:

> Hearing the actual speech of Malcolm X enables the
> listener to discover the type of argument and logic
> employed by a hate peddler. The resulting effect is
> clearly heard in the background of this particular
> tape.
> [Bureau deletion] The listener can hear audience
> reaction in the background as Malcolm X stimulates
> his listeners to the release of their prejudices, griev-
> ances and wishes. Some of the content of the tape
> underlines the inhibitions and repressed attitudes of
> a segment of Negroes in general and of Charlotte
> Negroes in particular. These bitternesses are easily
> identified on the tape through crowd outbursts as
> Malcolm X underlines some of the causes of Negro
> unrest.
> This taped speech [Bureau deletion] shows
> clearly Malcolm X unites the individuals into emo-

tional entity, how he achieves rapport, reaches common understanding and responsiveness as he fuses individuals into a unit. . . . He continually throws irritants into an atmosphere of growing disapproval of the white race.

Malcolm X uses his skill as a speaker to direct emotions and hatreds of his audience toward white people whom he sets up as a scapegoat for Negroes, described by him as a people severed from their racial heritage.[2]

Lest anyone dare to suggest that Malcolm's nationalist ideas were the reason for this official attack on him, we are reminded that this same agency, less than six months later, would, in the words of Deputy Director (and one-time heir apparent to Hoover) William Sullivan, "mark" the Rev. Dr. Martin Luther King Jr. as "the most dangerous Negro in the future of this Nation."[3] Was King, too, a "hate peddler?" Hardly. Messrs. X and King were both organizers of their people; they were thus deemed enemies of the state, and every phone call, every letter, every room they frequented was under the electronic and human eyes of U.S. government spies. The issue wasn't either of these men—it was the Black movement. Because the FBI was concerned about preserving white supremacy, anyone who wanted to organize Black people to resist their repression was deemed an enemy, and targeted for their political actions and ideological beliefs.

It's good to remember Malcolm for the positive lessons that continue to radiate from his life. It is also good to remember that this government opposed him and his colleague, Rev. Dr. King, using every resource, fair and foul, to destroy them and their movements.

Next time you see a stamp, remember.

48

SOLDIERS OF MISFORTUNE

June 19, 2003

Every politician worth his or her salt speaks sweet words of endearment about the young soldiers on the periphery of the American Empire.

They're "brave," "courageous" and "defenders of 'our' freedoms."

Everyone in power seems to be basking in the glow of spring love for "our" young warriors, but if time teaches us anything about the praises of politicians, it is that such sweet words last about as long as cotton candy in an April shower.

If we are honest, and if we look at things from the perspective of political leaders, we see that soldiers are but instruments of state power. They're seen as, say, a queen bee "sees" a drone: they are expendable.

How can we come to any other conclusion in light of the way veterans of military engagements past are treated, not by protesters who may oppose their imperial violence, but by the state that employed their services?

Soldiers of World War II were subjected to dangerous exposure to radioactive materials, causing uncounted effects in thousands of people over generations. The veterans of Vietnam were exposed to the ravages of Agent Orange, yet found their enemies not in grass and mud hooches in the subtropics of Asia, but in the Veterans' Administration hospitals, the chemical companies and the politicians who represent their interests, who rejected their health concerns for at least a generation. When thousands of men and women went to the (first) Gulf War, they experienced serious, life-threatening illnesses that were called Gulf War Syndrome. Who opposed their concerns, assuring them that it was "just in their minds"? The same folks who opposed the concerns of their predecessors!

The raging protests of Vietnam forced the government to deep-six the draft (which had been unpopular since the Civil War) and institute what they claimed was an "all-volunteer" service. Yet, who volunteers—and why?

Studies have shown that low income levels and chronic unemployment are important elements in why some people opt for military service. Slick, computer-generated ad campaigns promise thousands of dollars for college, and emphasize individuality under the "Army of One" pitch. When one has few prospects of a career in an economy driven by recession and bears the demoralizing weight of a dead-end job (if one is able to get one), the ads on TV can prove irresistible. The Philadelphia-based Central Committee for Conscientious Objectors considers the military's present recruitment efforts a "poverty draft."

The Jessica Lynches of the world, surviving in the low-growth economic battlefield of West Virginia, find the military a viable, stable option in an unstable civilian economy. How many people in the services would be there if education was truly affordable? Or if the economy was out of recession?

As Congress passes resolutions praising the troops, the very same House of Representatives moves to cut some $25 billion from veterans' health benefits over the next decade. The love of politicians seems ever so fickle these days. Meanwhile, more and more public dollars get funneled into the cavernous maw of the military-industrial complex.

As this happens, we see the economic underpinnings of war.

Wars are not waged on behalf of the many, but for the few, those few who can and will benefit from the ravages of war—oil companies, defense industries and the like. How can this most recent war be for the benefit of a people who overwhelmingly opposed it, in unprecedented numbers? Least of all are wars fought for those who fight in them.

These are drawn, overwhelmingly, from the ranks of the poor and the working classes, those who can find no space in a tight economic environment. They fight abroad because they are exhausted from the never-ending fight at home—for a decent, affordable education, for decent housing, for a job with some degree of longevity.

They are fighting to survive against a truly ruthless enemy—those who run America's economy.

BLACK AUGUST

July 18, 2004

*Among these large bodies, the little community of Haiti,
anchored in the Caribbean Sea, has had her mission in the
world, and a mission which the world had much need to
learn. She has taught the world the danger of slavery and
the value of liberty. In this respect she has been the greatest
of all our modern teachers.*
— Honorable Frederick Douglass,
former U.S. Minister to Haiti
Lecture on Haiti, January 2, 1893,
Quinn Chapel, Chicago

It was a sweaty, steaming night in August when a group of
African captives gathered in the forests of Marne Rouge, in Le
Cap, San Domingue. It was 1791.

Among these men was a Voodoo priest, Papaloi Boukman,
who preached to his brethren about the need for revolution
against the cruel slave-drivers and torturers who made the lives
of their African captives a living hell. His words, spoken in the
common tongue of Creole, would echo in the annals of history,
and cannot fail to move us today, 213 years later:

The god who created the sun which gives us light,
who rouses the waves and rules the storm, though
hidden in the clouds, he watches us. He sees all that
the white man does. The god of the white man inspires him with crime, but our god calls upon us to do
good works. Our god who is good to us orders us to
revenge our wrongs. He will direct our arms and aid
us. Throw away the symbol of the god of the whites

who has so often caused us to weep, and listen to the voice of liberty, which speaks in the hearts of us all.[1]

The Rebellion of August 1791 would eventually ripen into the full-fledged Haitian Revolution, lead to the liberation of the African Haitian people, bring about the establishment of the Haiti Republic, and end the dreams of Napoleon for a French American empire in the West.

Two centuries before the Revolution, when the island was called Santo Domingo by the Spanish Empire, historian Antonio de Herrera would say of the place, "There are so many Negroes in this island, as a result of the sugar factories, that the land seems an effigy or an image of Ethiopia itself."[2] Haiti was the principal source of wealth for the French bourgeoisie. In the decade before the Boukman Rebellion, an estimated 29,000 African captives were imported to the island annually. Conditions were so brutal, and the work was so backbreaking, that the average African survived only seven years in the horrific sugar factories.

In 1804, Haiti declared independence, after defeating what was the most powerful army of the day: the Grand Army of France.

Haiti's Founding Father, Jean-Jacques Dessalines, proclaimed at the Haitian Declaration of Independence, "I have given the French cannibals blood for blood. I have avenged America."

With their liberation, Haitians changed history, for among their accomplishments were these:

a) Haiti was the first independent nation in Latin America;
b) Haiti became the second independent nation in the Western Hemisphere;
c) Haiti was the first Black republic in the modern world;

d) Haiti was the *only* incidence in world history of an enslaved people breaking their chains and defeating a powerful colonial force using military might.

What did "Independence" bring? It brought the enmity and anger of the United States, which refused to recognize its southern neighbor for 58 years. In the words of South Carolina Senator Robert Hayne, the reasons for U.S. non-recognition were clear: "Our policy with regard to Hayti is plain. We never can acknowledge her independence. . . . The peace and safety of a large portion of our Union forbids us *even to discuss* [it]."[3]

In many ways, Black August (at least in the West) begins in Haiti. It is the blackest August possible—revolution, and resultant liberation from bondage. For many years, Haiti tried to pass the torch of liberty to all of her neighbors, providing support for Simón Bolívar in his nationalist movements against Spain. Indeed, from its earliest days, Haiti was declared an asylum for Blacks who had escaped from their white enslavers and a place of refuge for any person of African or American Indian descent.

On January 1, 1804, President Dessalines would proclaim: "Never again shall colonist or European set foot on this soil as master or landowner. This shall henceforward be the foundation of our Constitution."

It would be U.S., not European, imperialism that would consign the Haitian people to the cruel reign of dictators. The United States would occupy Haiti and impose its own rules and dictates. Haitian anthropologist Ralph Trouillot would observe that the long and hated occupation "improved nothing and complicated almost everything."[4]

Yet that imperial occupation does not wipe out the historical accomplishments of Haiti. During the darkest nights of American bondage, millions of Africans, in America, in Brazil, in Cuba, and beyond, could look to Haiti, and dream.

FORTY YEARS IN THE WILDERNESS

August 13, 2003

It's been 40 long years since the much-heralded "March on Washington." Almost half a century—and what is our condition today?

Our communities are ravaged from crumbling poverty, crumbling schools, bumbling politicians and brutal cops. Our culture has been ghettoized by increased corporate exploitation and the destruction of a sense of community. While hip-hoppers sing of playin' gangstas, the state engages in legalized gangsterism against Black folks.

At the very time that Reverend Martin Luther King was making a speech about his Dream in Washington, the FBI was waging a secret war against Rev. King and anybody else who questioned the status quo. Within weeks of his speech, FBI agents were plotting how to place a good-looking woman in his offices to lure him into a sex scandal. In January 1964, the FBI's #2 man, William Sullivan, announced: "We regard Martin Luther King as *the most dangerous and effective Negro leader in the country.*"

They tried to find a "safe" Negro leader to "replace" him, for they saw him as too "radical." Four years later he would be gone.

Reverend King perhaps dreamed of many things as he tried to peer into America's future, but I doubt he foresaw the grim reality that we live in now; I doubt he saw this dark, cheapened future that is bleaker than *Blade Runner* for millions of Black youth who are barely tolerated, if they are lucky, and all but ignored as they are shuttled into stationary slave ships (prisons) where ignorance and racism is the rule, brutality and hopelessness the norm, and where, thanx to the "good brotha"

Bill Clinton (who someone called the first Black president!), education is, under his 1994 crime bill, virtually illegal. Forty years later, prisons are increasingly the only Black communities where public housing is maintained; 40 years later, and Death Rows, North and South, are disproportionately Black; 40 years later, and still white judges and juries sentence Blacks to eternities in Hell; 40 years later, and still white (and now Black) cops wild on Black youth—male *and* female!—beating, choking, shooting and torturing them with impunity. Forty years, and while there may be thousands of Black politicians, there is precious little Black political power, and much of that lies trapped within the cage of Democratic politics where promises are many but actions are few.

As Florida proved overwhelmingly, just 'cause you got a Voting Rights Act don't mean you got voting rights. It may have been Rev. King's crowning achievement, but for tens of thousands of Blacks, it's little more than a dead letter. Under the conditions of this faltering economy, tens of thousands of Black youth go into the U.S. military not to fight, but to find funding for a decent college education. Instead, they become cannon fodder for insane propaganda wars like the Iraq adventure, in defense of an empire that doesn't give a damn about them.

Meanwhile, it's 40 years later, and Black America, which once was a deep reservoir of hope, has become a stagnant pool of despair. It is not enough for us to gather to praise the past; our challenge is to mobilize the people to transform our negative and deadening present.

It is not enough for us to rap and clap about battles won in the glorious past; it is necessary to mobilize the people to win the battles that are facing us today.

It is not enough for us to erect a monument that marks what transpired here some 40 years ago; monuments have a way of being forgotten, as this new generation has all but forgotten what came before them. They can't help it—when you talk about an American Dream, they can't see it, because of the nature of the American nightmare. They look out upon an America that is utterly ready to exploit them but has never learned how to love them; they look out on an America that never wanted to educate them, but will not waste an opportunity to incarcerate them.

They look out at an America that is as alien to them as it was to their forefathers two score years ago, who were sharecroppers and dirt farmers, and didn't have the vote. They suffer from a poverty of the spirit.

They look back into the mists of time, 40 years ago, and wonder—what is there to celebrate?

THE ILL-ADVISED IRAQ ADVENTURE
November 8, 2003

As the deaths begin to mount and opposition grows to the ill-advised Iraq adventure, we are assured by voices raised in the corporate media that "we" must all "stay the course," for surely the "light is becoming visible at the end of the tunnel."

To someone who lived during the Vietnam War, such assurances are, to say the least, disquieting. They are echoes that hark back to another time, another experience, another war.

Such echoes "assure" us that the essential natures of government and congresses are unchanged, or perhaps worsen over time.

At the very beginning of the Iraq attacks, voices of the Anti-War movement claimed that this was chillingly similar to the infamous Gulf of Tonkin resolution in Vietnam, when the administration, the Congress and the press conspired to create a false *casus belli* to spark the U.S. war machine. Headlines blared about the "brutal attack" on U.S. naval vessels by "cunning communists" assaulting Americans in an "unprovoked" attack.

It took the better part of a generation to unravel the fact that the war was waged based on a lie.

This time, as before, the United States claims to be "bringing democracy" to the benighted Iraqi people, and also "saving" them from a "brutal dictatorship." Conveniently, the fevered warnings of "weapons of mass destruction," which nudged a cowardly Congress into delivering unprecedented powers into administration hands, are casually forgotten. America is instead bringing "freedom" to the Iraqi people.

Uh, huh.

I've often wondered why African Americans have been a

frequent and visible presence in the anti-war movements that have sprung up in this period, unlike during the Vietnam War. One thinks it is the deep cultural understanding that Blacks bring to this question, given their own historical experiences in the United States.

Blacks know that there were millions of Americans who spoke about "freedom" and "liberty" for centuries without once thinking about *Black* freedom and liberty. They know, as a deep lesson of history, that their ancestors were dragged here in shackles by people who swore that they were doing it "for their own good." They know from bitter experience that while Americans may say one thing, they mean something quite different. They *know* this.

Few made the case as brilliantly as Frederick Douglass, who condemned the U.S. Constitution as deeply imperfect:

> Liberty and Slavery—opposite as Heaven and Hell— are both in the Constitution; and the oath to perform that which God has made impossible. . . . If we adopt the preamble, with Liberty and Justice, we must repudiate the enacting clauses, with Kidnapping and Slaveholding; . . . The Constitution of the United States:—What is it? Who made it? For whom and for what was it made? Is it from heaven or from men? . . . [W]e hold it to be a most cunningly-devised and wicked compact, demanding the most constant and earnest efforts of the friends of righteous freedom for its complete overthrow. It was "conceived in sin, and shapen in iniquity."[1]

The great American abolitionist and journalist William Lloyd Garrison would echo Douglass's comments, calling the U.S. Constitution "a covenant with death, and an agreement with hell."

The U.S. occupation of Iraq will end, one way or another.

The only question is when, and perhaps how. The American people will look back on this presidential adventure as folly. They may mourn the costs, or even ignore them. They will claim to "learn" from it, and then quickly dispatch it into the dark recesses of national memory. Soon, all too soon, it will be history, that most hated and ignored of subjects to Americans. Perhaps a new generation will dust off the dry tomes of the past and wonder, once again, how did such a thing come to pass?

Americans, perhaps more than other people, look less to the past to glean lessons. They are impatient and forward-thinking, with tomorrow on the radar scope; yesterday is all but forgotten.

They are thus ripe for the plucking when politicians unleash the fear card, to launch them once again into hell.

DEMOCRACY, DICTATORSHIPS AND EMPIRE

December 28, 2003

There is a profound contradiction at the heart of American political life: the claim to be a democracy, and the bitter struggle to deny that status to almost everyone else in the world, *all in the name of "bringing democracy" to the world.*

If there is one constant in American past and present history, it is the determination of the powerful elites in this country to impose their will upon that of other nations, against the wishes of the majority of people in foreign nations.

The American Empire utilizes force, brutal and terrifying, to intimidate the populations of other nations, and this, when alloyed with the mesmerizing power of the corporate press, serves to whitewash what is actually taking place.

When one looks at the present situation in Iraq, where the United States (on behalf of the whole world, we are assured) invades a sovereign nation, *which has not attacked the U.S.*, topples its government, bombs cities, and installs a puppet regime, we are assured (once again) that this is done for the Iraqis and *not* for U.S. corporations.

We have been here before—scores of times.

In 1915, the United States invaded nearby Haiti, ostensibly to deal with "violence" on the island. It dealt with it by bringing more. The U.S. Marines forced the Haitian Legislature to select the candidate the U.S. invaders wanted as president. When Haiti refused to declare war against Germany, the Americans dissolved the Haitian legislature! The Americans then pushed through a sham referendum for a new Haitian constitution— one far less democratic than the instrument it replaced. As for the so-called "referendum," under U.S. bayonets it passed by a ridiculous 98,225 to 768.

When Haitian nationalists rose up to oppose the northern invader some years later, the United States let loose a bloodbath, killing some 3,000 Haitians in the infamous Cacos Rebellion. George Barnett, a U.S. Marine general, would complain, "Practically indiscriminate killing of natives has gone on for some time." Barnett found this violent episode "startling."[1]

American troops put these proud people, who had forced two European powers (France and England) to surrender, in shackles on road crews, and dismantled Haitian homesteads to make room for large plantations. As Piero Gleijeses observed, "It is not that [President] Wilson failed in his earnest efforts to bring democracy to these little countries. He never tried. He intervened to impose hegemony, not democracy."[2]

Indeed, this is not a Haitian tale alone, for the U.S. invaded Cuba four times, Nicaragua five times, Honduras seven times, the Dominican Republic four times, Haiti twice, Guatemala once, Panama twice, Mexico three times, and Colombia four times—in the 36 years from 1898 to 1934 alone!

It went not to plant democracies, like they're some kind of tobacco plant, but to *remove* democracies, to prop up dictators, and to support repression.

Iraq is an inheritor to a grim and dark history that began in the Americas, spanned the Caribbean, and touched the region before. It brought the ignominious reign of the Shah to the "peacock throne" of Iran, tossing out a democratically elected president, Mohammed Mossadegh. Mossadegh's great offense? He dared to nationalize the vast oil resources of Iran. For this affront to the American oil merchants, the United States imposed the brutal and repressive dictatorship of the Shah, Reza Pahlevi, who turned the nation into a private fiefdom and a torture chamber. Indeed, it was hatred of the Shah that launched the Iranian Revolution and put the Ayatollah Khomeini in power there.

Similar forces are mobilizing in the Persian Gulf today to wipe out the Western-backed dictatorships that sit above unhappy, unstable quasi-states.

Americans, if they have any inkling of history, can no longer claim ignorance when it happens again.

53

"FLAWED INTELLIGENCE"

January 30, 2004

The formal war in Iraq has been over for months now, but the Occupation has not brought peace.

Now, after almost a year of fire, death and carnage, come the first signs of the truth, as a former weapons inspector, David Kay, announces to reporters and members of Congress, "We were almost all wrong."[1]

The deeply politicized weapons inspector announced that there were no weapons of mass destruction, the *casus belli* of the Iraq war, but it was, after all, a pretty good thing to wage war against the Hussein regime, because he was a "bad guy." As for President George W. Bush, he was not to blame, for he received "bad intelligence."

Amazing.

The function of a president, it seems to me, is not to "receive" but to decide; to exercise judgment; to use reason and balance in a world where missteps can cause global explosions. But Bush the Lesser isn't to blame. The CIA got it wrong, if Kay is to be believed.

The grim and unmistakable truth is that the president sits in the big chair to make important, life-and-death decisions. War is certainly one of the biggest decisions any political leader has to make. Bush blew it.

But Bush Lite isn't alone; the members of Congress, who voted away their constitutional responsibilities to their liege— er, I mean, president, are also to blame, for at a time when the nation needed real debate around such questions as these, Congress punted, and, in my view, failed.

Nor is that all. The nation's corporate media performed poorly in the weeks and months leading up to the Iraq War, as well as afterward. They acted largely as billboards and mega-phones for the administration, echoing and parroting whatever drivel came out of Washington, and added martial music and sexy graphics to make it sound and look better.

Who recalls the shoddy treatment accorded to the ex-weapons inspector Scott Ritter, who was essentially run off of network and cable news programs because he wouldn't address issues not related to the war?

According to one major U.S. news outfit, Ritter was "radio-active" because he wouldn't deign to discuss a slur thrown at him. Ritter, along with William Rivers Pitt, wrote a splendid little book that virtually predicted that no weapons would be found. *War on Iraq: What Team Bush Doesn't Want You to Know* debunks the whole range of Bush claims regarding Iraq's threat to its neighbors, the Kuwaiti invasion, and yes—weapons of mass destruction—which Ritter asserts were 90 to 95 percent destroyed after the first Gulf War of 1991. His co-author, Pitt, summarized the duo's arguments nicely:

> The case for war against Iraq has not been made. This is a fact. *It is doubtful in the extreme that Saddam Hussein has retained any functional aspect of the chemical, nuclear, and biological weapons programs so thoroughly dismantled by the United Nations weapons inspectors who worked tirelessly in Iraq for seven years.* This is also a fact. The idea that Hussein has connections to fundamentalist Islamic terrorists is laughable—he is a secular leader who has worked for years to crush fundamentalist Islam within Iraq, and if he were to give weapons of any kind to al Qaeda, they would use those weapons on him first.[2]

The American people should have known these facts be-fore their sons and daughters became cannon fodder for the Bush Regime in a war of occupation in Iraq. They should have known these things before 500 Americans and perhaps (we don't know exactly, because no one has counted!) some 10,000 Iraqis lost their lives. That they did not is testament to the failure of the corporate media, which serves Power, not the People.

Mao Tse-Tung used to say that "war is politics, by other means." The Bush Regime has waged war for its own political ends: the ability to say they did it, even against overwhelming world opinion. The Iraqis are but chess pieces in a globalist strategy of U.S. dominance over much of the region. But there is no peace, for there has been no justice.

54

IN THE SHADOW OF *BROWN*

April 29, 2004

It has been half a century since *Brown v. Board of Education* became law, the racial segregation of public schools was outlawed, and desegregation was ordered "with all deliberate speed."

When *Brown* was first decided, I was not yet born. Yet, despite the law that ruled segregation unconstitutional, my elementary, junior high, and high schools were institutions with over 95 percent—perhaps 98 percent—Black populations. Whites, whether as teachers or students, were quite rare, over a decade after *Brown* became law.

Years later, in my private studies, I learned that *Brown* wasn't decided because of the educational needs or violated rights of Black citizens, but because of the ideological needs of the U.S. government, which was trying to present a false face to the Third World, much of which was horrified at the images of dark-skinned people brutalized by racist cops for trying to get a decent education.

In 1952, U.S. Secretary of State Dean Acheson submitted a letter to the U.S. Supreme Court noting that "the continuation of racial discrimination is a source of constant embarrassment to this government . . . and it jeopardizes the effective maintenance of our moral leadership of the free and democratic nations of the world."[1]

Brown, then, was a propaganda victory, designed to defeat rhetorical attacks from the communist countries, which argued that the United States was a violent, racist nation.

It has been over 50 years since *Brown*, and ghetto schools from coast to coast, from North to South, are as segregated as they were in 1953. They are segregated not by law but by practice, as a class; poverty-stricken, they have few resources, increasingly poorly trained, poorly paid and demoralized teachers, and few educational expectations or outcomes of excellence.

Brown may be law on the books, but in the lives of millions of dark-skinned kids, it's barely an asterisk. It is meaningless.

The brilliant legal scholar Derrick Bell has long argued that *Brown* represents a prime example of what he calls "interest convergence," or an occasion when Blacks may benefit, but in order to do so, whites must benefit. Thus, under *Brown*, almost half of Black educators, especially in the South, lost their jobs. Whites were hired to replace them and also employed in the swell of private white academies that sprang up in opposition to the *Brown* decision.

Today, schools are but training grounds for prisons, and in an age of computerization and increasing outsourcing, they are struggling to find economic and social relevance. Writer Jonathan Kozol has written tellingly and touchingly of the deplorable conditions of urban schools, which are Black and Brown sinkholes of societal rejection, yet little has changed.

Members of the political elite love to kiss babies when they run for office, or even to offer empty words about "our children" when discussing them, but from coast to coast, "from sea to shining sea," urban public schools are places not of learning or of refuge, but of societal rejection and dismissal.

Their conditions and lack of sufficient resources reflect the subtle truth that they are engaged in a war against ignorance and forgetfulness about them and their futures. They are citizens, yes—youthful citizens who may be safely ignored, for they have no voice and no vote in the system.

Nothing is expected of them. They are consigned to the bitter fringes of the ghetto cash economy of all against all for sheer survival.

Let the bourgeoisie and the Black middle class celebrate *Brown*. Meanwhile, let the rest of us ignore it.

55

WHO "WE" ARE

May 29, 2004

When is a nation?
—Wole Soyinka, *The Open Sore of a*
Continent, 1996

With his dramatic, somewhat poetic turn of phrase, the Nigerian playwright and scholar-activist raises a question that resonates far beyond the borders of his West African homeland.

His question asks, almost in poetic code, "What do we mean when we claim the relationship of nationality?" "What binds us together?" And ultimately, "Who are 'we'?" In times of crisis, conflict and controversy, we learn that the "we" used by leaders is often different from the one used by people who live in a shared polity. In the United States, when a politician spoke of "we," for centuries that term meant "citizen," and thus by custom, law and definition, white men of property.

It therefore excluded the vast majority of human beings who shared the nation-space: women (who were probably the majority); Indians; Africans; poor, propertyless white men; and, at times, Catholics, Jews and Mormons.

From the earliest days of the U.S. Republic, Chinese were legally excluded from citizenship. In 1790, in fact, just months after the ratification of the U.S. Constitution, Congress would limit naturalization to "any alien, being a free white person who shall have resided within the limits and under the jurisdiction of the United States for a term of two years."[1] For the next 150 years, people who were Hindus, Sikhs, Mexicans, Japanese, Syrians, Arabs, Polynesians and many others were defined as non-whites by law, and therefore denied American citizenship, the right to vote, the right to a passport, and the right to testify in court (especially against whites!).

It took decades of struggle, and hard-fought social movements, to move the bar from such a ludicrous definition of citizenship. For many Americans, that bar has never moved. Who we *are*, then, is not who we were, for the notion of American citizenship is a changing thing; it is built by the struggles of many.

Yet it is also true that, far too often, the dark mirror of who we are can be seen in the color photos emerging from the gulags of Abu Ghraib prison in Iraq.

We are addicted to humiliating the weak.

We are hierarchical (meaning we follow the orders of those in power, even if the order is evil).

We are unfeeling to the pain and terror of others (especially if the Other is perceived as non-white, such as Arabs).

Much has been made of the Abu Ghraib photographs that spawned this scandal, yet how many of us know that several of the accused actually sent photos to their friends who were stateside, apparently proud of how they treated the cowering "towel-heads" in Iraq?

Another truth about who "we" are? We are racist.

That's the America that emerges from the glorious army of the republic, which is often touted as the greatest exemplar of racial peace and harmony in the nation.

It doesn't matter that perhaps a third of that army is African American and Hispanic, or that perhaps 15 percent of U.S. Army personnel are female. If we have learned anything, it is that ideas, ways of looking at the world, cross racial, linguistic and gender barriers. Members of institutions adopt certain ways of looking at those deemed Others.

Today, after September 11, Arabs and Muslims are Others.

Thus the horrific racist, depraved, humiliating treatment of those in Abu Ghraib. They are Other; Else, less than . . .

and therefore, subjected to treatment that can only be deemed barbarous.

Abu Ghraib is *us*.

56

"TRUE AMERICAN VALUES"

June 8, 2004

Such practices do not reflect our values.

—G.W. Bush

After the guilty plea of U.S. Specialist Jeremy Sivits to charges arising from the torture scandal at Abu Ghraib prison in Iraq, the shaping of the whitewash is almost clear.

Sivits has apparently made a deal that both he and his bosses can live with: the tortures, both physical and mental, of Iraqi detainees took place because of the actions of the "little guys," not the brass, for, in his words, "If they saw that was going on, there would be hell to pay." Sivits thus clears the higher-ups and gets a break by way of a "special" court-martial, as opposed to a "general" one, which dramatically lessens his possible sentences.

In fact, as we've learned from the International Committee of the Red Cross (ICRC), torture has been documented in U.S.-controlled prison camps in Iraq since at least March— of 2003. Over a year ago, the ICRC president met with U.S. Secretary of State Colin Powell and National Security Adviser Condoleezza Rice, as well as Deputy Defense Secretary Paul Wolfowitz, to insist that the U.S. government cease the systematic torture of people in their Iraqi prisons. According to the *Baltimore Sun*, Powell said he fully briefed President Bush about these ICRC reports.

The government, after the ICRC findings, announced through U.S. Defense Secretary Donald Rumsfeld that the United States would not be bound by Geneva Conventions, as it was involved in a war against terror, and the regular rules need not apply. Moreover, it selected a man named Lane

McCotter, a private prison company executive, to run the now-notorious Abu Ghraib gulag on the outskirts of Baghdad. The United States chose a man who worked for a company under investigation by the U.S. Justice Department following brutality charges against it: Management & Training Corporation.

Before his career at M&T took off, McCotter headed the Utah state prison system, until a scandal forced him to resign from his post in 1997. A naked prisoner had been shackled to a chair in one of his prisons for 16 hours, until he died. Working for the prison was a psychiatrist who wrote prescriptions for drug addicts and whose medical license was on probation. When McCotter joined M&T, it was the nation's third-largest private prison company, with 13 prisons and an unenviable record of brutality. Whatever can be said of McCotter, it can't be said that he wasn't qualified for the violence and depredations that would emerge at Abu Ghraib. Who better to run this colonial outpost of barbarity than one who ran internal gulags, both for the State and for the Dollar?

In a January 2004 interview, McCotter announced that Abu Ghraib "is the only place we agreed as a team was truly closest to an American prison."[1] And so it was, with violence, brutality, beatings, torture and state-sanctioned sadism. It is, preeminently, America's cultural gift to the people of Iraq. It demonstrates U.S. domination, U.S. repression, U.S. violence and U.S. contempt.

In December 2003, U.S. Lt. Col. Nathan Sassman gave the *New York Times* a unique insight into the mindset of U.S. occupation forces when he said: "With a heavy dose of fear and violence . . . I think we can convince these people that we are here to help them."[2]

The pictures from Abu Ghraib (those that Americans have been allowed to view, that is) have certainly shown the "heavy dose of fear and violence." The United States has launched this mad, imperial exercise to gain a beachhead on the shores of Dar ul-Islam (the realm of Islam) from which to pluck the duck—ripe fruits of oil wealth from the earth.

In the name of "freedom," Americans have supported dictators, only to discard them when they outlived their usefulness (think Noriega, the Shah, etc.). They, like every empire before them, are bound by the chains of avarice and economic interests. This is what a petro-war looks like.

57

ANOTHER RONALD REAGAN, ANOTHER AMERICA

June 9, 2004

For God's sake, let us sit upon the ground, And tell sad stories of the death of kings . . .
—William Shakespeare, *Richard II*

The recent passage of the 40th U.S. president, Ronald Wilson Reagan, into eternity has sparked a media frenzy, as well as a ruling-class attempt at historical revisionism that repositions him as a virtual reincarnation of Abraham Lincoln. Lincoln was cast as the Great Emancipator; Reagan, the Great Communicator.

There are many, however, both within and without the United States, who have a far different view of the Reagan years. They saw behind the actor to the scriptwriters, who often toiled in the shadows of Wall Street and who supported the former California governor from his earliest days, when he began to betray his class. Reagan's ascension to the presidency came after a career as an FBI snitch, when, as head of the Screen Actors Guild, he named names to the nefarious J. Edgar Hoover of those suspected of being "Reds." His political career was built upon this foundation of betrayal of the class he was born into, his fellow workers in Hollywood, his former political party, and those "fellow Americans" who had the misfortune to be born without silver spoons in their mouths.

As California Governor he supported a vicious war against the Black Panther Party and the entire Black Liberation movement, to curry favor with the core of his political support, white nationalists. He sparked the deepening of the poisonous prison-industrial complex that continues to ricochet across America.

His allegiance to Wall Street, and his antipathy for poor and working-class Americans, can best be seen in the economic policies that favored the former and beggared the latter, by the transfer of public monies from social programs to fund the military-industrial complex, in a plan to spend the former Soviets into the ground. This he did, but it also sent the U.S. economy into freefall.

As scholars Frances Fox Piven and Richard Cloward noted in their classic study *The New Class War*, Reagan's policies amounted to an "attack on the welfare state," seeking to undermine labor and the poor, to the benefit of the wealthy. Reagan launched incessant assaults on all sorts of social programs, for, as Piven and Cloward explained: "The income-maintenance programs are coming under assault because they limit profits by enlarging the bargaining power of workers with employers."[1]

Reagan was indeed an actor, one whose performance attracted the support of people who voted against their own interests.

But perhaps the greatest tragedy of the Reagan era may be the deep suffering of the poor and working people of Latin America. There, Reagan unleashed a terrorist army of psychopaths who ravaged the nations of Nicaragua, El Salvador, Honduras and beyond. Reagan, ever the actor, tried to paint the so-called Contras as "freedom fighters," whom he likened to "our Founding Fathers." They were, in fact, mostly members of the dreaded Guardia Nacional, the former Nicaraguan dictator Anastasio Somoza's henchmen, who were described by the Colombian diplomat Clara Nieto as "nothing more than gangs of terrorists and assassins."[2]

The Reagan administration, stung by critics, rushed to change the image of the Contras and used the CIA to create a nicer-seeming Contra movement. It unleashed a group that waged U.S.-supported atrocities against the country. This group, called by some the "Key Biscayne Mafia," erected "its own courts, its own prisons, its own torture chambers and clandestine cemeteries where it buried those it executed," according to Nieto.

This U.S.-supported echo of "our Founding Fathers" threw corpses into the river and operated terror centers where, Nieto writes, "Women were raped daily."[3] To fund the Contras, his administration broke the law. Their goal, according to Reagan, was to get the Nicaraguan government to "say 'Uncle.'"

There may be millions in the "other America," América Latina, who view the passing of "The Great Communicator" far differently from the version reflected in the media, but they are invisible.

58.

AMERICA: INDEPENDENT?

July 3, 2004

Once again, Americans will gather at parades, in parks, in bars and at home to celebrate the Fourth of July holiday, a date marking American Independence.

Politicians will add heat to the summer air with lofty, lying oaths to "the People" about freedom, liberty and "the American way." President George W. Bush (whom writer and critic Arundhati Roy deliciously calls "Bush the Lesser") will doubtless give a variation of his threadbare stump speech, about "freedom" or "American values" or some other kind of blather that some extremely well-paid aide has written for him to poorly deliver. Americans, delirious on the "day of independence," will exercise their freedom by getting drunk and eating until they pass out from the carbo-protein load.

Several days ago, the U.S. Supreme Court decided the long-awaited *Hamdi v. Rumsfeld* case and *Rasul v. Bush*, dealing with multinational detainees held in the Guantánamo Bay U.S. naval brig. In *Hamdi*, Supreme Court Justice Sandra Day O'Connor wrote, for the court's majority, "We have long made clear that a state of war is not a blank check when it comes to the rights of the nation's citizens." The majority opinion added, "The threats to military operations posed by a basic system of independent review are not so weighty as to trump a citizen's core rights to challenge meaningfully the government's case and to be heard by an independent adjudicator."

The *Hamdi* and *Rasul* opinions seem to open the courthouse door to hundreds of people accused of being so-called "enemy combatants" by the Bush administration. The rulings caused an explosion of praise from the media elite and others,

• *175*

such as lawyers and law professors, who praised the Court as the greatest protectors of U.S. liberty against tyranny.

Lost in the applause, however, was a ruling endorsed by a majority (five members) of the Court: the government can detain Americans—such as Vasser Hamdi, who is, after all, an American citizen—because of the U.S. president's declaration of "enemy combatant" status, and the congressional resolution supporting the president, made after September 11.

Several days before Independence Day, the nation's highest court ruled that Americans can be detained without trial and without charges, for an undetermined period of time, as long as a habeas corpus writ, an order summoning the defendant to court, was available at the time of arrest.

I don't know about you, but I find this breathtaking.

Americans are about as "free" as the president allows them to be. Happy Independence Day!

"Independence" in a nation where more than two million people—men, women and children—are held in prisons. The most imprisoned people on earth!

Happy Independence Day! Where, for Black Americans, driving, jogging, walking and standing still on your own doorstep—while Black—is far too often a capital crime.

Happy Independence Day! Where "independence" of the mind, by a true, liberating education, is virtually impossible for millions of Black, Brown and poor white kids—in the richest nation in the history of the world.

Happy Independence Day! When the government, under the so-called "Patriot Act," can rifle through the notes, files and papers of people, at will.

Happy Independence Day—indeed.

Americans can celebrate "independence day," but they can't celebrate independence. The government is increasingly intrusive, growing more and more so every single day.

We would do well to heed the wisdom of the great German

writer Johann Wolfgang von Goethe, who observed: "None are more hopelessly enslaved than those who falsely believe they are free."

59·

WHAT WOULD
THOMAS PAINE THINK?

August 18, 2004

The voting is over in Venezuela, and the U.S.-supported right wing lost—badly. Over 60 percent of Venezuelans voted to keep President Hugo Chávez in power, despite the opposition of the wealthiest segments of Venezuelan society.

Venezuelan society is one of extreme contrasts of rich and poor. Sixty-seven percent of Venezuelans live in poverty; 35 percent live in extreme poverty.

The opposition to Chávez came from those like owners and managers of Coca-Cola, where workers were intimidated and fired for voting against an earlier recall. The main economic support of the anti-Chávez movement came from—guess where?—the man who owns Venezuela's subsidiary of Coca-Cola, billionaire Gustavo Cisneros, the guy who also owns the nation's largest TV network, which has been on an anti-Chávez campaign for years.

Chávez has enemies among the wealthy because he has supported using Venezuela's vast oil wealth to try to rectify the nation's staggering social problems. Some three-quarters of Venezuelans are unemployed or work on the margins in the informal economy.

In the view of the very wealthy, the resources of the nation should be privatized and sent along the usual routes—north. They are not social resources but private ones, to be owned and sold. They deeply oppose Chávez's plan to share the wealth.

What Chávez is trying to do is deepen a kind of social revolution among the poor, using the name and nationalist spirit of the greatest Venezuelan of them all—Simón Bolívar—to rally and mobilize Venezuelans for *bolivarismo*, in strong support of the nation against the imperialists to the North.

That's why he is being demonized in the Western and corporate media. Prepare for more of it—soon. For while the voting may be over, the battle to exploit Venezuela's natural resources ain't.

An early American revolutionary, Thomas Paine, wrote in his 1791 classic, *Rights of Man*, about the kinds of guys who stir up conflicts in nations for their own ends. Two hundred years later, he seemed to be talking about Americans when he wrote:

> That there are men in all countries who get their living by war, and by keeping up the quarrels of Nations, is as shocking as it is true; but when those who are concerned in the government of a country, make it their study to sow discord, and cultivate prejudices between Nations, it becomes the more unpardonable.

When Paine scribbled these words, he was probably criticizing his birthplace, England. He was always critical of what he saw as imperial arrogance, and of England's attempts to stir up enmity between America and France.

What would this radical writer and anti-imperialist think of the American Empire, with its armies in more than 120 countries?

What would Paine think of the nefarious Central Intelligence Agency, whose main job is to "sow discord" among nations?

What would this American revolutionary think of the Rebirth of Rome on the Potomac?

What would he think about an America that tried, unsuccessfully, to spark a coup in Venezuela several years ago, because oil companies and money men didn't want that country to spend its national wealth on the nation's poor? Would he find in Señor Presidente Chávez, and his struggle to empower the poor, an enemy or an ally?

The United States has consistently treated its neighbors in Latin America like something on the bottom of one's shoe—as something repellent. It has treated them the way Rome treated Carthage, or Greece, or Britain.

This is not an America that Paine would recognize or support.

In fact, if he were alive, he'd still be a revolutionary, but one determined to oppose this new empire, the Empire of Wealth and Greed—the Empire of Capital.[1]

60

VOTING FOR YESTERYEAR: ALABAMA DREAMIN'

December 9, 2004

Much has been written and said about the recent elections, and about the "values" driving certain segments of the nation to the polls.

Hidden in the steamy land of Alabama, voters were poised to begin the 21st century by voting to repeal a part of the state's constitution that dated back to the 1954 *Brown v. Board of Education* case. Shortly after *Brown* was decided, ordering desegregation in the nation's public schools, political leaders in Alabama had moved to enact new amendments to the state constitution that starkly opposed the Supreme Court decision. The amendments read as follows:

> Separate schools shall be provided for white and colored children, and *no child of either race shall be permitted to attend a school of the other race.*
>
> To avoid confusion and disorder and to promote effective and economical planning for education, the legislature may authorize the parents or guardians of minors, who desire that such minors shall attend schools provided for their own race, to make election to that end, such election to be effective for such period and to such extent as the legislature may provide.
>
> But nothing in this Constitution shall be construed as creating or recognizing any right to education or training at public expense, nor as limiting the authority and duty of the legislature in furthering or providing for education, to require conditions or

procedures deemed necessary to the preservation of peace and order.[1]

The voters were asked to repeal this obviously unconstitutional and, indeed, racist language from Alabama's state constitution by voting for Amendment 2. According to Alabama press reports, 1.38 million votes were cast in the vote on Amendment 2, and the opponents, led by former State Supreme Court Chief Justice Roy Moore, won the day, by 1,850 votes.

That means that legalized racial segregation is still a part of Alabama's constitution.

Under Alabama law, any vote margin less than one-half of one percent activates an automatic recount. No matter the result of the recount, that Amendment 2 could lose at all, in November 2004, gives us deep insights into the thinking of some of the modern American electorate.

While opponents of the repeal charged that it would open the door to new, higher taxes for education by what Justice Moore and his followers called "left-wing judges," many believe it really reflects what it seems to reflect—deep and abiding racist feelings in the hearts of white Alabamans toward their Black fellow citizens. (I mean, c'mon, how many "left-wing judges" do you think are in Alabama? Two?) Of course, this is but one state, a relatively poor Southern state (only seven states have a lower annual per-capita personal income than Alabama's $22,946), but how many of us would have predicted that a repeal of such overtly unlawful constitutional provisions would have lost in 2004?

There is within the American soul a deep wish to go back to the old days, often called the "good ole days," when things were not good for millions of people born in this land. Feelings such as these no doubt fueled the vote for George W. Bush, as well as other conservatives. This viewpoint, which is at the heart of white nationalism, longs for a mythic halcyon past, a past of whiteness. We don't like to admit this these days, but it is the truth. We are supposed to be living in a "color-blind" society, one where race does not matter and we all enjoy the same rights, immunities and privileges.

The great W.E.B. Du Bois, in (one of) his classic(s), *Black Reconstruction* (1935), wrote about the American predilection to rewrite history with nice, sweet lies:

> One is astonished in the study of history at the recurrence of the idea that evil must be forgotten, distorted, skimmed over. We must not remember that Daniel Webster got drunk but only remember that he was a splendid constitutional lawyer. We must forget that George Washington was a slave owner . . . and simply remember the things we regard as creditable and inspiring. The difficulty, of course, with this philosophy is that history loses its value as an incentive and example; it paints perfect men and noble nations, but it does not tell the truth.

We should not be surprised at what happened in Alabama. It is but an echo of our history.

61.

WHEN THE PRISON GOES INTERNATIONAL

April 2, 2005

Thanks for your kind invitation to join the "Attica to Abu Ghraib" Conference: *Ona MOVE!*

When we think about the atrocities of Attica and the abominations at Abu Ghraib, we are sometimes caught searching for a common denominator. What could it be?, we wonder, as we look at the brutal state assault on both prisoners and staff at Attica [in 1971], and the human rights violations and, yes, torture, that marked American behavior at Abu Ghraib prison in Iraq.

The commonalities, however, are more than first meets the eye. Of course, they are both prisons (but that's obvious). They both came to public consciousness through the actions of people who were prison guards. And they both were, initially, defended by the state with a flood of lies.

What matters least, really, is that they occurred in different countries. They both happened in the same empire. What marked the differences between them is the critical element of time, and even this quality does not speak well of things to come. For, as time is the difference, yet it tells us how far things have fallen, how the 30 years between Attica and Abu Ghraib have marked a coarsening of American character and a brutishness in imperial defenders.

Attica opened up an era of prison reform across much of the nation and fueled the movement to attempt to eradicate the most depraved elements of the nation's repressive prison systems. The Abu Ghraib revelations were met by quasi-official justifications, government obfuscation and the incredible spectacle of right-wing pundits likening the torture and human rights abuses there to "college pranks." The humiliation of naked Arab men was compared to the field displays of cheerleading squads!

There is, of course, another monstrous difference: the architects of Abu Ghraib, and high-level defenders of torture, have been rewarded by higher and more prestigious posts in government. In a nutshell, torture pays! We have not spoken of the pivotal American issue of race. Without prisoners actively advocating Black liberation, there would have been no Attica. The tortured, maimed and humiliated prisoners at Abu Ghraib were targeted by the U.S. Army because it sought to intimidate and eliminate people who were trying to fight to free their country from foreign occupiers. In other words, they were fighting for their own national liberation. In an empire, which picks puppets for other nations, this is not acceptable. It wasn't acceptable under the Roman Empire, the British Empire or its North American successor, the American Empire.

To this latest global incarnation of the White Nation, Arabs are but sand niggers to be beaten into submission and obedience. It is the refusal to accept this status that is fueling what the U.S. media calls "the insurgency." There is another element that arises from the evidence: American cruelty. Big Black, the late veteran of Attica, told stories of the torture and beatings that he endured, naked and held under gunpoint. It is an eerie precursor to the treatment of Arab prisoners at Abu Ghraib. Nor is it mere coincidence that some of the most brutal, most vicious actors at Abu Ghraib were U.S. Reserves who, in their civilian lives, were prison guards. How else could they learn it? One of the most infamous was a man from supermax prison SCI-Greene in southwestern Pennsylvania, named Charles Graner. Recently his ex-wife came forward to tell of the terrors to which she was exposed daily. She said Graner promised to cut her into little pieces, and that no one would ever find her body.

Welcome to U.S. "corrections" as the Prison Nation goes global.

LYNNE STEWART SPEAKS

May 15, 2005

Attorney Lynne Stewart has a long and distinguished career as a radical lawyer who has worked on cases that most lawyers look down their noses at.

Today, for taking on the case of the blind Egyptian cleric Sheikh Omar Abdel-Rahman, a man charged with inspiring the first bombing of the World Trade Center, and for trying to defend his case publicly, Stewart, along with her colleagues and co-defendants, professional Arabic translator Mohammed Yousry and paralegal Ahmed Abdel Sattar, stands convicted of aiding and abetting terrorism.

At the heart of the case, almost unbelievably, are prison regulations called Special Administrative Measures (SAMs), which are designed to isolate prisoners. Stewart and the other lawyers signed these regulations, never thinking that the state would use these rules, put in place by the U.S. Bureau of Prisons, to interfere with legal representation of their client.

Of course, they were wrong, and in a recent interview Stewart explained what lay behind the convictions:

> I really do think there was a pervasive fear out there.
> I think that the government—you know, when we talk about fascism, we talk about textbook fascism, but really it's an emotion more than anything else— and I think that the jury bought into "we have to protect the country, and the way to do that is to back the government." You know, it's classic to say, "If we do what the government tells us, if we do what the government thinks best, then we will be safe." Which raises that other question, doesn't it, about

whether an empire abroad can ever have a democracy at home.[1]

Stewart explained the alleged basis of the SAMs violation:

After Sheikh Omar was convicted, he was sent to the middle of America and that wasn't good enough for the government, so they imposed on him these very harsh prison regulations. . . . He was only allowed one phone call a month to his family and one a week to his lawyers, and that was it. He was not allowed to communicate with the media at all. And there were various other things as well: no outside visitors who were not family, not even for religious reasons. So these very, very restrictive regulations were put in place. And then the lawyers, all of us, myself, Ramsey Clark, Abdeen Jabara, we all were asked to sign on that we were aware that he was under those and that we would abide by them. But it was our thinking: well, of course, these prison regulations cannot interfere with the legal work. And so as a result we did what we thought we had to do for the client, that is, keeping him advised of those events and things that would influence his case and be important for him to know and understand. . . .

[So] they put these very harsh regulations; one of them included the media. And, of course, what I did was I made a press release just as we had been doing for the last four years. And it was only after September 11th that this act, which had been done in 2000, suddenly became actionable in the government's eyes. I always like to talk about, you know, they're moving the line. You know they talk about I crossed the line, but they moved the line after September 11th, and then they moved it again, of course, to get this conviction by bringing in all sorts of extraneous, but very prejudicial, things.

"Prejudicial," like a videotape of the notorious Osama bin Laden being shown to the New York jury!

With such tactics as these, we should be surprised that we were surprised, that she, Yousry and Sattar were convicted.

Stewart, Yousry and Sattar are planning vigorous appeals, and Stewart has been supported by groups such as the National Lawyers Guild and the National Association of Criminal Defense Lawyers.

Some of the more tony and wealthy law firms have been somewhat slower to support Stewart, but even conservatives like Judge Andrew Napolitano, in a *New York Times* op-ed piece, called the convictions a "perverse victory in the Justice Department's assault on the Constitution." Napolitano, a frequent Fox News contributor, wrote: "In the good old days, only Congress could write federal criminal laws. After 9/11, however, the attorney general was allowed to do so. Where in the Constitution does it allow that?"[2]

Well said. But to paraphrase Tina Turner, "What's the Constitution got to do with it?" The law is an instrument of politics and power.

Lynne Stewart transgressed *politically*, not legally, and the trial was but a formality. The U.S. Constitution, like the Declaration of Independence, is endlessly invoked but often ignored when it comes to how courts really rule, and how life is really lived. It's up to people, folks like you, to organize to make change a reality. Words on paper have never sufficed.

Support Lynne Stewart, Mohammed Yousry and Ahmed Abdel Sattar!

63

WHITEWASHING WHITE CRIMES

May 28, 2005

Abu Ghraib. Guantánamo. Bagram. Diego García . . .
Words have power, and what these words evoke is precisely what American policy makers want to evoke: terror.

The international human rights group Amnesty International recently called the infamous Abu Ghraib prison in Iraq "the gulag of our times."

The reference to the torture chambers and repressive Siberian prisons of the old Soviet Union, marked by the term "gulag," was remarkable. It was also correct.

Predictably, White House mouthpieces dismissed the report as "ridiculous," saying that they brought "liberty" to the people of Iraq. Also remarkable, and in a perverse way, correct. In 2004, U.S. Major General Geoffrey Miller, the American commander in charge of detentions and interrogations at Abu Ghraib prison, conducted a press tour of the dreary facility to proudly announce newly renovated sections of the joint, which he dubbed "Camp Redemption" and "Camp Liberty."

At the height of the Civil Rights movement, while Black and white youth tried to register voters in the Deep South, they faced naked white terrorism from the Ku Klux Klan and police (who were often one and the same). In movement offices throughout the region could be found posters with the following message:

There's a street in Itta Bena called Freedom. *There's a town in Mississippi called Liberty.* There's a department in Washington called Justice.

Words like "liberty," "freedom" and "democracy" are just words.

In Iraq, and in America, they are often used to mask the truth that lies behind them.

The spring 2005 issue of *Covert Action Quarterly* has a harrowing article by law professor Marjorie Cohn, who draws the dotted lines between the torture, brutality, humiliations and repression of Abu Ghraib and the White House, the Department of Defense and other U.S. government agencies. Using sources like Seymour Hersh's book *Chain of Command: The Road from 9/11 to Abu-Ghraib*,[1] Cohn leaves little question about how high the crimes of Abu Ghraib rise. She also cites a CIA analyst who went to Guantánamo in the late summer of 2002 and, after interviewing 30 detainees, "came back convinced that we were committing war crimes in Guantánamo."

And, of course, it's not just there.

Think of the thousands of people thrown in Abu Ghraib by the Americans. The Red Cross has documented that *70 percent to 90 percent* of those people were there by mistake. There in that hellhole, by mistake, where rape, sodomy with foreign objects, the use of unmuzzled dogs to bite and severely injure handcuffed prisoners, and beating prisoners to death have all been documented. Women prisoners have begged their families to smuggle in poison so that they can kill themselves, to escape the humiliations they have suffered.

A military consultant with ties to Special Ops told Seymour Hersh that war crimes were committed in Iraq with utterly no repercussions. He asked rhetorically, "What do you call it when people are tortured and going to die, and the soldiers know it, but do not treat their injuries?" The consultant replied, "Execution."[2] The White House would call this "liberty."

Months ago, I wrote that if anyone would be punished for the actions at Abu Ghraib, it would be low-level people, those with the least power.

I have no expertise in Iraq or the Middle East, particularly. But I know a thing or two about prisons, and about whitewashes.

It is not in the least surprising that the United States would export the worst features of its prison culture abroad.

These are Bush's prisons, Rumsfeld's prisons, Gonzalez's prisons; *these are America's prisons*, and those who are tortured, raped, humiliated and traumatized have this done in your name.

Who will solve these war crimes?

64

SUPREME COURT JUSTICE CALLS SYSTEM "BROKEN"

August 7, 2005

It was something of a surprise to hear a radio report that a Justice of the U.S. Supreme Court, John Paul Stevens, harshly criticized the American death penalty and called the criminal justice system "broken."

That doesn't happen often.

It reminded me of the late Supreme Court Justice Harry Blackmun, who in 1994 issued a stirring dissenting opinion in a case called *Callins v. Collins*, in which he vowed to no longer "tinker with the machinery of death."

While Stevens apparently didn't go as far as his late colleague, his comments seem to echo Blackmun's observations.

Unfortunately, as with Blackmun, it is doubtful that Stevens's comments presage a wholehearted repudiation of the U.S. death penalty scheme.

In summarizing Blackmun's view, international law scholar and attorney William A. Schabas recently wrote in his book *The Death Penalty as Cruel Treatment and Torture*:

> The endeavor was a failure; it was not possible to eliminate arbitrariness from imposition of the death penalty, and consequently any capital punishment statutes breached the guarantee against cruel punishment found in the Eighth Amendment. Justice Blackmun said the Court had already virtually conceded that fairness and rationality could not be achieved in the administration of the death penalty, in *McClesky v. Kemp* (a case decided in 1987).[1]

But what Blackmun said, no matter how moving and rare, was not law. It was but a footnote to the law, a hope that one day, a majority of the Court would agree with him.

Stevens has apparently begun the trek toward agreement, although he isn't quite there yet. There is a vast difference between making a public speech and writing a judicial opinion. It is more to convince four other justices to agree with you.

That day is not yet here.

I wish it were otherwise, but—*c'est la vie*—there it is.

The current politics of the nation, joined with the ages of many sitting justices, also does not support the theory that such change is remotely imminent.

It is also true that, from the very year that the U.S. death penalty was reinstated in *Gregg v. Georgia* (1976), the Supreme Court has erected, maintained, expanded, repaired and endlessly "tinkered with" the U.S. death machinery. It is their creation, which, like a Frankenstein monster, lumbers on and on.

In the *Callins* case dissent, the late Justice Blackmun noted, as he neared his retirement:

> [D]espite the efforts of the States and courts to devise legal formulas and procedural rules to meet this daunting challenge, the death penalty remains fraught with arbitrariness, discrimination, caprice and mistake. . . . [T]he problems that were pursued down one hole with procedural rules and verbal formulas have come to the surface somewhere else, just as virulent and pernicious as they were in their original form.[2]

Eleven years after *Callins*, another Justice appears to agree (at least partially). In another 50 years, who knows?

Justice Blackmun, nearing retirement and knowing his days were dwindling down to few, issued an impassioned plea for change. A decade later, another Justice inches toward his view, as he, too, must surely contemplate retirement, and the great demise.

So the System is broken.

That much, many people have come to know.

Shall we continue to "tinker with the machinery of death"?

65.

ROSA PARKS, CLAUDETTE COLVIN
AND JO ANN ROBINSON

October 25, 2005

The death of civil rights icon Mrs. Rosa Parks, at the age of 92, has become a national event, with media outlets running retrospectives about the Montgomery Bus Boycott, which sparked the rise of the late Rev. Dr. Martin Luther King Jr. and the birth of the modern Civil Rights movement.

This, in this moment of familial and social loss, is yet a good thing, for it teaches and reminds the young of how things were in an America that they did not live in. Mrs. Parks rightly deserved the accolades and honors heaped upon her for the great and noble role she played in a mass movement that touched the lives of millions.

Yet, unless one reads the work of Black and radical historians, we would not know that Mrs. Parks wasn't the first Black woman who refused to give her seat to a white man, nor the first to be arrested for refusing to do so.

In December 1955, an organizer of the Women's Political Counsel, Jo Ann Robinson, went into action within hours of Mrs. Parks's arrest, working the phone tree and then writing a leaflet that went out throughout the city, which read:

Another Negro woman has been arrested and thrown in jail, because she refused to get up out of her seat on the bus for a white person to sit down. It is the second time, since the Claudette Colvin case, that a Negro woman has been arrested for the same thing. This has to be stopped. Negroes have rights too, for if Negroes did not ride the buses, they could not operate.

Three-fourths of the riders are Negroes, yet we are arrested or have to stand over empty seats. If we do not do something to stop these arrests, they will continue. The next time it may be you, or your daughter, or mother. This woman's case will come up on Monday. We are therefore asking every Negro to stay off the buses Monday in protest of the arrest and trial. Don't ride the bus to work, to town, to school, or anywhere on Monday. You can afford to stay out of school for one day if you have no other way to go except by bus. You can also afford to stay out of town for one day. If you work, take a cab, or walk. But please, children and grown-ups, don't ride the bus at all on Monday. Please stay off all buses Monday.[1]

Without Jo Ann Robinson's activism, who would know of Rosa Parks? What if she, or her Women's Political Counsel, had done nothing? What if she hadn't activated the phone tree, or written and then distributed this leaflet, and what if Black folks in Montgomery, by the hundreds, thousands and more, hadn't responded to those leaflets?

People build movements one by one, in tens, hundreds, thousands and eventually millions, and Claudette Colvin, this poor woman, lost not only her seat and her dignity but was later tossed in a mental institution. Few remember this woman's name. Yet her contribution, which would set the stage for Parks, was immense, and none of us can deny the power of Montgomery and how it electrified the nation.

On Thursday, December 1, 2005, a number of organizations, unions and activists are calling for a Rosa Parks 50th Anniversary Nationwide Strike, to shut the war down. On that day, they're calling for no school, no shopping, no work, not only to mark Rosa Parks's refusal to give up her seat, but as a nationwide strike against poverty, racism and war. Organizers include the Million Worker March movement, the Troops Out Now Coalition, Black Workers for Justice and a wide, diverse group of organizations and leaders.

When asked about the bus boycott, Parks said, "The only thing that bothered me was that we waited so long to make this protest." It's been 50 years since her heroic stand in Montgomery against the racist system of segregation. Today, in the brutal aftermath of Hurricane Katrina, it is past time for protests against poverty, racism and the scourge of war. People joining together make movements.

66

WHAT KIDS ARE REALLY LEARNING IN SCHOOL

November 26, 2005

On November 2, 2005, kids across the nation joined protests organized by The World Can't Wait, which called for walkouts to support the demand for an end to the Bush Regime.

One of those who answered the call was a 10th grader named Geovany Serrano. A student at L.A.'s Belmont High, Geovany passed out fliers and tried to organize his fellow students to support the walkout. When administrators learned of the plan, they launched an attack on the youth, grabbing him, blasting him with pepper spray and arresting him! He was hauled into the infamous Los Angeles Police Department's Rampart Station, taken to Juvenile Hall and fingerprinted.

This 10th grader is now under house arrest, forced to wear an ankle bracelet, simply for trying to organize his fellow students in opposition to the Bush Regime. Guess what *this* kid has learned about "constitutional rights" of free speech, free association, and the rights to assemble and protest?

Despite these events, Geovany has definitely learned some important lessons, ones that never would've fit a classroom. He wrote recently:

> Look at the war in Iraq. There are jails where there are people that the government just wants to disappear. They have them there and are torturing them and putting them on leashes. They're bombing the sh-- out of people's houses. . . . When I first got into this it hit me so hard. It's hard to go back to living a regular day, knowing that there are people that are

being killed and victimized by the system is so difficult. Is that the world I want? No, I don't want none
of that.[1]

At Granada Hills High, another student was hauled into
the Dean's office for wearing a World Can't Wait sticker on
his T-shirt. When the Dean told him to remove his T-shirt
because school wasn't the place for voicing political beliefs, the
student replied, "If you want me to take off the sticker, then I
have to take everything off as well." He promptly stripped to
his skivvies, and told the Dean: "You can take my clothes and
my sticker, but!—you can't take what I believe in my heart."

What teacher wouldn't give her right arm to have students so committed and involved in the world around them?
Students who dare to care more about the world they'll inhabit
than what they'll wear to the prom?

At L.A.'s Reseda High, student leader Sara Escuerdo was
slapped with a two-day suspension for organizing a walkout
and threatened with arrest for possession of World Can't Wait
stickers! She was also threatened with transfer, until hundreds
of outraged parents and teachers deluged the principal's office
with calls of protest. Escuerdo wrote on worldcantwait.com:

We owe it to the millions of people that are getting
tortured, getting murdered, and suffering around the
world to do this. Resist or Die—It has come down
to that slogan. . . . Right now, the future is in everybody's hands. It is up to us. The question is what
kind of world do you want to live in? Will you accept
everything this regime stands for? If you don't, then
you must join this movement.

The great behavioral psychologist Carl Rogers once said
that the function of school is to provide "learning to be free."
What do you think these kids are learning from admin-

istrators, from cops, from adults? How to be free? Or how to obey?

The writer Derrick Jensen, in his book *Walking on Water: Reading, Writing and Revolution*, wrote what he learned as a young student:

> I learned to not talk out of order, and not to question authority—not openly, at least—for fear of losing recess time, or later of losing grade points. I learned to not ask difficult questions of overburdened or impatient teachers and certainly not to expect thoughtful answers. I learned to mimic the opinions of teachers, and on command to vomit facts and interpretations of those facts gleaned from the textbooks, whether I agreed with the facts or interpretations or not. I learned how to read authority figures, give them what they wanted, to fawn and brownnose when expedient. In short, I learned to give myself away.[2]

Is this what we want our students to do? To learn how to kneel, "brownnose," obey—or to be free?

These brave and compassionate kids, high-schoolers, many of whom will be called upon quite soon to join the imperial army to fight for presidents, princes and oil barons, are also doing some serious "teaching." They are teaching us all about freedom, the truest freedom—to resist!

It is a valuable lesson that millions of kids (and older folks) should learn well, before it is too late.

THE ONGOING WAR AGAINST WORKERS: THE TWU STRIKE

March 1, 2006

It only lasted for three days, but it lasted long enough to exhibit the scuffles and scars of war.

It was a spark for another round in the eternal war between labor and capital. It was a war between those who work and those who hire.

When the New York Transport Workers Union (TWU) went out on strike [in December 2005], their action sent shock waves across the country and rattled the rulers. Immediately, like a slave-driver who claims he was "betrayed" by "his people," New York's mega-billionaire mayor, Michael Bloomberg, unleashed an ugly verbal missile at those who demanded a fair contract under which to work.

In the minds and mouths of the Bloombergers, TWU strikers were: "Thugs!"

The corporate press joined the slander, with one well-known fishwrapper blaring in a banner headline, JAIL 'EM!

Them's fightin' words. And they reflect, with a richness and clarity rarely seen, the true nature of this war: a class war.

Local 100 of the TWU is a predominantly Black, Latin@ and immigrant union, and the ugly war of words, spun by the masters of the nation's media machines, were as raw as they were racist.

When an unruly mob of cops converged on City Hall to lambaste the city's first Black mayor (David Dinkins) as a "washroom attendant," and sprinkled in other racist references to local Black leaders, one needed to search far and wide to find references to the cops' behavior as "thuggish."

The city and the Metropolitan Transportation Authority used the Taylor Law, which disallows such strikes, to demand that local courts return crippling fines against any striker.

But some leading TWU members pointed to the history of the early Civil Rights movement, specifically the experience of the late Rosa Parks, who broke unjust laws to spark a mass movement.

Can the Taylor Law be just, when it leaves workers at the mercy of management, when it forces them to accept substandard contracts, when it requires ruinous givebacks? While the corporate press channeled the negativity of their bosses, strikers reported that average working-class and poor folks supported their efforts, for many understood that this was a stand to strengthen workers generally, and to beat back the hands of greed that have been choking unions all across the country.

As for the Taylor Law, why would anyone even try to pass such a law, which clearly disadvantages labor? The very fact of its existence proves the political betrayal on the part of politicians who supported it, lobbied for it and voted for it.

The Taylor Law is a weapon of the rulers, and a whipping for the workers. It strips them of their only real instrument of social power—the ability to refuse their labor. Since when is that a crime?

Well, to the rich, it is. Karl Marx said that the law "is but the will of one class made into a law for all."

It is a machine, just as the law made segregation legal and criminalized Black freedom and dignity. The same law demanded that Blacks take the back of the bus. That same law outlaws the right of those who labor to withhold their labor, as well as to better their condition and that of those who follow them.

Such a law must itself be outlawed! But it won't be, if the people rely on the politicians to do so.

That law can be unmade only by the concerted actions of the people, by workers' power, supported by others in every area of work and life.

Even though a recent contract was approved by the TWU leadership, the proposed pact was reportedly rejected by a majority of union members.

These front-line workers want to put an end to givebacks, and compromises, and labor bowing to capital and its puppet politicians. Labor wishes to fight for their class, and for their many and varied communities who are supported by their efforts.

To make a change, labor must fight for it!

68

FBI SURVEILLANCE

March 15, 2006

As these words are written, reports are emerging about the FBI surveillance of the Pittsburgh-based Thomas Merton Center, a pacifist anti-war group named after the late Trappist monk and writer Thomas Merton (1915–1968).

The news of surveillance of the center, discovered after the center's lawyer filed a Freedom of Information Act request, reminded me, once again, that the more things change, the more they remain the same. Reading from the newly released documents under the heading of "anti-terrorist" surveillance, one must be reminded of the efforts of the FBI in the late 1960s, when, under the guise of "anti-communism," peace groups were subjected to relentless surveillance.

Indeed, according to Frank Donner's exhaustive book *The Age of Surveillance*, the abilities of a single FBI informant (who also spied for the Washington, D.C., Metropolitan Police), one Robert Merritt, showed this tactic's dangerous potential. Merritt spied on at least 28 separate political, social and radical groups. Among the overtly anti–Vietnam War groups were the Anti-War Union, the Coalition of National Priorities and Military Policy, and the People's Coalition for Peace and Justice.[1]

Among the other groups subject to informer surveillance, the author lists the Academy of Political Science, the American Civil Liberties Union, the American Friends Service Committee, *The Advocate* (a publication of the National Law Center at Washington University), the Black People's Party, the Children's March for Survival, Common Cause, *The Furies* (a radical feminist publication), Community Bookstore,

206 • FBI Surveillance

the D.C. Statehood Party, the Howard University Committee to Free Angela Davis, the Tenants' Rights Workshop, and Rap, Inc. (a local drug rehabilitation program), among other groups.

What this shows us is that anybody and everybody was suspect, and subject to infiltration by informants and surveillance by the government.

Here we go again.

And again, thanks to the utility of fear, we are seeing how virtually silent people are in this asphyxiation of the alleged constitutional rights of the People.

When the Thomas Merton Center is under surveillance because of government suspicion of ties to terrorism, then we are seeing the outer limits of the arrogance of power.

Secret prisons, secret prisoners, gulags of torture and death in the Caribbean, Afghanistan and Iraq, black sites in Eastern Europe—and silence?

Every age is its own. It would be silly to hope for the rebirth of the 1960s in this day and time. And yet, the time will surely come when children will look to their parents and grandparents and ask, "What did you do, Mommy, when dictatorship came?"

"What did you do when people were thrown into torture chambers?"

"What did you do when people were sent overseas to be tortured?"

"What did you do when the Congress betrayed the Constitution?"

What did you do?

What are you doing?

Fear immobilizes; that is its intent. But hope opens up, as spring opens up the earth.

Don't re-create the 1960s. Make this moment, this day, this era, one of speaking out against the Empire. Make it a time for joining together with others who share your fears, and your hopes.

Make it an age of marching against the madness that assaults our senses. Make it a chance for change, or it will be with us forever.

69.

GM AND THE GLOBAL WAR
AGAINST WORKERS

April 9, 2006

As GM slices away hard-won workers' rights and protections, French youth amass in the millions to protest their government's latest neoliberal assault on their rights. At stake is not just the affected workers. At stake is the struggle of all workers, everywhere, for they are being attacked to open up attacks against all other workers in the industrialized states.

For if GM can do it, which business can't?

GM is one of the biggest, if not *the* biggest industrial concern on earth.

In 1999, it was the largest-grossing business in the United States, with over $199 billion dollars in annual receipts. By 2005, even though GM slipped to third (after WalMart and Exxon Mobil), the carmaker netted $192.6 billion (that's billion, with a *b*) in annual receipts.

When you see a behemoth like GM urge buyouts of some 30,000 people, and a similar attempt by subsidiary Delphi to let some 18,000 workers go, it's not because these concerns aren't making enough money—it's that they don't want to share that massive wealth with workers.

The corporate press has been spinning this story as if its copy was written on Wall Street. In a way, it was. For the nation's press is a corporate entity, and it looks at the world not from the perspective of their readers, viewers or listeners but from the perspective of its stockholders.

The watchword is "profit," "profit," and more "profit." What is important isn't the needs of working people; they are sidebars to the story. What is important is the stock price.

Is it any wonder that people are shedding their addiction to newspapers by the day? We have been deluged with stories of the impending bankruptcy of Delphi in its ongoing dispute with the United Auto Workers (UAW). How many of us have read about the suit filed by Appaloosa Management LP? Appaloosa, which owns 9.3 percent of Delphi stock, is seeking to intervene in the bankruptcy case, arguing that the auto parts company has used wrong and misleading data to make its bankruptcy claim.

The rights of workers have been won by hard and bitter labor struggles, from the 1930s onward. They won what were supposed to be ironclad promises, sealed in contracts, to protect their interests. Now, those contracts are being broken. Pensions? Forget about it! "Take this dough," the businesses say, "and get outta here." They do so because the labor movement is now moribund, after years of tying their hopes to the false promises of the Democratic Party. The Party, like its alleged adversary (Republicans), has taken so much dough from the corporate elite that it is but an agency at their beck and call.

How many politicians have you heard protesting the treatment of GM workers? How many have you heard condemning GM's attempt to buy out, sell out and sell short the workers, many of whom have devoted decades to the company?

Don't hold your breath!

GM wants to wash out a generation of workers, only to hire a new generation of workers at about half the wage, with few (if any) benefits.

In France, the resistance of the government to budge on no-fire demands demonstrates the increasingly global nature of this neo-liberal, anti-worker trend.

Labor activist Marty Glaberman, in his book *Punching Out*, was always critical of the contract, which, he argued, took powers from workers and granted them to business. He wrote:

The contract is a contradictory thing. To begin with,

it records the gains by the workers, the wages, the hours, the right to representation. Putting these gains in a contract makes them secure, or so it appears. But for every advance made in the contract a price must be paid. The fundamental cost was the reestablishment of the discipline of the company. The contract gave to the company what the workers had taken away—the right to organize and control production. The complete recognition of a grievance procedure meant the establishment of a structure of red tape where the worker lost his grievance. To end the constant battle over members, the union won the union shop and the dues checkoff—and paid by removing the union another step from its membership.[1]

The GM/Delphi moves prove it's time for the unions to fight back, rather than continue the same old losing strategies. The only solution is to use its labor power, and STRIKE!

70

SILENCE OF THE LAMBS

May 14, 2006

The recent report that the nation's largest phone companies turned over data on millions of Americans is less surprising than the somewhat muted response it has evoked.

If polls are to be believed, nearly 70 percent of those polled find nothing objectionable in the secret tracking of phone calls by the National Security Agency (NSA).

Without directly challenging the accuracy of such polls, the simple facts that folks aren't up in arms, marching on the White House like angry cinematic villagers, torches in hand, on the tracks of a Frankenstein monster, is stunning. The relative silence of Americans—not pundits, who are paid to have an opinion—but of average folks on this earth-shattering issue, suggests that it may be true.

What does this say about Americans? It suggests that people have incredible faith in the government, or are so immobilized by fear that they welcome virtually anything the state advances, as long as it promises safety.

Some will say this is a natural response after 9/11.

Yet this didn't begin on 9/11.

Illegal government spying on Americans has a long history in this country, occasioned by the fears unleashed during the Cold War. However, even in the 1970s, when such spying was uncovered, the result was not an end to such practices, but a transfer to another file, under another pretext. One need only read Frank Donner's 1981 book *The Age of Surveillance.*[1] This documented history is long, clear and undeniable.

Yet most Americans neither know, nor seem to want to know, about what happened then, or what's happening now.

That great French observer of America Alexis de

Tocqueville saw these qualities in Americans over 150 years ago, writing in his 1835 classic, *Democracy in America*:

A nation that asks nothing of its government but the maintenance of order is already a slave at heart—the slave of its own well-being, awaiting but the hand that will bind it. By such a nation the despotism of faction is not less to be dreaded than the despotism of an individual. When the bulk of the community is engrossed by private concerns, the smallest parties need not despair of getting the upper hand in public affairs. At such times it is not rare to see upon the great stages of the world, as we see at our theaters, a multitude represented by a few players, who alone speak in the name of an absent or inattentive crowd: they alone are in action whilst all are stationary; they regulate everything by their own caprice; they change the laws, and tyrannize at will over the manners of the country; and then wonder to see into how small a number of weak and worthless hands a great people may fall.[2]

As the White House and its lapdog press peddle the potion of fear and beat the drum for more war, the alleged "guarantees" of the Constitution are shredded like tissue paper, daily. Wars based on lies; U.S. torture chambers in Guantánamo, in Iraq, in Afghanistan; secret CIA prisons in Eastern Europe, North Africa and beyond; and now the tracking of millions of calls of Americans.

Something is broken in Babylon, yet all we hear today is the silence of the lambs.

BEFORE GUANTÁNAMO OR ABU GHRAIB—THE BLACK PANTHERS

May 24, 2006

Long before the words Guantánamo and Abu Ghraib entered common American usage as reference points for government torture, there were several young Black men who knew something about the subject.

The year was 1973, and among 13 "Black militants" arrested in a New Orleans sweep were three men: Hank Jones, John Bowman and Ray Boudreaux. The three were beaten, tortured and interrogated by New Orleans cops, acting on tips supplied by San Francisco police. The men were stripped, beaten with blunt objects, blindfolded, shocked on their private parts by electric cattle prods, punched and kicked, and had wool blankets soaked in boiling water thrown over them. Under such torture, the three gave false confessions in the shooting of a San Francisco cop in 1971.

The charges were eventually thrown out after a judge in California found that the prosecution had failed to tell a grand jury that the confessions were exacted under torture. Today, over 30 years later, Jones, Bowman and Boudreaux have again been called before a grand jury, to try to resurrect what was dismissed in 1976. Imagine what these men thought when they heard about the U.S. government torture chambers in Guantánamo, or Abu Ghraib in Iraq. The names may have been different, but the grim reality was the same. Today, these men have formed the Committee for the Defense of Human Rights to try to teach folks about what happened so many years ago, and what is happening now.

Their living example teaches us that history repeats itself, but in worse, more repressive forms. That's because their first conflicts with the state took place under the aegis of the since discredited Counterintelligence Program (COINTELPRO). That program, after the famous Church Committee hearings in the Senate, was declared illegal and a violation of the Constitution. Today, thanks to a Congress weakened by corporate largesse and frightened by 9/11, the same things that were illegal in the 1970s have been all but resurrected and legalized under the notorious USA PATRIOT Act. What we are seeing, all across the nation, is the emergence of what the late Black Panther Minister of Information Eldridge Cleaver called "Yankee Doodle fascism": the rise of corporate and state power to attack dissidents and destroy even the pretension of civil rights. I say pretension because the events I discussed earlier happened in 1973, yet none of the torturers, the violators, the criminals in blue, were ever sanctioned for their violations of state, federal and indeed, international law, to this day. Not one.

Think of this: the murderers of Fred Hampton Sr., those malevolent minions of the state who crept into his home and shot him dead (as he slept!) have never served a day, a minute, a second in jail for this most premeditated of murders, planned at the highest levels of government.

The roots of Guantánamo, of Abu Ghraib, of Bagram Air Force Base, of U.S. secret torture chambers operating all around the world, are deep in American life, in its long war against Black life and liberation.

Is it mere coincidence that the most notorious guard at Abu Ghraib worked right here, in the United States; here, in Pennsylvania; here, in SCI-Greene prison, for over six years before exporting his brand of "corrections" to the poor slobs who met him in Iraq?

Back in the 1960s and 1970s, Panthers and others spoke about fascism, but it had an edge of hyperbole, of radical speech, to move people beyond their complacency. Several years ago, a political scientist who studied fascism on three continents came to some pretty sobering conclusions.

According to Dr. Lawrence Britt, fascist states have 14 characteristics in common. They are, briefly: 1) powerful nationalism, 2) disdain for human rights, 3) scapegoating to unify against "enemies," 4) military supremacy, 5) rampant sexism, 6) controlled mass media, 7) national security obsession, 8) government religiosity, 9) rise of corporate power, 10) suppression of labor, 11) anti-intellectualism, 12) obsession with punishment, 13) deep corruption and cronyism, and 14) fraudulent elections.[1]

How many of these features are reflected daily in the national life of the United States? What happens abroad is a grim reflection of what has happened here, albeit quietly. The tortures of Jones, Bowman and Boudreaux won't be featured stories on *Nightline*, nor on (supposedly "liberal") National Public Radio. (Remember the characteristic of "controlled mass media"?)

What happens overseas has its genesis in the monstrous history of what happened here: genocide, mass terrorism, racist exploitation (also known as "slavery"), land-theft and carnage. All of these horrors have been echoed abroad, shadows of hatred, xenophobia and fear, projected from the heart of the Empire outwards.

If we really want to change the dangerous trend of global repression, we must change it here first. For only then can the world breathe a deep sigh of relief.

KATRINA: ONE YEAR LATER

August 24, 2006

The evocative power of one word is amazing: Katrina.

It resonates like a klaxon in the dark of night, an alarm that quickens the pulse, forces sweat from the armpits, and causes the heart to beat at a rapid pace.

It is as much name as it is nightmare; but it is more.

It is revelation, the brief moment when lightning turns the night sky into brightest day, until the ears echo with the roar of thunder.

For decades, at least since the high points of the Civil Rights movement, or the heyday of the Black Liberation movement, U.S. Blacks were able to live with the illusion that while things were far from perfect, they were getting better.

We were (to quote the theme song from the situation comedy *The Jeffersons*) "movin' on up" to places of power, respect, prestige and responsibility.

There were hiccups, of course, but racism, that great monster, Leviathan, was receding into its dark cave—perhaps for good.

Then came Katrina.

In a flash, in an hour, in a day, in a week, we saw with our own eyes the loss, the waste, the death, and perhaps worse, the dismissal of Black life by virtually every agency of local, state and federal power, and the media as well. For if the state was deadly by ignoring Black suffering, the media was deadly by its poisonous attention, and its perversion of the truth.

The media gave the state license to ignore, to disappear, to downplay and to discard Black life, for, in its twisted, racist coverage, Blacks were savages, and thus unworthy of saving.

If U.S. Blacks had any illusions, the dark, fetid waters of

Katrina washed them away. Nationalism, citizenship, belonging to the White Nation were lies. The waters of Katrina cleared the crust of sleep from our eyes, and taught us that if you're Black and poor, you're utterly on your own.

With the death of this illusion of nationalism, we learn that we are Rwanda, we are Burundi; we are united in our Blackness, our social isolation, our savage distancing from the very definition of humanity.

We are them.

A year has passed, and yet disaster remains.

Over half the city, over a quarter of a million people have not returned to the Crescent City. The Lower Ninth ward, the hub of Black poor and working-class New Orleanians, has neither running water nor electricity today.

Between fighting the government and fighting the insurance companies, tens of thousands of people are still fighting for money to rebuild their homes and lives.

And lest we trip about whether Katrina unveiled differences of class or race, scholar Michael Eric Dyson addressed the conundrum in his book *Come Hell or High Water: Hurricane Katrina and the Color of Disaster*:

> Class certainly loomed large in Katrina's aftermath. Blacks of means escaped the tragedy; blacks without them suffered and died. In reality, it is how race and class interact that made the situation of the poor so horrible on the Gulf Coast. The rigid caste system that punishes poor blacks and other minorities also targets poor whites. Concentrated poverty doesn't victimize poor whites in the same way it does poor blacks. For instance, the racial divide in car ownership . . . partially reflects income differences between the races. However, as if to prove that not all inequalities are equal, even poor whites are far more likely to have access to cars than poor blacks. In New Orleans,

53 percent of poor blacks were without cars while just
17 percent of poor whites lacked access to cars.[1]

Katrina, standing alone, is a beautiful name. But it may be
many years before it stands alone again.

For it is an event now of historic proportions, one that
impacts all that flows from it, like a war, like a massacre, like a
hurricane that transforms terrain, that shatters landscapes, that
explodes myths of who we thought we were.

NO SAFE AGE

December 3, 2006

It's boys' night out, and a group of brothers are having a bachelor party at a neighborhood club. One of them is particularly thrilled, because his marriage to the woman he loves is just hours away.

But he will never marry, because a pack of wild undercover cops will execute him, unleashing a deadly rain of 50 bullets on him and his friends.

The crime? Cruising While Black. Sean Bell, unarmed, was 23.

And the corporate media merely explains it may've been a case of "contagious" shooting—one cop fires, two cops fire, three cops . . . get the picture?

It's a kind of social illness, like alcoholism.

But neither Sean Bell, Trent Benefield nor Joseph Guzman was armed. According to some reports, one of them *said* he was armed.

Like the madmen who launched a preemptive war on the unsubstantiated suspicion of weapons of mass destruction, undercover cops launched an urban preemptive war on unarmed young Black men, reportedly based on unsubstantiated suspicions. *Fifty shots.* Death, and serious injury.

No cell phones, no wallets, no threatening candy bars—for such trifles are no longer deemed necessary. In America, Blackness is sufficient.

Even maleness isn't required, as shown by the recent shooting of an elderly woman who allegedly allowed a drug dealer to use her home. Katherine Johnston, having lived almost nine decades, was shot to death while trying to defend her Atlanta home after it was attacked by undercover cops.

According to a neighborhood snitch, he never claimed her house was a drug site, despite police pressure to do so. No significant quantities of drugs were found at the home. What was *her* crime? Trying-to-Survive-to-90 While Black?

What's more dangerous—drugs, or armed undercover cops kicking in doors allegedly on drug raids?

Police suspicion, it seems, is a weapon of urban war. Several years ago, writer Kristian Williams noted a case in which a whole community was held under siege, because of police suspicion. In his remarkable 2003 book *Enemies in Blue: Police and Power in America*, Williams recounted an amazing story:

> The racial politics of police suspicion are well illustrated by the North Carolina State Bureau of Investigation's "Operation Ready-Rock." In November 1990, forty-five state cops, including canine units and the paramilitary Special Response Team, [laid] siege to the 100 block of Graham Street, in a black neighborhood of Chapel Hill. Searching for crack cocaine, the cops sealed off the streets, patrolled with dogs, and ransacked a neighborhood pool hall. In terms of crime control, the mission was a flop. Although nearly 100 people were detained and searched, only 13 were arrested, and one of them convicted. Nevertheless, and despite a successful class action lawsuit, the cops defended their performance and no officers were disciplined.
>
> When applying for a warrant to search every person and vehicle on the block, the police had assured the judge, "there are no 'innocent' people at this place. . . . Only drug sellers and drug buyers are on the described premises." But once the clampdown was underway, they became more discriminating: Blacks were detained and searched, sometimes at

gunpoint, while whites were permitted to leave the cordoned area.[1]

How many of the armed maniacs who shot Johnston, Bell, Guzman or Benefield will ever see the inside of a cell? How many will reach the confines of Death Row?

We *know* the answer—because we've seen this movie before. . . . Paid leave (which amounts to paid vacations), a whitewash of an investigation, and a "they-were-doing-their-jobs" is all that ever happens.

It's a damned shame.

74·

DECOLONIZATION: THE INFLUENCE OF AFRICA AND LATIN AMERICA ON THE BLACK FREEDOM MOVEMENT

January 23, 2007

The struggle for Black freedom in the 1960s and 1970s was deeply influenced by freedom struggles elsewhere in the world.

That influence found various forms, from the indirect, as through African Americans reading seminal works by revolutionaries in African and Latin American decolonization struggles, to the direct, as when Black Americans made personal contact with such popular struggles, which deeply touched, informed and moved them toward looking at the national Black freedom struggle through a newer, wider lens.

One should never underestimate the extent to which people involved in imperialist wars are often radicalized by that role, and made into anti-imperialists.

During the Vietnam war, Blacks in the U.S. Army, observing the fundamentally racist nature of the conflict, found startling similarities between the repression visited upon Blacks in the United States and that exerted on Vietnamese people fighting for their own national independence.

Black veterans returning from the war often told folks stateside about small but powerful acts of solidarity between African Americans and Vietnamese people. Heard in many a Black barbershop was the tale of a night raid on a U.S. Army camp perimeter, where the Black guardsman would be left untouched, while the white guardsman would have his throat slit.

Many people who had a background in the U.S. Empire's service later joined the Black Panther Party. Kwando B. Kinshasa, a member of the New York Panther 21, wrote in the group's collective autobiography about his experiences while in Guatemala:

> I arrived in Guatemala City, and the Guatemalans were in the middle of a revolutionary war, a war that is still going on. Right on to the Guatemalan revolutionaries! My political education progressed so far while I was in Guatemala that by the time I left two-and-a-half years later I was on the verge of being kicked out by the reactionary government in power, not to mention the Americans there who didn't like my friendships with known revolutionaries. *I entered the country a very apolitical Negro marine, and came out a dedicated black revolutionary.* I made it a point to learn all I could about our Latin American and black brothers in Central America; and those brothers whose friendship I gained made it a point to educate this black marine from America. At the time, there were only ten blacks from the U.S. in Guatemala, but the population itself is about 80 per cent Mayan, 10 per cent black, and 10 per cent a mixture of European and Mayan and black.[1]

There can be no real discussion of the impact of the global wars against colonialism (or European conquest, control and exploitation over large swaths of Africa, Asia and Latin America) without reference to the work of Dr. Frantz Fanon, a young Martinique-born physician who, finding racism in France and its then-colony in Algiers, joined the Algerian Revolution and wrote works that rippled across several continents. Of all of his works (at least those translated into English) perhaps none was more influential than his masterwork, *The Wretched of the Earth*.[2] It was this volume, which a young junior college student named Bobby Seale gave to his fellow student, Huey Newton, that became a deep influence in the formation of the

Black Panther Party.[3] Few have captured Fanon's significance
with more clarity than former Black Panther Party Central
Committee member Kathleen Neal Cleaver, who wrote:

> His books became available in English just as waves
> of civil violence engulfed the ghettos of America,
> reaching the level of insurrection in the wake of the
> assassination of Dr. Martin Luther King, Jr. in 1968.
> Fanon died in 1961, a year before Algeria obtained
> the independence he had given his life to win, but his
> brilliant, posthumously published work *The Wretched
> of the Earth* became essential reading book for Black
> revolutionaries in America and profoundly influenced
> their thinking. Fanon's analysis seems to explain and
> justify the spontaneous violence ravaging Black ghet-
> tos across the country, and linked the incipient in-
> surrections to the rise of a revolutionary movement.
> The opening sentence of *The Wretched of the Earth*
> said, "National liberation, national renaissance, the
> restoration of nationhood to a people . . . whatever
> may be the headings used or the new formulas intro-
> duced, *decolonization is always a violent phenomenon.*"
> Fanon's penetrating dissection of domination was
> compelling to Blacks fighting in America; it provided
> a clearly reasoned antidote to the constant admoni-
> tion to seek changes peacefully. Fanon explained how
> violence was intrinsic to the imposition of White co-
> lonial domination, and portrayed the oppressed who
> violently retaliate as engaged in restoring the hu-
> man dignity they were stripped of by the process of
> colonization. His analysis of the tortured mentality
> of the colonized person and the therapeutic nature
> of fighting to destroy colonial domination provided
> radical Blacks in America with deep insights—into
> both their own relationship to a world-wide revolu-

tion underway and to the profound kinship between their status in America and that of colonized people outside America.[4]

Cleaver's analysis could not be more key to the thinking of the time, even as Fanon seemed to go some lengths to distance the Black American struggle from the national liberation struggles of African states. For, while Blacks in America felt a "need to attach themselves to [an African] cultural matrix," Fanon opined, "every culture is first and foremost national," and therefore Blacks in the United States, the Caribbean and Latin America had distinctly different challenges from those confronting their continental African cousins. Yet, if the objections were somewhat different, the problem they faced had undeniable similarities. Fanon wrote:

> Their problem is not fundamentally different from that of the Africans. We have seen that the whites were used to putting all Negroes in the same bag. During the first congress of the African Cultural Society, which was held in Paris in 1956, the American Negroes of their own accord considered their problems from the same standpoint as those of their African brothers.[5]

Throughout his book one found references that could hardly but echo Black souls:

> The mass of the people struggle against the same poverty, flounder about making the same gestures and with their shrunken bellies outline what has been called the geography of hunger. It is an underdeveloped world, a world inhuman in its poverty; but also it is a world without doctors, without engineers and without administrators. Confronting this world,

the European nations sprawl, ostentatiously opulent. This European opulence is literally scandalous, for it has been founded on slavery, it has been nourished with the blood of slaves and it comes directly from the soil and the subsoil of that under-developed world. The well-being and the progress of Europe have been built up with the sweat and the dead bodies of Negroes, Arabs, Indians, and the yellow races.[6]

When Seale gave Newton a copy of Fanon's text, Newton was so intrigued that he read it, then reread it six times. Fanon's work, the writing of Chinese revolutionary leader Mao Tse-Tung and works by Ernesto "Che" Guevara, a pivotal figure in the Cuban Revolution, deeply influenced Huey's thinking, and through him, the Party that he led. In his 1973 work *Revolutionary Suicide*, Newton explained:

We read these men's work because we saw them as kinsmen; the oppressor who had controlled them was controlling us, both directly and indirectly. We believed it was necessary to know how they gained their freedom in order to go about gaining ours. However, we did not want merely to import ideas and strategies; we had to transform what we learned into principles and methods acceptable to the brothers on the block.[7]

Seen in this light, perhaps it is not surprising that when the Black Panther Party sought to open its international office, it did so in Algiers, North Africa.

This office served as a kind of quasi-embassy of the African American Freedom movement, where Panthers and their allies met with revolutionaries from around the world. Kathleen N. Cleaver would later write that the villa, situated within the "revolutionary diplomatic community" there, served as an "information center" providing "news about revolutionary developments with the United States to their associates in Algiers and receiving information from all movements represented in Algiers."[8]

The national liberation movements in Africa, Asia and Latin America had a deep impact on the thinking of Black revolutionaries in the United States from a wide variety of social movements. Indeed, thanks to the organizing efforts of Fred Hampton (the martyred Black Panther leader in Chicago, Illinois), groups inside the United States like the Young Lords Party (which began as a Puerto Rican street gang, was radicalized and became a socialist political party organization), the Patriot Party (composed of young, radical whites), and the Brown Berets (Chicanos) began raising socialist, revolutionary and anti-imperialist themes in their domestic communities. In the branches from the western part of the United States, Party members worked with groups like I Wor Kuen (Asian American radicals) and the Red Guard (primarily young Chinese American radicals) who did similar organizing.

The Black Freedom movement, especially that segment struggling for national independence and true political autonomy, was a movement as home-grown as oak trees, yet it was profoundly influenced and impacted by other liberation movements in other areas of global struggle.

While decolonization did not bring the results hoped for by many (especially African) nations, the reasons for this may be found in the works of Fanon, who, in *The Wretched of the Earth*, warned of the scourge of neo-colonialism, or colonialism under the guise of a domestic so-called "bourgeoisie." As Fanon warned with his typical prescience:

> In under-developed countries, we have seen that no true bourgeoisie exists; [this] is only a sort of little greedy caste, avid and voracious, with the mind of a huckster, only too glad to accept the dividends that

the former colonial power hands out to it. This get-rich-quick middle class shows itself incapable of great ideas or of inventiveness. It remembers what it has read in European text-books and imperceptibly it becomes not even the replica of Europe, but its caricature.[9]

We see from this lamentable fact that the Black freedom struggle has much work to do, both here and abroad.

75

PRESIDENT OR PRIEST?

June 6, 2007

It is almost a year and a half before elections, and already we have been treated to the spectacle of a parade of politicians promising virtually everything to everybody now, with yet more promises of better, sweeter things to come.

On what passes for the left and right of acceptable U.S. politics, a plethora of candidates have proceeded to pronounce their religious beliefs, and their tacit unbelief in science—especially evolution.

Of course, in the United States one is free to believe or not believe in a given religious dogma. One is free to speak of it or not.

But there is something fishy when politicians speak of their faith to use it as an advertising tool, a campaign sign of the soul, so to speak. What is rarely heard is how their religious belief relates to the health, education and welfare of the poorest millions, who still dwell in the unseen crevices of American society. What is rarely heard is the state and fate of those called "The Least of These."

What is rarer still, is mention of peace.

Poverty and peace are off the agenda. Instead, there is the muscular religion of smiting one's enemies, or jailing one's opponents, or using the power of the state to enforce one's religious code upon others, especially those who are of a different belief. There is the aura of holy war wafting over the heads of the assembled throng, as they try to outdo each other in false piety and the promotion of what amounts to a theocracy. This is done not because any of the given political figures actually believes in their stated faith, but because they all know that a large number of people in the United States do believe in faiths, and they want to capture their votes.

How could one claim to believe in a faith that preaches peace while practicing war?

How can there be claims to justice when there is injustice, torture and planning for new imperial adventures?

Presidents make poor priests.

That's because the interests of priests are supposedly spiritual, while the interests of presidents are mostly temporal. When either meddles in the other's realm, it almost inevitably leads to chaos.

In the United States, the fastest-growing religion is Islam, with adherents numbering in the millions, across a broad ethnic and racial spectrum. Although the current president is in power (at least in part) because of a majority of their votes, can it be said that he has represented their interests?

In a nation of Christians, Muslims, Jews, Sikhs, Buddhists, Hindus, Sufis, Hare Krishnas, Confucianists, Seventh-Day Adventists and an almost uncountable host of others (as well as millions who believe in no faith), whom does the president represent?

76

1967: YEAR OF FIRE, YEAR OF RAGE

July 18, 2007

1967: In that brief recitation of time we find history's echo of an era of rebellion, resistance, fear and hope.

It was emblematic of what we have come to call the "long hot summer." For in 1967, cities across the nation went up like kindling, fires waved their reddish-orange fingers into the night air, and white fear, usually echoed in the corporate media, gave voice more to fancy than to fact. Reporters wrote stories based not on their knowledge, but on their suppositions (come to think of it, not very different from what passes for the media today, huh?).

Cities exploded like popcorn on an oily griddle: Roxbury first, from June 2 to 5; then Tampa, Florida; days later, Cincinnati erupted; before two weeks passed, Buffalo, N.Y., had a rebellion.

Of course, many here know that Newark went into rebellion in the midst of these events. From July 12 to 17, almost half the city was the site of the rebellion. More than 1,500 people were injured; 1,300 were arrested; 26 were killed. Newark came to stand for the Watts of the East Coast, the symbol of how widespread was the fever of Black discontent.

Of course, folks in the Garden State know that Newark wasn't alone. It lit the flame that spread to New Brunswick, Englewood, Paterson, Elizabeth, Palmyra, Passaic and Plainfield, New Jersey.

Before the fires were extinguished in Newark, the sparks flamed in Cairo, Illinois; then Durham, North Carolina; then Memphis, Tennessee; then Minneapolis!

Before the month passed, Detroit exploded, bigger than Newark, with federal troops, not National Guard (as was usually the case), called out to attempt to quell the rebellion. Some 43 people died in Detroit alone.

And the month of July 1967 still had not passed.

What were the sparks, and how do we look at that era, four decades later? The sparks were those that caused rebellion and conflict virtually anywhere in the country, and that still mark our present.

Police mistreatment, brutality and violence against Black people.

If we think that this was a distant reality, we need only look at 1992, when the Rodney King verdicts of acquittal came down. Hell, we ain't gotta go to L.A., for just days ago, a few miles north of Newark, we saw the police beating of two Black lawyers, Michael Tarif Warren and his wife, Evelyn. Their beatings came as they tried to stop the cop beating of a handcuffed Black youth outside a McDonald's restaurant in Brooklyn.

So much for how times have changed.

The question isn't whether repression has changed (cause we know it hasn't), but whether our forms of resistance have changed. The answer, of course, is an unequivocal yes. For change only comes when people fight for it. To quote our honored ancestor, Frederick Douglass, "Power concedes nothing without demand. It never has, and never will."

People didn't rebel all across America during 1967 for a Black boxing champ. They didn't rebel because they wanted a Black mayor. They didn't rebel because they wanted Adam Clayton Powell returned to his seat in Congress, or because they wanted a Congressional Black Caucus.

They rebelled because they wanted Power: the power to better their lives. They also wanted an end to the violent repression of the cops.

Out of that year of fire and rebellion came the first National Black Power Conference, where people from all walks of life tried to grapple with ways to gain true, social, cohesive communal power.

Shortly thereafter came several other such conferences, in various cities, among them and perhaps best known the National Black Political Assembly in Gary, Indiana, in 1972.

It is almost painful to read what those delegates decided there, and to contrast it with our miserable present. It shows us, in ways we cannot deny, how some things simply have not changed.

In the Gary Declaration, the following words were used as part of the call:

> Let there be no mistake. We come to Gary in a time of unrelieved crisis, for our people. From every rural community in Alabama to the high rise compounds of Chicago, we bring to this Convention the agonies of the masses of our people. From the sprawling Black cities of Watts and Nairobi in the West to the decay of Harlem and Roxbury in the East, the testimony we bear is the same. We are witnesses to social disaster.[1]

The Gary Declaration went on to decry the woes of unemployment and the impact it had on Black lives, especially for Black youth. It critiqued the failure of the prison system and pollution in the environment, and called for Gary to become an important part of the Black Liberation movement.

It recognized something that we (or many of us) seem to have forgotten: "The American system does not work for the masses of our people, and it cannot be made to work without radical, fundamental change."

It also called for a Black independent politics, not a dependence on either of the major political parties.

That dream, the fruit of the year of fire and rage, is—40 years later—as distant as Mars. As cultural workers, poets, organizers and activists, Amiri and Amina Baraka have tried to be forces for social change in the city, and both have made deep and lasting impacts on Newark, but for most of us, the Rebellion of 1967 seems to be the rebellion betrayed. For while it may be said that there are certainly more Black politicians now than then, is there truly more political power?

Have Black politicians come to represent the system, or their constituencies?

The answer is written in the spreading fields of "desperation" that dot our communities all across the land.

The educational system converges to destroy young minds, not enlighten them. There is a need, now more than ever, to add new life to the spirit of rebellion and resistance in our people's long march to liberation.

Let us commit ourselves to serve that grand objective.

77

THE LATEST BATTLE IN THE WAR AGAINST THE POOR

September 19, 2007

For a growing number of people all across the country, homes are becoming an endangered species.

In many cities, the forces of gentrification are weighing not only on home-buyers but on renters, for as the price of housing property increases, so does the price of rental property in a market that is bursting through the roof.

For many, the bubble has burst.

Just as Congress made bankruptcy more difficult to obtain, the adjustable-rate mortgage (ARM) industry has garnered billions from young folks eager and willing to join the ranks of property owners.

But, like the spring-loaded top of a mousetrap, the ARMs snapped shut, and as subprime lenders now depart the market, the effects are rippling throughout the economy. In a sense, there is a perverse logic to this gambit, for it comes just as the national economy began to adjust to the de-industrialization of big cities, which spelled the end of good-paying jobs for a generation.

For a brief moment, there seemed to be a window of hope offering affordable homes for many folks who thought ownership was beyond their reach. As soon as they reached for the brass ring, however, the booby-trap popped: foreclosure.

In Buffalo, the city plans to raze more than 5,000 abandoned houses, relics of a time when the city was a magnet for manufacturing.[1]

In Philadelphia, North, South and West Philadelphia renters are being squeezed to make room for yuppies, and homes, when they are built, are for buyers, not renters.

In New York City, homeowners are spending from 30 percent to 50 percent of their income to pay for the mortgage. The prices, even of rents, drive people from Manhattan, from Brooklyn and from Queens into the Bronx.[2]

In San Francisco, homes for the poor are becoming rarer and rarer.

In cities across the country, working-class Blacks are being forced, by the inability to make ends meet, to leave the cities of their birth and familial memory. In South Philadelphia, renter Victoria Fernandez told a reporter for the *Philadelphia Tribune* that poor Black folks were on their own. "The government don't care about us," she exclaimed. "We vote, but do we have a say? No."[3] Her family has lived in that city's Black community for generations, but the city looks to young, white entrepreneurial types, or students, to buoy the city's taxes and fortunes. Victoria Fernandez explains, "It ain't never been fair for poor people. We're drowning."

In New York, the nation's financial capital (or capital of capital), foreclosures are becoming almost routine. Ismena Speliotis, executive director of New York Acorn Housing, described the conditions facing low- and moderate-income folks in the city, and of homeowners: "We've seen a huge increase in defaults and foreclosures in Brooklyn, in East New York [and] East Flatbush," she said.

This is the latest front in the continuing war against the poor. That it comes at a time when the nation's political leaders have spent hundreds of billions of dollars on a war that was as unnecessary as it was stupid, is nothing short of a crime against humanity. For what does it matter if the Dow Jones Average or the NASDAQ is breaking new records, if homeowners are facing imminent foreclosure, renters are fleeing cities, and both are facing the invisibility of homelessness? For whom is the economy working?

For the poor, it's just another kind of war.

THE PERILS OF BLACK POLITICAL POWER

August 6, 2008

As we are on the eve of what may be the most powerful Black achievement in U.S. history, it would be well to examine the history of Black political leadership in this country. Most historical researchers look to the 1967 election of Carl Stokes (1927–1996) as Mayor of Cleveland, Ohio, as the emergence of Black political power in major American cities. Many Blacks saw this as the beginning of an age of freedom for our people. From the 1960s to now, we most certainly have been disabused of that notion.

For while Black political leadership has surely been a source of pride, it has not been a source of Black political power. That's because, as agents of the state, those leaders must defend the interests of the state, even when this conflicts with the interests of their people.

For example, let's look at the experience of Mayor Stokes.

Shortly after taking office, Stokes appointed former U.S. Army Lt. Gen. Benjamin O. Davis Jr. as his public safety director (a kind of super police chief). Lt. Gen. Davis, fresh from the rigors of Vietnam, ordered 30,000 rounds of hollow-point (or dumdum) bullets, items in violation of the laws of war.

The object of his ire? The Cleveland branch of the Black Panther Party and a local office of a Panther support group, the National Committee to Combat Fascism. In August 1970, Gen. Davis resigned from the post and criticized Mayor Stokes for not giving him sufficient support in his battle against radicals (like the Panthers). Stokes, the more politically adroit of the two, made Davis look bad for ordering ammo that violated the Geneva Conventions, but Stokes's personal papers revealed meetings between the two men, and their agreement on dumdums as appropriate arms to be used against Panthers.[1]

Just because he was a Black mayor didn't mean he wasn't dedicated to destroying a Black organization. Indeed, in times of Black uprising and mass discontent, Black mayors seem the perfect instrument of repression, for they dispel charges of racism.

If Barack Obama wins the White House, it will be a considerable political achievement. It will be made possible only by the votes of millions of whites, most especially younger voters. This does not diminish such an achievement; it just sharpens the nature of it. But Black faces in high places does not freedom make.

Power is far more than presence. It is the ability to meet people's political objectives of freedom, independence and material well-being.

We are as far from those objectives as we were in 1967.

79

BEATING BACK BATSON

September 6, 2008

For those who follow court opinions, few can ignore the U.S. Supreme Court's 1986 *Batson v. Kentucky* decision. Essentially, it prohibited the state from removing Black jurors for racial reasons. It rewrote the rules from the *Swain v. Alabama* case (1965) in which the court required complainants to show systematic discrimination over a number of cases, over a period of years. Needless to say, such a challenge was beyond the resources of most people, so relatively few complaints were lodged, and even fewer were successful. It is hard to resist the suspicion that this was merely judicial lip service to a principle that was easily ignored in the breach.

For it took over a generation, over 20 years, for *Swain* to be overruled by *Batson*, and now *Batson* is beginning to bear an eerie resemblance to its unworkable parent, because courts have been loath to grant relief, and have either created new rules or simply ignored its dictates.

We see this at work recently in a number of cases, among them *Com. v. (Robert) Cook.*[1] In this case, the prosecutor used 74 percent of his strikes to remove 14 Black jurors. Incredibly, the Philadelphia Court of Common Pleas initially found that even this didn't constitute a prima facie case of discrimination. Later, it found a prima facie case but ruled that the prosecutor put forth sufficient race-neutral reasons for exclusion, and therefore did not violate *Batson*.

Recently, the Pennsylvania Supreme Court agreed, even though the prosecutor couldn't recall why he removed two Black jurors—in other words, couldn't articulate a justification. Now remember: *Batson* states that the improper removal of one juror violates the constitution. One, not 14.

And here's the kicker. The prosecutor in Mr. Cook's case made a training video in which he taught his fellow prosecutors how to violate *Batson*—and how to lie about it to judges. But perhaps the then-prosecutor, Jack McMahon, didn't need to work that hard, for courts would take up the slack. Where the prosecutor can't remember a reason, the court will invent one.

This is especially egregious in this case, for the man who wrote the opinion was the DA when McMahon made the tapes, but now sits as Chief Justice of the court. Can you spell "conflict of interest"? Did he recuse himself? (What do you think?) For over a decade, Pennsylvania courts have painted McMahon as the bad guy, a kind of rogue prosecutor, and most of his convictions have been reversed (except Cook's)—but McMahon wasn't, and never should've been, the issue. For he was simply describing the pattern and practice of the office, and training his colleagues in techniques used over years of trials.

Mr. McMahon was putting into words what ADAs[2] did to get convictions. Does that mean his office sought a fair and impartial jury? In McMahon's words, "Well, that's ridiculous. You're not trying to get that." In fact, McMahon explained, their jobs were to get the most "unfair" jury possible. And in many cases that meant getting as few Blacks to serve on the jury as possible.

Batson is as empty as *Swain* was, for if they don't want to give it up, any reason will do. They proclaim ideals of fairness that bear no relationship to the real process happening daily in courtrooms all across America.

That would be, to quote McMahon, "ridiculous."

80

THE TIME FOR TROY DAVIS IS NOW

October 22, 2008

As these words are written, Troy Davis's life may be measured in hours, if Georgia has its way.

His case is proof positive of how easy it is for a state to send someone to the death house, and how hellishly difficult it is to fight one's way out.

His case is ripped throughout with false testimony, with 80 percent of his trial witnesses now admitting as much. Of nine people who testified at trial, seven have recanted, saying they were forced by the cops to lie.

One of them, Jeffrey Sapp, swore in an affidavit, "The police came and talked to me and put a lot of pressure on me to say 'Troy said this' or 'Troy said that.' I got tired of them harassing me, and they made it clear that the only way they would leave me alone is if I told them what they wanted to hear. I told them that Troy told me he did it, but it wasn't true. Troy never said that or anything like that."

But these recantations have fallen on deaf judicial ears, both in Georgia and in Washington. Indeed, there has never even been a hearing on these recantations. In another era, Davis would've had a new trial. But that was before the draconian Anti-Terrorism and Effective Death Penalty Act of 1996 (signed into law by Bill Clinton, by the way), which makes it increasingly difficult for judges to grant relief—or even to get hearings.

In fact, even the state court judge, Georgia Supreme Court Justice Leah Ward Sears, in her dissenting opinion, noted that the bar has been set so high for granting a new trial that no one could meet it.

Not even Troy Davis—an innocent man.

If Troy Davis is to be saved, it will take the People to demand it!

WELFARE FOR THE RICH

October 22, 2008

Stimulus package. Bailouts. Banking rescues.

It has been generations since we've witnessed scenes such as these.

Government officials spin like jacks, proclaiming a policy one day, only to renounce it the next. The Dow Jones Industrial Average rushes up and spirals downward in a matter of minutes, and offers a visual, measurable reminder of the volatility of the market.

Money is dumped into failing financial houses, failing banks and private companies in an attempt to "prime the pump," we are told.

Companies that have been icons for over a century fade away like dew in the morning sun. And this ain't just national; it's global.

A year ago, British banking giant Northern Rock fell into a crisis. For months, the government sought to persuade private investors to take a bite, but there were no takers. In February, the institution was nationalized, and the government pumped in 87 billion British pounds to keep it afloat. The bank was salvaged, but thousands of its employees were fired.

The Northern Rock debacle, coupled with the $700 billion bailout, has set off alarm bells among the investor class. One billionaire investor, Jim Rogers, was quoted thus: "America is more communist than China is right now. You can see that this is welfare of the rich, it is socialism for the rich—it's just bailing out financial institutions. This is madness, this is insanity, they have more than doubled the American national debt in one weekend for a bunch of crooks and incompetents. I'm not quite sure why I or anybody else should be paying for them."[1]

What makes it even more surreal is how politicians hurl charges at other politicians of "socialist!" Ignored is the socialism accorded to the wealthy bankers and houses of high finance.

Of course, this isn't anything like real socialism at all.

For the working class, the working poor, and millions in the middle, this economic crisis is a terrifying portent of things to come. They know that hard times will only get harder.

They wish they had some of the "socialism" that has been lavished on the rich.

ISRAEL

November 1, 2008

The roots of the problem? It is impossible to discuss the current crisis in the so-called Middle East without examining the history that led to the creation of Israel and the role of what is often called, mistakenly in my view, the international community. Long before Israel became a geo-political reality, discussions were had in London and in New York about giving displaced Jews land to settle in. These discussions led to what is known as the British Declaration of Mandate over Palestine.

For many history-minded Palestinians, September 11 rings bells completely unrelated to what happened in New York in 2001. That date, in 1922, marked the British government's proclamation of its mandate. Shortly prior, in 1917, the British government had issued the Balfour Declaration, named after British Foreign Secretary Arthur James Balfour, which promised a national home for the Jewish people. Balfour ordered the seizure of Arab land to grant to European Jews. It is telling that Balfour didn't offer any British land for such a project. Some years ago, when he was Britain's foreign secretary, Balfour said: "In Palestine we do not propose even to go through the form of consulting the wishes of the present inhabitants of the country. . . . Zionism, be it right or wrong, good or bad, is rooted in age-old traditions, in present needs, in future hopes, of far profounder import than the desires and prejudices of the 700,000 Arabs who now inhabit that ancient land."

A recent book by British journalist Robert Fisk cited the views of the historian George Antonius, who as early as 1938 wrote about the future of blood, loss and war that would befall Israel and the region if the Jewish faith were placed there.

Fundamentally, Antonius spoke about the inherent injustice in the British colonial plan:

> The treatment meted out to Jews in Germany and other European countries is a disgrace to its authors and to modern civilization. But posterity will not exonerate any country that fails to bear its proper share of the sacrifices needed to alleviate Jewish suffering and distress. To place the brunt of the burden upon Arab Palestine is a miserable evasion of the duty that lies upon the whole civilized world. It is also morally outrageous. No code of morals can justify the persecution of one people in an attempt relieve the persecution of another. The cure for the eviction of Jews from Germany is not to be sought in the eviction of Arabs from their homeland; and the relief of Jewish distress may not be accomplished at the cost of inflicting a corresponding distress upon an innocent and peaceful population.[1]

Those remarkable words were written in 1938. But historians don't guide history. They write it, long after it's passed. Of course, after a U.N.-brokered partition and the withdrawal of the British after a blistering campaign by Jewish terrorists, the state of Israel was born on May 14, 1948. One need not look to the Jewish, Christian or Islamic scriptures to find the injustice that lies at the heart of this matter. As the United Nations and Britain, in their roles as imperial overlords, gave rise to this problem, they cannot be the authors of a viable solution. From its birth to its present state as U.S. proxy, Israel has not known peace in its 58 years of existence. It is a military state, defined as much by its persecution of the indigenous people of the land as by the persecutions in Europe that led to its founding. It has led to the present-day power relation, which marks Israel as a ruthless aggressor in the region, with few friends now and fewer in the foreseeable future.

Scholar and former U.S. diplomat William Polk, in his 1991 book *The Arab World Today*, wrote: "The powerful view the weak as irresponsible, violent, untrustworthy, and illegal, and as either actual or potential terrorists, while the powerless see those in power as tyrants who are using the apparatus of the state and the law unfairly and mercilessly to strip them of their possessions, their security, indeed, their very humanity."[2]

Such roots can only lead to bitter fruits.

FROM FRANTZ FANON
TO AFRICA WITH LOVE

December 25, 2008

As the economies of the West and East tumble, tremors may also be felt in African economies, as heightened food prices push populations to the breaking point, near starvation. In country after country, the struggle for life becomes even harder, and it seems as though leaders are more remote than ever.

Whenever I read of economic or ethnic strife in any part of Africa, I'm reminded of Dr. Frantz Fanon, the ethno-psychiatrist born in the Caribbean island of Martinique, who became a revolutionary working on behalf of the Algerian Revolution and wrote the masterpiece *The Wretched of the Earth*.[1]

Fanon's work was widely read on three continents and is still worthy of study, not least because the insightful thinker predicted how African rulers would rule if they didn't unite the continent's various peoples and failed to develop truly independent and socialist governing systems. Many African postcolonial leaders, trained as they were in Eurocentric schools, sought to replicate the instructed theories in African societies, which could only result in disaster. Fanon is cutting when he describes the role of these Eurocentric African leaders who were attempting to re-create little pieces of Europe in their former colonies:

> In underdeveloped countries, we have seen that no true bourgeoisie exists; there is only a sort of little greedy caste, avid and voracious, with the mind of a huckster, only too glad to accept the dividends that the former colonial power hands out to it. This get-

rich-quick middle class shows itself incapable of great ideas or of inventiveness. It remembers what it has read in European textbooks and imperceptibly it becomes not even the replica of Europe, but its caricature.

When leaders were trained in capitalist colonizing economic theory, the most important lesson they learned was how to re-create colonialism, how not to destroy it.

Many African nations have been riven by deadly and destructive ethnic clashes, such as Kenya, Nigeria, Rwanda, Mauritania and beyond.

Fanon wrote in *Wretched* that the "national bourgeoisie . . . which has totally assimilated colonialist thought in its most corrupt form, takes over from the Europeans and establishes in the continent a racial philosophy which is extremely harmful for the future of Africa."

Thus, long inculcated into the European practice of "divide and conquer," African leaders exploit ethnic differences— so-called "tribalism"—to stir the pot between communities. So, Hutus fight Tutsis, Zulus fight Xhosas, Kalenjins fight Kikuyus and on and on, while communal unity seems like an unattainable mirage. While people think of their ethnic identities, few think of national identities, and fewer still think of what African unity really means.

Divided into clans, Africa remains ripe for the plucking by the new colonialists, who see it as a vast stealing ground, from which resources can be looted with relative ease. Fanon foresaw this half a century ago. Nkrumah tried to organize against it. But, regrettably, we are where we are.

It is almost painful to read Fanon today, over 40 years after his publications (in English), so accurate and cutting is his analysis. Yet the truth remains that many African states have Black presidents and prime ministers who preside over systems that are tied with a thousand chains to the old colonial powers, which continued under new management the old exploitative relationships.

Indeed, in *Toward the African Revolution*,[2] Fanon wrote of the global significance of the imperialists' murder of Patrice Lumumba, the first democratically elected president of the Congo:

> Africa must understand . . . that there will not be one Africa that fights against colonialism and another that attempts to make arrangements with colonialism. . . . Our mistake, the mistake we Africans made, was to have forgotten that the enemy never withdraws sincerely. He never understands. He capitulates, but he does not become converted. Our mistake is to have believed that the enemy had lost his combativeness and his harmfulness. If Lumumba is in the way, Lumumba disappears. Hesitation in murder has never characterized imperialism. Look at Ben M'hidi, look at Moumie, look at Lumumba. Our mistake is to have been slightly confused in what we did. It is a fact that in Africa, today, traitors exist. They should have been denounced and fought. The fact that this is hard after the magnificent dream of an Africa gathered together unto itself and subject to the same requirements of true independence does not alter facts. . . . Let us be sure never to forget it; the fate of all of us is at stake in the Congo.

In February and March, several African states had food riots—or should we say "hunger riots"? Some countries have sold staples at lower cost in special stores. Other countries have reached almost apocalyptic levels of hyperinflation such that their currency is virtually worthless.

In general—at least as of several months ago—the following were equivalent to one U.S. dollar: in Algeria, 65 dinars; in

Côte d'Ivoire, 420 francs; in Nigeria, 118 nairas; in Tanzania, 1,396 shillings; in Malawi, 140 kwacha. Only in one African country, Ghana, was its New Cedi equal to a dollar.

Half a century after most African states gained independence, the continent is still a social, economic and political basket case. Fanon, if he were still alive, would weep.

84

WITH JUDGES LIKE THESE

February 2009

In Pennsylvania's Luzerne County there are nine judges of the Court of Common Pleas. Two of them just pled guilty to a conspiracy to convict and sentence juveniles to a private prison, so the judges could get kickbacks from the prison's builders and owners. According to published accounts, Judge Mark A. Ciavarella and Senior Judge Michael T. Conahan sent hundreds of boys and girls to the private facility and pocketed some $2.5 million in kickbacks.

This was accomplished not merely because of the venal greed of the judges, but because virtually none of the children were provided with legal representation. When the Philadelphia-based Juvenile Law Center filed a petition in the Pennsylvania Supreme Court calling the county's practice of adjudicating and sentencing some 250 kids to jail without legal representation unconstitutional, the state's highest court denied the petition on January 8, 2009.

To make matters even worse, recently filed criminal information states that the two judges used their power and influence in the county to defund the county juvenile facility, precisely as they were steering kids to the private jail. (Boy, talk about privatization!)

Nearly a month later, the state's highest court changed its mind, vacating the denial. What transpired in the interim? Well, for one thing, the two judges provisionally pled guilty to federal charges of wire service fraud.

Hundreds of children get socked into jail, after demonstrably unconstitutional proceedings with no legal representation, and the state's highest court doesn't even raise an eyebrow.

The media reports on this outrage, and the Pennsylvania

Supreme Court expresses little interest. This is the nature of judging these days, when even kids are expendable fodder for the prison-industrial complex.

Luzerne County is the state's 10th-largest county, with just over 300,000 souls. At least 22 percent of its judges have admitted being corrupt, in the sordid business of selling the freedom and well-being of poor children for profit.[1]

85

THE *OTHER* INAUGURATION
CELEBRATION

March 9, 2009

For millions of people, both in America and abroad, the inauguration of a Black person as President of the United States was a moment of transcendent history, one of meaning and significance, that suggests real change in a nation that has long labored under its racist history.

This was perhaps best evidenced by the vast number of people who swarmed Washington to be part of such a day.

But for half a dozen men at Pennsylvania's Camp Hill prison, in its Special Management Unit (SMU), the day will be remembered quite differently. For that day marked a fit of beatings, electric stun-gun (and stun-shield) shocking, kicking, punching and other such treatment, accompanied by a rash of racist slurs by white guards against Black prisoners.

According to the Pittsburgh-based Human Rights Coalition (HRC), guards and staff launched an attack timed to the inauguration, to send the message, "F—k a historical day, y'all always going to be niggers!"

In an extensive six-page report sent to members of the press, the HRC's "Fed Up!" chapter documents assaults and threats against six men that day: David Smith, Gary Tucker, Damont Hagan, Ronald Jackson, Willie Robinson and Jamar Perry. Some of these men were threatened with death for daring to file suits in courts against their treatment in the unit.

On the morning of the inauguration, one high-ranking guard reportedly announced over the public address system, speaking of Obama, "He may have won, in my eyes he's still a nigger." He also stated: "There will be no showers or yard today. We are going to show you niggers who runs this SMU."[1]

Men were handcuffed, sprayed with hot pepper mace in the face, blinded, stripped naked and beaten in retaliation for exercising their alleged constitutional right to file a civil rights suit in an American court, on the very day that Barack H. Obama was taking the oath of office, telling the assembled throng before him and the nation and world viewing it remotely, that "we do not torture."

86

BLACK CITIZENSHIP

September 1, 2009

For nations, as with people, life's road offers many turning points.

For the United States, Reconstruction offers one such turning point, and the road not taken spelled not just a century of continued oppression for millions of Africans (one hesitates to call them African Americans, for they could hardly be called citizens except in the most tangential sense), but also sent the nation down a spiral of smallness, meanness and hypocrisy.

This era marked America as surely as did any war, for in fact there was a war—a war against Black freedom, Black autonomy and the very notion of Black citizenship in the national polity.

That Reconstruction was ended, in the face of lofty words in the U.S. Constitution promising citizenship rights, voting rights and civil equality before the law, proved that something else was animating state power rather than the written law. This was, of course, the unwritten laws of white supremacy and Black subordination—laws that, although unwritten, sucked down as heavily as gravity on the lives, aspirations and dreams of Blacks for generations.

For over a century, then, the U.S. Constitution was a dead letter; all promise, no performance. Nor is this merely the writer's opinion.

In the 1971 work *Black Resistance: White Law*, constitutional law scholar and historian Mary Frances Berry wrote that whether before or after 1965 (or before or after the Civil War), the federal government interpreted the Constitution only in ways that supported white supremacy, and when Blacks were harmed, the Constitution had no utility nor applicability. Barry, in her volume's preface, states:

> Before 1865, in addition to aiding in the suppression of slave revolts, the national government ignored or approved—on constitutional grounds—white mob violence directed at blacks and their few white supporters even when local officials participated in the violence. Those blacks who did not become involved in conspiracy and rebellion before the Civil War were not necessarily "docile"; they lived in the grip of a system of violent control institutionalized under the Constitution. The years since Reconstruction, when blacks became nominally free, are littered with incidences of white riots against blacks, burnings of black homes and churches, and lynchings, while federal and local law enforcement agencies stood idly by. And while federal law enforcement disregarded white violence, pleading lack of jurisdiction under the Constitution, it endorsed and contributed to rigorous campaigns of surveillance and control of rebellious blacks, using "constitutional" military force against them with impunity.
>
> Whether its policy was action or inaction, the national government has used the Constitution in such a way as to make law the instrument for maintaining a racist status quo. Law and the Constitution in the United States have been a reflection of the will of the white majority that white people have, and shall keep, superior economic, political, social and military power, while Black people shall be the permanent mudsills of American society.[1]

87.

UNION BUSTING

April 30, 2010

Not since the infamous PATCO action of the 1980s, the Reagan-era attack on the air traffic controllers union, have we seen such an open assault on a union as has happened to hundreds of workers at Rio Tinto, the California open-pit mine owned by the global conglomerate in Boron.

On a brisk morning in January 2010, Rio Tinto bosses locked out nearly 600 workers, all members of Local 30 of the ILWU (International Longshore and Warehouse Union), and brought in a scab crew waiting in the wings. The lockout came because the workers rejected an unconscionable collection of union givebacks that essentially nullified not only previous contract agreements, but federal and state laws in support of labor and human rights standards.

At a time when politicians cry crocodile tears at miners' funerals, the livelihoods and living standards of real, living miners (and their families) like the hundreds locked out of Rio Tinto get barely a whisper.

Not surprisingly, Rio Tinto, a wily corporate giant, chose a time of near collapse of the economy to try to hammer its laborers. Nor is Rio Tinto hurting, having posted a $16 billion pre-tax profit in 2008. The mega-corp owns mines in Papua New Guinea, in Namibia in Africa, and throughout Asia. When the original contract expired in 2005, Rio Tinto responded by offering an agreement that would've, among other things, cut full-time jobs to part-time jobs, reduced pay at will, sent jobs abroad by outsourcing at will, required the union to pay the company's fees and penalties if Rio Tinto violates any state or federal labor law, and the like.

Many of these proposals were designed to push union buttons, to force it to oppose any agreement. For the company's objective wasn't agreement—it was domination, the power of the employer to crush the employee, the power of wealth to smash a union.

But ILWU Local 30 is fighting back, supported not only by its International but by shipping and maritime unions around the world. Workers in Australia, New Zealand, Poland, South Africa and Canada have supported their efforts.

For this is not just an assault on workers at Rio Tinto; it's an attack on all workers and their very right to organize.

88

TEA PARTY OR OCCUPY MOVEMENT?

October 19, 2011

As the Occupy movement gains steam and inspires similar protests worldwide, defenders of the so-called Tea Party have decried the Occupy activists as "law breakers," "radicals," and even "un-American" (unlike themselves, of course).

One imagines that such objections, coming from Tea Partiers, are meant to contrast Occupy activists not only with themselves, but with the original groups of Americans who made the term "Tea Party" history.

In this version, they were nice, law-abiding folk, engaged in a little, oh, patriotic disagreement.

Suffice it to say, it didn't exactly happen that way.

The late, great historian Howard Zinn, in his groundbreaking *A People's History of the United States: 1492-Present*, recounts the Tea Party as a great event not only of rebellion, but of law-breaking. Imagine the worth of crates of imported tea, broken into and tossed into the Boston Harbor. The property of local merchants—destroyed. Why? Because of the taxes added on, which made Americans angry at such high prices for something they considered a staple. It was also a thumb in the eye of the British.

The British government responded to this provocation by passing Parliament's Coercive Acts, closed down Boston's port, dissolved the local colonial government, and brought in armed troops, virtually establishing martial law.

Now, which contemporary group more closely resembles their American ancestors? The Tea Party or the Occupy movement?

And lest we miss the big lesson, women played a pivotal role in these protests as well. John Adams's wife, Abigail, wrote of a "coffee party" led by nearly 100 women who, angry at the high coffee prices at a Boston store, marched down to the warehouse, and demanded the "stingy" merchant surrender his keys.

Abigail describes what the women did with the merchant:

> [O]ne of them seized him by his neck and tossed him into the cart. Upon his finding no quarter, he delivered the keys when they tipped up the cart and discharged him; then opened the warehouse, hoisted out the coffee themselves, put it into the trunks and drove off. A large concourse of men stood amazed, silent spectators of the whole transaction.[1]

"Law-breakers"? "Radicals"? "Un-American"?

Well, they broke the law, certainly, for, during colonial days, English law ruled. Were they radicals? Probably.

Were they un-American?

They destroyed private property. They reacted to the rich getting richer by looting their warehouses.

Sounds pretty American to me.

89

TO MY BRETHEN AND SISTAS ON THE ROW

December 18, 2011

It has been barely a week since I departed Death Row, yet I cannot help but look back, for many of you are in my heart.

I may no longer be on Death Row, but because of you Death Row is still with me. How could that not be so, when I've spent more years of my life on Death Row than in "freedom"? Or, spent more time on Death Row than with my family?

I write to tell you all—even those I've never met—that I love you, for we have shared something exceedingly rare. I have shared tears and laughter with you, that the world will neither know nor see. I have shared your anguish when some judge shattered your hopes and spat disappointment, or when some politician sought to use you to climb to higher office.

We have seen time and disease take some of our people off the Row. We have seen several choose their own date to die, cheating the hangman via suicide (William "Bill" Tilley, Jose "June" Pagan).

But, Brothers and Sisters of the Row, I write not of death, but of life.

If I can walk off, so can you.

Keep rumblin', keep fightin', keep rockin'. Check out your Mills issue.[1]

But there is more. Live each day, each hour, as if it is the only time there is. Love fiercely. Learn a new thing. A language. An art. A science. Keep your mind alive. Keep your heart alive. Laugh!

Look at each other not as competitors, but as fellow travelers on the same red road of life.

No matter what the world says of you, see the best in each other and radiate love to each other. Be your best self.

If you are blessed to have family, send your love to them all—no matter what. If you have a spiritual family or faith, practice it fully and deeply, for this links you to something greater than yourself. No matter what, Christian, Muslim, devotee of Judaism, Hinduism, Krishna Consciousness, Buddhism or Santería (or MOVE).

This broadens you and deepens you.

I have been blessed to have many of you as my teachers, and my students. Some have been my sons; some have been my brothers. Yet I see all of you as part of my family.

Take heart, for the death penalty itself is dying. States and counties simply can't afford it, and politicians who run on it are finding fewer and fewer buyers. Juries (especially in places like Philly) are increasingly reluctant to vote for death, even in cases where it appears inevitable.

Sisters on the Row, while we have never met, my heart has felt your tears as you are forcibly separated from your children, unable to hold or kiss them. In many ways, as women, your anguish has been the worst, as your loves and sensitivities are deepest. My words to my brothers are yours as well: Keep mind alive. Keep hearts alive. Live. Love. Learn. Laugh!

I know you all as few outsiders do. I've met artists, musicians, mathematicians, managers, jailhouse lawyers and stockbrokers.

I've seen guys who couldn't draw a straight line emerge as master painters (Cush, Young Buck); I've seen guys come from near illiteracy to become fluent in foreign languages; I've met teachers who've created works of surpassing beauty and craftsmanship (Big Tony).

You are all far more than others say of you, for the spark of the infinite glows within each of you.

You are on Death Row, but what is finest in you is greater

than Death Row. So care for each other. Not in words, but in the heart.

Think good vibes on each other.

Lastly, don't rat. (If ratting was so cool, they would've beat me off the Row). Keep rumblin', 'cause your day is coming.

FOR A REVOLUTIONARY BLACK HISTORY MONTH

February 21, 2012

As we once again approach February, the papers and TV stations will feature programming that shows more Black faces than usual. Some will show movies, some documentaries and some will feature history in celebration of Black History Month.

Undoubtedly, Martin Luther King Jr.'s epic "March on Washington" speech will be sampled, its grainy, black-and-white videotape the very symbol of a bygone era, and its key catchphrase, "Thank God Almighty, we're free at last!" a haunting and ironic mockery of the real state of most of Black America.

One tape that invariably will not be shown is one of the final press conferences of the nation's first—and perhaps only—Black U.S. Supreme Court justice, Thurgood Marshall, aged and ill, yet with the presence of mind to announce, "I'm still not free."

For millions of Black Americans, this Black History Month, while perhaps rich in symbolism, comes amidst the greatest loss of collective assets in our history—crippling joblessness, haunting home foreclosures, public schools that perform more mis-education than education, rabid police terrorism and perhaps the highest Black incarceration rates in U.S. history, with all that entails.

That we have Black History Month at all is due to the Black Freedom movements of the 1960s and the dogged persistence of Black historian Carter G. Woodson, who began his efforts with Negro History Week back in the 1920s! Yet it begins, as do all struggles for progress, with the movement.

If Black mothers and grandmothers and later Black schoolchildren hadn't followed King, we wouldn't know his name, except perhaps as a historical footnote. For without followers there is no movement—and thus no progress.

The late, great Marxist revolutionary historian C.L.R. James, in his finest work, *Black Jacobins*,[1] a history of the Haitian revolution, illustrates how the leadership—including Gen. Toussaint L'Ouverture—tried repeatedly to betray the revolution only to face two immovable forces: the racist recalcitrance of the French government of Napoleon, who wanted to restore slavery, and the militancy of the Black soldiers, who pushed onward to revolution.

The point? People make history by mass movements, often ones that go faster and further than the leaders want. And masses make and sustain revolutions—often against "leaders" whose every instinct is to betray them. In a foreword to one of the many editions of *Black Jacobins*, James reminds us that "it was the slaves who had made the revolution. Many of the slave leaders, to the end, were unable to read or write."[2]

But they sure knew how to fight.

Haitian General Jean-Jacques Dessalines won the last major battle of the Haitian revolution, the Battle of Vertières, in November 1803, against Napoleon's troops, then the most powerful army on earth, and strung up a few of the French officers.

Africans by the tens of thousands broke their chains, and though penniless, hungry and scarred by the ravages of bondage, found weapons and the will to fight for freedom against the defenders of slavery: France, Britain and Spain. They beat them all, because their hunger for freedom was greater than anything.

ANYTHING.

And by so doing they changed world history.

They shattered French dreams of an American empire and enabled the U.S. to double in size after its purchase of Louisiana from Napoleon.

They also did what no "slave" army had ever done in modern or ancient history. They defeated an empire.

That is revolutionary Black History—and it deserves to be remembered during Black History Month.

9 1 .

MEMORIES FOR MAROON

May 12, 2012

His name is almost legendary: Russell "Maroon" Shoatz, an affiliate of the Black Panther Party, an activist and Black revolutionary.

My teenage memory is sparse about him, other than what I read in the paper, which is largely disbelieved. As a member of the Black United Liberation Front, I prepared a leaflet in his support, calling for letters to be written to him.

Occasional news flashes intervened, but such reports became increasingly rare, and his name faded into the mist of memory, except for his family and closest comrades. Until 1995, when I was transferred to Greene's ominous Death Row, folks assumed I knew him, although we'd never met. Again, we saw each other sparingly, until a cool day, perhaps in 1998, when we were near each other in the "yard"—actually, the "cage"—separated only by two walls of fencing. He praised my newest book, *Faith of Our Fathers*,[1] a study of African American and African spiritual traditions. I was thrilled that he'd read and enjoyed it.

The next time I saw and really talked to him was Friday, December 9, 2011, around 7 a.m., the day after I left Death Row. We both tried to ignore the biting sub-freezing temperatures, wearing T-shirts and boxers under thin, flimsy orange jumpsuits, with "yard" lasting only an hour.

Even though not formally on "the Row," I unconsciously expected two hours of yard, but Maroon knew better. He launched into an analysis of the Occupy movement that left me stunned with his brilliance, insight and succinctness. I thought to myself, "Whoa! This guy has thought long and deeply about this; I've got to sharpen up my game!"

According to Maroon, this new formation showed how technology has transformed not only communications, but organizing itself. It cut out the middleman—went straight to the potential activist and convinced him or her to engage or disengage. He explained that this new social medium gave impetus to organizing in Tahrir Square, Cairo, but also in the U.S.-based Occupy movement. Organizing would never be the same, he said.

For three frigid mornings on C Pod, Maroon and I met for just under an hour, and I left impressed each time. For here was a man who was arguably one of the longest-held Black political prisoners in America—with the possible exception of former Black Panther Chip Fitzgerald of California—unquestionably one of the longest-held men in Pennsylvania's solitary, kept for over 30 years. And although he was nearly 70 years old, his mind was as sharp as a cactus, informed, analytical, intuitive, acute.

Three days—three hours—and then I was gone.

Maroon—writer, historian and theorist—remained, as he does to this day. His loving family continues to fight for his release from the tortures of "the hole" by making people aware of the plight of Maroon.

92.

BEYOND TRAYVON: WHEN THE
PERSONAL AIN'T POLITICAL

July 21, 2012

The Trayvon Martin case is rightly the straw that broke the camel's back, for it shows, with unusual clarity, how Black life is so easily trivialized.

But it is not alone in this endeavor.

How the corporate media have responded to this tragedy is its own form of trivialization: a feeding frenzy of sheer spectacle, the exploitation of emotion, and endless, directionless discussion, leading less to light than to commercials.

For the media explores the episodic, while it ignores the systematic.

Thus, Trayvon's case attracts the lights and videos, but the many, many others who fall, especially to police violence, draw little interest.

Absent from most discussions is the targeting of a system that cages more people than any in history. Lost from the orgy of spectacle are the hidden faces of mass incarceration that impacts millions.

For, while attention to the episodic elicits tears, contemplation on the systematic brings the challenge of change.

If "Stand Your Ground" gets repealed, it does not change the system that treats many, many youths as expendable.

Several months ago, by just one vote the Supreme Court condemned the practice of sending juveniles to life terms in prison without possibility of parole.

Of all the jurisdictions in America—indeed, in the whole, wide world—Pennsylvania ranked first in juvenile life incarcerations. *First.*

But juveniles aren't only the targets of the prison industry, they face shuttered schools, rampant joblessness, and the fear and loathing of their elders.

They face tomorrows of emptiness.

They face the faceless fury of a system that damns them to half-lives at their birth.

Trayvon is one; they are many.

93

THE *REAL* JOHN CARTER

August 17, 2012

Several months ago a science-fiction flick was released featuring a superhuman fighting nasty aliens on a forbidding planet somewhere in the cosmos. As a sci-fi fan, I confess interest, but I never heard of the title character, John Carter. (I later learned that the story was based on the lesser-known works of Edgar Rice Burroughs, known for the Tarzan books.)

In fact, as the movie was seeking an audience, another John Carter was facing a deadly force—prison guards armed with weapons of mayhem. Carter was locked in a prison cell as it was being pumped full of pepper spray.

This John Carter had spent over half his life in Pennsylvania prison cells following a robbery-murder conviction after he was certified by the courts as an adult despite his juvenile age. Irony after irony abounds, for this John Carter seems to have predicted his own demise in a letter he wrote to members of the U.S. Congress seeking passage of a bill outlawing juvenile life terms. In his June 2009 letter, John Carter wrote the following:

> Now years go by as I struggle to evolve and mature within a cell I now view as my casket. Some days I'm hopeless . . . some days I'm focused. But every day I realize that after 14 years I am no longer growing. . . . I am deteriorating . . . emotionally . . . physically, psychologically, and spiritually. Instead of living, I simply exist until my heart stops beating, my lungs stop breathing, and my soul is called into the next life. I ask myself on occasion—is this the form of damnation other human beings wish upon troubled

youth? Are we in a society that believes in a forgiving God, but the same society will turn around and be UNFORGIVING to a child's trespass?[1]

Witnesses from the "hole" at Rockview Prison say John Carter barricaded himself in his cell and armored guards attacked the cell, pumping at least three canisters of pepper spray into the windowless, enclosed area—not only burning his eyes, mouth and nose, but depriving him of any usable oxygen.

When the door was breached, guards rushed in using electrified stun shields to subdue him, repeatedly. Those in view said the 35-year-old man was carried out with his knees and head dragging on the ground.

His friends called him "J-Rock." But his name was John Carter on state documents recording his death on April 26, 2012.

The real John Carter was a juvenile lifer who was sentenced at 16 years old under a law that the U.S. Supreme Court recently ruled was unconstitutional in *Alabama v. Miller.*

Irony of ironies. "J-Rock" never lived to see it.

94

ENDING SOLITARY CONFINEMENT

September 5, 2012

Brothers and Sisters! *¡Hermanos y Hermanas!* Comrades! Thank
you all for coming together here.

You may think that you know something about solitary,
but you don't. You may have a loved one in prison who has
experienced it and told you about it.

But still I say, you don't know it.

You know the word, but between the word and the reality,
a world exists.

You don't know that world.

But the closest we may come is to say it must be like life on
another planet. One where the air is different, where the water
is different, where wildlife and flora and fauna mean different
things.

For, just as you know the word "torture," you don't know
how it feels. Solitary *is* torture.

State torture.

Official torture. Government-sanctioned torture.

Some may call that hyperbole, or exaggeration.

But I've lived in solitary longer than many—most, perhaps—Americans have been alive. I've seen men driven mad
as a hatter by soul-crushing loneliness. Who have sliced their
arms until they looked like railroad tracks. Or burned themselves alive.

This isn't something I've read about in psychology books
or newspaper reports. I've seen it with these eyes looking on
as I write these words. I've smelled the blood. I've smelled the
nauseating stench of the smoke.

Why? Because human beings are social creatures; and solitary confinement kills that which is human within us.

Why did these men do these things (to themselves)?

We can't really know, but if I could guess I'd say they simply wanted to feel. To feel something. To feel as if they were alive.

I've seen men beaten while handcuffed, shocked with Tasers and electrified shields, and gassed with pepper spray—really a form of liquid cayenne pepper, which inflames the eyes, nasal passages and mouth.

As America embarks on its second century of mass incarceration, breaking every repressive record ever made, it's also breaking every record in regard to solitary confinement: locking up, isolating and torturing more and more people, for more and more years.

As I've noted elsewhere (in my book *Live from Death Row*,[1] for example), in 1890 the U.S. Supreme Court, in the case *re Medley*, held that solitary confinement for a man on Colorado's Death Row was unconstitutional. In a sense, over a century later, the law has lurched backwards!

Today, such an idea would be laughable, if not unthinkable. According to some estimates, there are more than 100,000 people in solitary across the country. I happen to believe this is a conservative estimate. But no matter the number, the reality is stark: under international law, solitary confinement is torture.

Period.

And if it happens to one man, one woman, or one child, it is torture nonetheless, and a crime under international law.

That's because such a policy has one primary purpose: to destroy human beings by destroying their minds.

Is it cruel and unusual, and thus violative of the Eighth Amendment to the U.S. Constitution? Apparently this was so in the 1890s, but not so in the present, probably because of who was in prison then—and who is now.

It may surprise you to know that at the end of the 19th century, Blacks were a distinct minority of American prisoners, and while numbers certainly swelled post-slavery (to build the prison contract-labor industry—really slavery by another name), the biggest bounce in Black imprisonment came in the aftermath of the Civil Rights and Black Liberation movements, when Black people, en masse, opposed the system of white supremacy, police brutality and racist juries.

And then—the Empire strikes back!

Indeed, never in the history of the modern world have we seen such a vast machinery of repression, and the United States is the world's undisputed leader in imprisonment of its citizens.

Neither China, Russia nor any other nation comes close. As scholar–law professor Michelle Alexander has aptly described it, the U.S. has reconstituted a "New Jim Crow."

And as prison populations explode, the law becomes increasingly more supportive of this repression and less tolerant of the notion of equal rights, or even equal access to courts. These factors have continued to be problems irrespective of whether under Republican or Democratic administrations. For repression is apparently bipartisan.

But all is not gloom and doom.

People have the power to transform their grim realities. All they have to do is fight for it. Organize.

When people get together—and fight together—they create change. They make change. If you want to shut down solitary confinement, you can do it. You've got to organize—and fight for it.

If you find the prison-industrial complex intolerable, then organize—and fight it.

This is not Pollyannaish, or pie in the sky.

This is as gritty and as down-to-earth as spinach.

It's as real as dirt. As real as steel. As real as blood. As real as life.

Whenever any social advance has happened, it's because people fought for it. Often against their own governments, for governments ever embrace the status quo.

During the U.S. Civil War, one of Lincoln's severest critics was Frederick Douglass, the fiery Black ex-slave and abolitionist. When Lincoln died a few years later, Douglass would both mourn his passing and laud his accomplishments. It was Douglass who said: "Power concedes nothing without demand. It never has, and never will." That lesson of our Ancestor is still true.

We must demand what we want—and fight for it!

Period.

If we want the closing of solitary confinement, we can make it happen.

If we want people like Delbert Africa, Mike Africa, Russell "Maroon" Shoatz, Janet Africa, Phil Africa, Janine Africa, Chuck Africa, Leonard Peltier, Jalil Muntaqim, Ed Africa or Dr. Mutulu Shakur freed, we can make it happen.

Really. Truly. But we gotta fight for it.

Movements make change. So let us build such a movement, one that shakes the earth! Don't rely on voting, for politics is but the cruel art of betrayal. Rely on working together and fighting for change.

For "*power concedes nothing without demand*"!

Build the Movement!

Let us go forth and make the change we want, for we are the hope of more people than we know—and people make change!

Ona MOVE! Long Live John Africa!

Power concedes nothing without demand! Down with solitary!

Shut Attica down!

Down with the prison-industrial complex!

95

OBAMA'S RE-ELECTION: WHAT IT MEANS, WHAT IT DOESN'T

January 20, 2013

For the second time in American history, a Black man takes the office of U.S. president—a feat not thought possible just a few years ago.

The re-election of Barack Hussein Obama to the nation's highest office is indeed a watershed moment and a tribute to a man who is a true master of the game of politics.

Few politicians could've prevailed against the headwinds bearing down upon him—a mobilized and highly motivated opposition, the monetary windfall of campaign riches made possible by the Supreme Court's *Citizen's United* ruling, and the candidacy of an exceedingly wealthy and utterly ruthless opponent, "Mitt" Romney.

Despite occasional setbacks, few politicians, Black or white, have had careers so blessed.

But the conditions of Black Americans could hardly be called blessed. By all the measurements by which we rank life, Blacks rank at the bottom, where life is a nightmare.

Health, education, employment, life expectancy, mortality, incarceration—you name it—the figures betray a life at the margins; lives at the bottom.

Moreover, it is unrealistic to expect any change for the better in four years—no matter who is president—nor what color he or she is.

Them's the facts.

It is a great and remarkable symbol that a Black person is elected—and re-elected—to the presidency.

It is a dazzling spectacle.

Yet it remains a spectacle.

The lives of everyday Black folk are just as grim as they were four years ago. They still must seek a way out of the prison-keep that is America.

A new, dark-skinned warden doesn't change that.

Education will still be a dizzying maze for millions of children who leave school bitter and uneducated.

The police are a repressive presence all day long, making life unbearable.

And behind it all stands what legal scholar Michelle Alexander calls "The New Jim Crow" (also the title of her book), a system of oppressive containment on a scale that the world has never seen.

A one-day celebration, and four more years of hell.

96.

MARTIN LUTHER KING: IN MEMORY AND IN LIFE

April 4, 2013

Dr. Martin Luther King Jr. gave his now-famous "Beyond Vietnam" speech at the Riverside Church 46 years ago, on April 4, 1967. A year later to the day of his Riverside address, on April 4, 1968, Dr. King was assassinated in Memphis, Tennessee. While the Riverside Church commemorates the speech yearly, last week's commemoration was special because it fell on a Thursday, the same day of the week that Dr. King was assassinated.

The program was titled "Honoring the Radical MLK." An edited version of this statement prepared by Mumia Abu-Jamal was published in the official program of the Riverside Church event.

—

I come today to praise Dr. Martin Luther King, not to berate him, for though he has become in our modern life perhaps America's only indigenous saint, it is useful to remember how utterly bedeviled he was in his final years of life, hounded as he was by the forces of the state. It is worthy for us to recall that the highest levels of government taped Dr. King's phone calls, monitored the privacy of his hotel rooms, steamed open his mail, and assigned anonymous informants to watch his every move. What we have forgotten in this era is how the second-highest official in the Federal Bureau of Investigation, one William Sullivan, wrote in a now notorious memo that Reverend Dr. Martin Luther King was "the most dangerous Negro in America."

How was he so?

You, of all people, the congregation at the Riverside Church, should know best, for it was here at Riverside's historic pulpit that Dr. King spake the words that, in FBI parlance, made him a "marked" man. Here he called his nation, the United States of America, "the greatest purveyor of violence on earth," and he condemned "militarism, racism and materialism."

King felt common cause with the peasants of Vietnam who were being bombed by the most powerful military in the world. To King, there was something not just un-Christian, but unseemly, when the wealthiest nation on earth unleashed an unprecedented level of violence on an industrially underdeveloped, agricultural society such as Vietnam. To King, follower of a poor Jewish carpenter, the worship of wealth amidst immense poverty in America deeply troubled him.

This is why the Reverend was marked by the state as "dangerous"—a socialist and a radical. This is why his fair-weather friends departed from him and denounced him in his greatest hour of need. Martin Luther King was an adversary of the military-industrial complex and the mammoth business interests that support it. This is why, like the crucified Jesus, state power marked him, quashed his voice, and gave him up to a violent death.

But King did not oppose war, materialism or racism purely out of ideological motivations. As a man and a child of God he felt these things cheapened people's relationship with one another and degraded the divine principle of life itself. He saw the dynamic of men fighting, bombing and killing other men, women and children as the ultimate sacrilege. King felt the pain of Vietnam because he truly believed in a *beloved community* . . . one without borders.

For these principled impulses, and for his words, he breathed his last, one year to the day after his Riverside address.

As we gather to remember Martin Luther King, we must ponder what this towering figure would say about the behemoth of modern-day mass incarceration, about stop and frisk, about the death penalty, about the bewildering violence of drones, and about the continuing hunger for wars abroad in our name.

We know that the true Martin Luther King does not dwell in statues, in ghetto streets bearing his name, or in schools where children are violated daily within buildings erected in his name. His true spirit dwells with the least of these, in communities of the poor worldwide, in ghettoes north and south, and yes, even in prisons.

In the revolutionary spirit of Dr. Martin Luther King, we remember him as he was, not as he has since become.

97

THE COMING ACQUITTAL OF TRAYVON MARTIN'S KILLER

July 8, 2013

By the time these words reach you, perhaps it will all be over.

"It" is the Zimmerman trial in Florida.

I have no idea what the ratings are for CNN (or CNBC, for that matter), but I'd bet it's pretty elevated for their usual summer viewership.

In this place, among the prison population, every man with a mouth wants to discuss the case.

In the chow hall. On the walkways. In the gym. On the yard.

Not even the buxom (and buttsome) beauties of "Love and Hip Hop" have garnered that much attention.

"Are you watching the trial?"

"Who do you think is gonna win?"

Questions bounce like basketballs, as all eyes are locked on this, the latest "trial of the century."

The trial of George Zimmerman for the homicide of unarmed 17-year-old Trayvon Martin has snatched a level of public attention that hasn't been seen since the mid-1990s—in other words, the O.J. Simpson murder trial.

I believe, frankly, that Zimmerman will be acquitted.

I may be wrong, but I don't think so.

I've never seen a defense lawyer utilize so skillfully the ju-jitsu-style techniques of witness flipping.

In all honesty, the state's prosecution witnesses became defense witnesses. And where the defense was adroit, the prosecutor bumbled and fumbled.

I may be wrong. I *hope* I'm wrong, but I don't think I am. We shall see.

98

PUERTO RICO: UNDER U.S. COLONIAL LAW

October 21, 2013

Greetings to Members and Delegates of the National Lawyers Guild in San Juan, Puerto Rico, for the Law for the People Convention.

As I thought about this event, I could not avoid thinking of the status of Puerto Ricans as part of the American Empire.

Puerto Ricans are, of course, American citizens by birth, but what kind of citizens? By U.S. law and custom, they are something other than most Americans, for though they may freely join the Army, they are forbidden (while on the island) from voting for a president, and, for that matter, forbidden from having their delegate to the U.S. House vote on matters outside of committee.

This distinction of Puerto Rico as a people separate from Americans surely had its genesis in its seizure from Spain in 1898, and thereafter, that idea was concretized in the U.S. Supreme Court's 1922 *Balzac v. Porto Rico* decision, which denied the right of Puerto Ricans to jury trials, saying, in essence, that they weren't ready for such an innovation. Lest any doubt my reasoning, please heed the following account from the opinion:

"The jury system needs citizens trained to the exercise of responsibility of jurors. In common law countries, centuries of tradition have prepared a conception of the impartial attitudes jurors must assume. The jury system postulates a conscious duty of participation in the machinery of justice, which it is hard for people not brought up in fundamentally popular governments to acquire at once. One of the greatest benefits is in the security it gives the people: through their role as jurors they can help prevent the arbitrary use or abuse of the judiciary system.

"Congress has thought that a people like the Filipinos or the Porto Ricans, trained to a complete judicial system which knows no juries, living in compact and ancient communities, with definitely formed customs and political conceptions, should be permitted themselves to determine how far they wish to adopt this institution of Anglo-Saxon origin."[1]

Apparently, Puerto Ricans (and Filipinos, it seems), weren't Anglo-Saxon enough to handle jury trials.

And while time has certainly changed (we note that the court now boasts a Puerto Rican justice), the imperial perspective of distinction, of difference, of deference owed the empire by the colony, yet remains.

For millions of Puerto Ricans, especially her political prisoners from the early 20th century to today, the right of national independence rates higher than second-class citizenship within the U.S. Empire. In 1950 and 1954, Puerto Rican independence fighters opened fire at President Harry Truman and members of Congress to emphasize their support for independence.

Lolita LeBron and Rafael Cancel Miranda, among others, spent decades in American prisons for their efforts.

A new generation of Independentistas emerged after the 1960s and the 1980s, and 11 were freed during the Clinton era, to buy support for Hillary Clinton's New York State Senate campaign.

Some, on principle, like Oscar López Rivera, remain in prison today, one of the longest-held political prisoners in the world.

We should not kid ourselves. Puerto Rico, though bedecked in finery, is a colony; moreover, as a jewel seized after an exhausted Spain was forced to withdraw after a losing effort to hold on to Cuba, it still isn't free.

Perhaps they are still not Anglo-Saxon enough.

99

"OF ALL OUR STUDIES, HISTORY BEST REWARDS OUR RESEARCH"

December 1, 2013

American history is longer, larger, more vicious, more beautiful, and more terrible than anything anyone has ever said about it.
—James Baldwin, December 21, 1963

It is an advantage, of sorts, to have been born when I was. For 1954 was the tail end of the Boomers, and on the brink of one of America's most rebellious eras of the 20th century—the 1960s. The year 1954 marked *Brown v. Board of Education*, the transformative anti-segregation education case (yet it didn't stop this writer from experiencing a primary and secondary education that was apartheid in everything but name).

It was a time of ferment, of psychological, societal, political, sexual and racial transformation, the ripples of which are still with us. America was facing its painful emergence from its own variety of apartheid, forced to do so by influences both external and internal. Inside the United States the civil rights and Black Power movements were shaking the state and corporate classes to the core. Externally, the repercussions thereof revealed the U.S. to be, centrally, a white supremacist state, at the very time when decolonization and independence movements raged in Africa and Asia.

Into this milieu appeared one of Black America's most dynamic leaders—Malcolm X.

To hear this man's voice, to read his life story, and to see his rise from the very depths of society to its representational heights was epic. The power and immediacy of his oration fired my blood with the necessity of revolution. He may have been a Black Muslim minister, but he was a modern-day Jeremiah, launching words of truth and power at the world's most powerful empire.

In that remarkable yet brief life, one literally saw the power of history at work. For the story of Black America (as taught by the Nation of Islam), took one of the most despised of men (one whose prison nickname was "Satan") and radically transformed him into one of the organization's most effective and energetic ministers.

For me and my generation of that era, to hear him speak was like listening to thunder. One could not help but be moved, outraged, energized—radicalized. I became, in my heart, a Malcolmite.

That influence, coupled with the April 14, 1968, assassination of Martin Luther King Jr. (his closest competitor for Black America's heart), would propel thousands of young men and women to join the nearest formation of the Black Panther Party. Indeed, this writer (in his 15th year of life) helped found and form the Philadelphia branch of that group.

That world of the 1960s may've passed into the river of history's flow, but it continues to pulse in the veins of the living present. For the Black Freedom movement gave life and energy to successive movements of the latter 20th century: the Women's movement, the Gay Rights movement, the Latin@ movement, and more.

We learn from these historical observances something vital: that movements have effects far beyond their own existence; they influence, inform, bleed into other spaces of life. Why? Because they live.

In Malcolm's life, the Nation of Islam became his site for learning—his school and university. This is not surprising, given the dearth of history taught to millions of Black children in the realm of public education.

Prisons are (by reputation) the abode of the ignorant, for

many of their citizens attended apartheid-held educational systems where the level of education was abysmally low.[1] And while there may be some truth to such reports, it is also true that for some prisoners, properly motivated, cells can become isolated spaces of learning.

Such was the case for Malcolm X.

Such too was the case for me, beginning as a child of two of the latter travelers in the Great Migration (both hailed from North Carolina), who saw education as the one acquisition that could not be taken by the forces of repression. Father may've reached the fifth grade of formal schooling (he was born in 1897), and Mother graduated high school in her sixth decade of life (she was born in 1924). And while they had decades of differences between them, their voices often joined in a singular message to their children, one hard-learned from life: "Boy, you better get yo'self an education: it's the only thing that the white man can't take from you!"

They left the southlands of their births in search of a better life, and in hope of the opportunity of a better education for their children. And although they no longer dwell among the living, their influence continues to resonate among those they bore.

But youth is the spirit of rebellion, and for me, as for many people of the 1960s, the voices of parents faded before the searing roar of revolution raging in the streets of America and through the hearts of the youth. That irresistible pull had a gravity all its own, and I left school without graduating. School seemed unreal—and worst of all, boring. But in this era, where free winds blew through many institutions, graduation was no barrier to college enrollment.

On the advice of an older man, I entered Goddard College, circa 1973. The call came again, and I answered its song, dropping out again.

But, as with Malcolm, education beckoned like a light in the midst of darkness. On Death Row, in a place designed to never let lights blaze, I returned to the college of my youth and, writing furiously (by hand, as typewriters were not permitted), caught up on my work and wrote a final project paper on the liberation psychology and theology of two revolutionary doctors of the 1960s–1970s: psychologist Ignacio Martín-Baró and psychiatrist Frantz Fanon. In a few years, I was able to finally complete my parents' dream of college graduation.

That hunger for education asserted itself yet again, and I promptly entered graduate school for a master's in the humanities. Those studies deepened and enriched my thinking on history, and taught me the theoretical value of primary and secondary sources to truly study and impart history.

But as Goethe has said (I paraphrase), "Theory is gray—until touched by the green tree of life."

Reading Gary B. Nash's groundbreaking *The Unknown American Revolution*,[2] one cannot but be deeply impressed by his research and usage of primary sources to rediscover history that has lain silent for centuries. Nash, a former president of the Organization of American Historians, has brought green life to the boughs and dry bones of days long gone.

Such work, with new information on virtually every page, can only inspire aspiring historians.

Reading such an unexpected wealth of revelation, the voice of Malcolm came to mind: "Of all our studies, history best rewards our research."

In the mind's silence, a voice is heard saying, "I want to do that." I shall endeavor to do so.

Here.

Now.

NATIONAL SECURITY AGENCY

December 17, 2013

Long before the name Edward Snowden became known, the National Security Agency (NSA) was involved in warrantless wiretapping and eavesdropping on people all around the world; yes, even Americans.

This was known and done repeatedly before Barack Obama assumed the presidency, and at the highest levels of government.

In his 2008 book *The Shadow Factory*, national security reporter James Bamford tells how the FISA court (its name an acronym for the Foreign Intelligence Surveillance Act) signed secret court orders without even reading them.

He quotes a former NSA intern who brought NSA requests to them. Now a prominent law professor at George Washington University Law School, Jonathan Turley recounts: "I was shocked with what I saw. I was convinced that the judge . . . would have signed anything that we put in front of him, and I wasn't entirely sure that he had actually *read* what we put in front of him."[1]

But even that was too much for the Bush administration, for after 9/11 they decided that the president was not bound by the Fourth Amendment to the U.S. Constitution. They informed the then-presiding judge of the FISA court, federal judge Royce Lamberth, that the president had decided to conduct warrantless surveillance.

Period.

Lamberth, at the meeting in the Attorney General's office, agreed to not even inform his fellow judges on the FISA court.

Secret courts. Secret decisions.

By October 4, 2001, it was a done deal. It has only grown since then.

The Snowden revelations have brought those measures to light recently, including the bugging of presidents, prime ministers and even German chancellor Angela Merkel.

Why? Because they can. They have the capability.

If you don't think they can be, or *are*, presently bugging Americans—well, you're being naïve.

This is the United States today—all ears—all the time.

MARTIN, WOMEN AND THE MOVEMENT

January 3, 2014

If Dr. Martin Luther King were alive today, he'd be 85 years old.

But he is not. Yet his ideas have deepened through the experience of movements, and perhaps more importantly, his inspiration remains.

For the Civil Rights movement has had a profound impact on the nation, the world and movements to come. But Martin, reared as he was in the bosom of a conservative, privileged, middle-class Baptist family, seemed ill-prepared for the topsy-turvy, hurly-burly battles of the era, when Blacks were compelled to struggle against their racial, class, gender and national oppressions.

Given his background of privilege, he found confident, outspoken, activist women hard to take. This was perhaps best seen in his interactions with activist-organizer Ella Baker. For, let us be clear: like many, perhaps most men, King was sexist and chauvinistic. As a man of his class, and his profession, he expected deference—especially from women.

Ella Baker, a brilliant and skillful organizer, was unable to defer to any of the spiritual and national leaders of the time. She opposed, on principle, the idea of charismatic leadership, preferring instead collective leaders drawn from their work among the people.

She was among the founders of the Southern Christian Leadership Conference (SCLC), founded the Student Non-Violent Coordinating Committee (SNCC), and had traveled the country organizing as field secretary for the NAACP. In

Baker's words, she knew she wouldn't make it as a leader among the ministers of SCLC, explaining:

> There would never be any role for me in a leadership capacity with SCLC. Why? First, I'm a woman. Also, I'm not a minister. And second . . . I knew that my penchant for speaking honestly . . . would not be well tolerated. The combination of the basic attitude of men, and especially ministers, as to what the role of women in these church setups is—that of taking orders, not providing leadership—and the . . . ego problems involved in having to feel that there is someone who . . . had more information about a lot of things than they possessed at the time. This would never have lent itself to my being a leader in the movement there.[1]

King felt "uncomfortable" around Baker, and other women of her type. She had a saying: "Strong people don't need strong leaders."[2] She also wasn't keen on building national organizations; she believed in building movements.

King, as a man transformed by the burgeoning movement around him, tried mightily to adapt to it, but it wasn't easy. For, like many men, King had a weakness for female flesh. He felt guilty about it, yes—but he indulged, for he couldn't say no. In this conflict between flesh and spirit, flesh inevitably won out.

Many of us associate Dr. King with his last big movement push: the Poor People's Campaign. When he accepted the invite of the National Welfare Rights Organization's executive director, George Wiley, to address their board, he experienced a rude awakening. For the NWRO board was staffed by women, and they felt offended, because they had advanced the idea of a poor people's campaign before the Southern Christian Leadership Conference.

When King sat down with the board, they shocked him

with their aggressiveness and their radical thinking. When King was given the floor, he stated his ideas and solicited their support. NWRO First Vice Chair Etta Horn asked him for his views on Public Law 90-248. King was dumbfounded. NWRO leader Johnnie Tillmon (a woman), told King that Horn "meant the Anti-Welfare Bill, H.R. 12080," passed by Congress the year before and signed into law by President Lyndon Johnson in January 1967. King again had no clue. Tillmon pressed her advantage, asking pointedly, "Where were you . . . when we were down in Washington trying to get support for Senator Kennedy's amendments?"

King, the leader of the movement, was helpless before welfare mothers at the top of their game. Johnnie Tillmon, seeing that he and his staff were getting defensive, said, "You know, Dr. King, if you don't know about these questions, you should say you don't know, and then we could go on with the meeting." King agreed, saying, "You're right, Mrs. Tillmon, we don't know anything about welfare; we're here to learn."[3]

And he did. He listened. He learned.

That learning reshaped, deepened and broadened his ideas. He outgrew many of his earlier notions and became increasingly socialist in his economic orientation, anti-capitalist, and, quite rare for the time among Black civil rights leaders, deeply anti-war.

While Martin, as preacher, might've brought women to church, it must also be said that women, as teachers, took him to school. For at the heart, at the very core of both church and the movement, were women. Their faith, their wisdom, their knowledge, their visions of a better tomorrow, fed those expressions and gave them life.

Martin's martyrdom may've ended his individual existence, but it did not still the movement. For movements spread, grow, deepen and develop. The Civil Rights movement gave space and life to the Black Liberation movement, the women's movement, the Latin@ movement, the gay movement—and beyond. That's because those democratic energies could not be repressed forever. When King burst through, he opened doors that had been soldered shut in American society.

One of the most radical of the Black liberation groups to sprout in the post-King period was the Black Panther Party, founded by two college students two years before King's assassination. Although there is no doubt the Black Panther Party was weighted with a decidedly macho image—what with the berets, the black leather jackets and, lest we forget, guns—it was most assuredly not an all-male collective. Indeed, quite the reverse is true.

The Black Panther Party had a majority of female members, and a good number of women led local sections or even captaincies in cities. Indeed, the Black Panther Party was the only formation of the era to have a woman in complete command of the group (under Elaine Brown).[4]

Was the Black Panther Party sexist? Yes, without question. But within a sexist society, who was not? If King, with all his extraordinary education and gifts, was trapped within the dark amber of sexism, what of men who had no such learning, who learned from the streets?

That said, the Black Panther Party leadership announced at this very time that it supported women's liberation—and gay liberation, to boot. Party co-founder Huey P. Newton mused, "Maybe they might be the most oppressed people in society." Frankye Malika Adams, from the Brooklyn chapter of the Party, said, "Women ran the Black Panther Party pretty much. I don't know how it got to be a male's party or thought of as a male's party." She knew what every male Panther knew, that despite what the newspapers reported, without women, who made sure the work got done, every day, the organization would not have lasted as long, or done as well, as it did. Period.[5]

Women form the core of movements. They organize, as did Ella Baker. They lead, as did Elaine Brown. They do the work to make organizations—and movements—work. And given the sexism extant in a capitalist society, it rarely gets reported, much less known.

But the simple truth is that revolution is woman's work. And man's work. It is the work of all of us, working as comrades. Kathleen Cleaver was a member. She joined the Party and today is a law professor working against the prison-industrial complex. Safiya Asya Bukhari was a college student who was intrigued by the Party's Breakfast for Children Program. When she was threatened by cops, she quit college, joined the Party and later ran the Party's East Coast organization from the Bronx headquarters. Still later, she led and commanded units of the Black Liberation Army before she returned to the ancestors.

Martin Luther King Jr. was made, both literally and figuratively, by women. They educated him, even when he didn't want to be educated. Again, as Baker stated, "Martin didn't make the movement; the movement made Martin."

Progressive and liberatory social movements are energized and sustained by the gifts women bring with them. They broaden our perspectives on issues of women, of gender, and of how, under capitalism, everyone living within the prisons of capitalism are exploited, atomized and made to war against each other.

Martin opened doors to rooms he did not know existed, but he did so with the hope that it would lead to greater social justice and fairness. In one of his later speeches before the Southern Christian Leadership Conference, King presented a synthesis of his ideas, calling for a radical restructuring of the entire system: "We are called upon to help the discouraged beggars in life's marketplace. But one day we must come to see that an edifice which produces beggars needs restructuring." He continued this questioning openly now, in ways he had done privately: "Who owns the oil? . . . Who owns the iron ore? Why is it that people have to pay water bills in a world that is two-thirds water?" The Martin Luther King of 1967 was a different man from the M.L. King of 1965, a deeper man. Such a man as would say this:

> A nation that would keep people in slavery for 244 years will "thingify" them, make them things. Therefore they will exploit them and poor people generally, economically. And a nation that will exploit will have to have foreign investments . . . and will have to use its military might to protect them. All of these problems are tied together.[6]

It is a measure of some irony that King couldn't bring himself to work more closely with one of the most talented organizers of the era: Ella Baker. For, some 30 years before her career as a civil rights organizer bloomed, she co-wrote, with colleague Marvel Cooke, a remarkable article published in the NAACP journal *The Crisis*, which revealed the venal nature of capitalism for poor Black women in Harlem. They wrote:

> Not only is human labor bartered and sold for the slave wage, but human love is also a marketable commodity. Whether it is labor or love, the women arrive as early as eight a.m. and remain as late as one p.m., or until they are hired. In rain or shine, hot or cold, they wait to work for ten, fifteen, and twenty cents per hour.[7]

This, the naked face of capitalism, where one sells one's flesh to eat, was an insight that Baker knew, but it took a lifetime for King to glimpse. Capitalism eats its own, for there are no Chinese walls or sacred barriers—it is buy and sell, money-trading as the highest value of life.

It shows us all how far the Movement has yet to go.[8]

103

LAND GRABS

March 19, 2014

With the annexation of Crimea to the Russian Federation, U.S. politicians have gone cuckoo, raising Cain about it, likening it to Hitler's seizure of Poland, with Americans snarling about violations of international law, about "land grabs."

Almost immediately, Americans and Europeans, citing threats of "regional destabilization," announced sanctions on Russia.

For Americans to crow about "land grabs" is, above all, an assault on U.S. history.

For how did America come to be, if not for vast land grabs from the so-called Indians, and later, from the Mexicans?

Was it illegal? Yep. Did it violate International Law? You betcha!

Treaties are pacts between nations. The United States violated so many treaties with Native nations that it's almost embarrassing to recount.

Remember Texas? It was part of Mexico, until the Americans rebelled. For almost 10 years it was its own country—the Republic of Texas—until 1845, when the United States annexed it.

Nevada? New Mexico? Arizona? Utah? Colorado? California? All of it was part of Mexico until the United States started a war to justify a land grab. By 1848, it was over, and more than half a million square miles of Mexico became part of the United States of America.

I'm not a scholar of Crimea—or of Russia for that matter.

But I do know that it was originally annexed by Russia in 1783. It remained Russian until 1991, when it was ceded to Ukraine.

300 · *Land Grabs*

Seen from this perspective, Russia had a better claim to Crimea than the U.S. had to northwestern Mexico. Shall the United States return the land it stole from Mexico? Shall it then return the millions of square miles it swindled from indigenous nations by violating international treaty law? The very question seems rather silly to us, doesn't it?

And yet in 1999, our neighbor to the north, Canada, carved out a vast swath of its Northwest Territory and returned it to the descendants of the indigenous, traditional people, the Inuit. It's called Nunavut—and it's roughly the size of the so-called Louisiana Purchase, the land that France sold to the United States, doubling its size overnight.

The very idea is crazy in the United States—giving back land.

In Canada, it's history.

104

BEATINGS

July 7, 2014

The scenes are, unfortunately, all too familiar.

A person is beaten ruthlessly, relentlessly, by a cop (or group of cops).

A video is released, and, at least initially, public sympathy flows to the beaten figure on the bottom.

Before long, however, the counter-narrative emerges: the beaten was belligerent, combative, resisted arrest—or, worst of all, was on drugs!

Then, the story goes away. Done!

In California, a 51-year-old grandmother is pummeled by a cop, who throws something like a dozen punches in bunches. He is hitting her like she's a man.

In occupied Palestine, a teenager, 15-year-old Tariq Abu Khdeir, is seen punched, kicked and stomped by black-uniformed cops, who then place the child, now beaten into a stupor, into a waiting vehicle.

The grandmother? Police say she was playing in traffic.

The teenager? Cops said he was with boys with knives.

Yeah. So they beat them.

The videos are chilling. They are Rodney King, without the batons. They are Delbert Africa, without the rifle butts.

And they are standard operating procedure.

It's what cops do.

Until people saw actual tapes of police in action, the police and the media were able to play it down.

But this is the age of social media.

And you see what you see.

Police in action, beating women and children—because they can.

THE HISTORIC ROLE OF JOURNALISM AMONG BLACK PEOPLE

July 29, 2014

When we consider the historic role of journalism among Black people, we are left with the deep conviction that, for Black people, the necessities of the time demand that activism must play a role in the performance of the profession.

It must be so, I argue, both then—in our not-too-distant past—and now, in our troubled present, for to neglect activism leaves our people at the not-too-tender mercies of a system that has demonstrated a kind of vehemence and animosity from which few populations in America have suffered.

For ultimately, a profession is just that—a claim to act a certain way in the world, according to certain stated norms and codes which a certain area of employment must abide by.

Except in the long history of Black America, we know better.

We must know, as did the esteemed Black journalist Frederick Douglass, that a constitution written on parchment would differ greatly from government and legal practice when it came to Black people. They were promises: promises broken and unfulfilled for over a century, after the Supreme Court decided in the *Plessy* decision that "separate but equal" was good enough. Black journalist Ida B. Wells-Barnett worked long and hard to bring light to the lies used to justify lynchings against Black people. So much so that, according to recent scholarship, she was shunned and avoided by leading lights of the early Civil Rights movement, who regarded her as "too militant, too outspoken."

Meanwhile, under the Hayes-Tilden gentlemen's agreement, white terrorism, perpetrated through lynching, was the peculiar American custom that wasn't spoken of in polite society. So, quietly (except for Ida B. Wells), Black bodies hung and burned by the thousands across America, the courts and law deeming it mere local custom, beyond their control.

When we enter the modern era, we see a panorama of Black pain that is as unprecedented as it is silent. I speak of mass incarceration, the targeting, imprisonment and criminalization of dark people in ways (and in numbers) the world has never seen. For decades.

And, until recent days, the silence—even among Black journalists—has been deafening. Recently the *New York Times* editorialized against it. How many Black newspapers have done so?

Why not? Professionalism? A false objectivity?

The late historian Howard Zinn for years decried the notion of professionalism. In a speech in Colorado in 2006, Zinn said:

"We all go into professions where you're supposed to be professional. And to be professional means that you don't step outside of your profession. If you're an artist, you don't take a stand on political issues. If you're a professor, you don't give your opinions in the classroom. If you're a newspaperman, you pretend to be objective in presenting the news. But, of course, it's all false. You cannot be neutral."[1]

In Zinn's words, "You can't be neutral on a moving train."

For journalists, the choices before you are actually quite clear. Follow the dictates of your bosses, or serve the interests of your people.

Black Americans, in the main, live life in a hell—daily. For them, freedom is a word, but prison is inevitability. For them, civil rights are a mirage, and daily humiliations are a certainty.

For all the powers of the state are arrayed against them.

They know this—as do we, but such lived realities rarely flow from our pens, our mouths, or our fingers.

So we write dross on the lifestyles of the rich and famous. Or some blathering from a politician.

While our people suffer.

The choice, for any journalist, should be clear.

106

THE MEANING OF FERGUSON

August 31, 2014

Before recent days, who among us had ever heard of Ferguson, Missouri?

Because of what happened there, the brief but intense experience of state repression, its name will be transmitted by millions of Black mouths to millions of Black ears, and it will become a watchword for resistance, like Watts, like Newark, Harlem and Los Angeles.

But Ferguson wasn't 60 years ago—it's today.

And for young Blacks from Ferguson and beyond, it was a stark, vivid history lesson—and also a reality lesson.

When they dared protest the state's street-murder of one of their own, the government responded with the tools and weapons of war. They assaulted them with gas. They attacked them as if Ferguson were Fallujah, in Iraq.

The police attacked them as if they were an occupying army from another country, for that, in fact, is what they were.

And these young folks learned viscerally, face to face, what the White Nation thought of them, their claimed constitutional rights, their so-called freedoms, and their lives. They learned the wages of Black protest. Repression, repression and more repression.

They also learned the limits of their so-called "leaders" who called for "peace" and "calm" while armed troops trained submachine guns and sniper rifles on unarmed men, women and children.

Russian revolutionary leader V.I. Lenin once said, "There are decades when nothing happens; there are weeks when decades happen."

For the youth—excluded from the American economy by

inferior, substandard education; targeted by the malevolence of the fake drug war and mass incarceration; stopped and frisked for Walking While Black—were given front-row seats to the national security state at Ferguson after a friend was murdered by police in their streets.

Ferguson is a wake-up call. A call to build social, radical, revolutionary movements for change.

107

EBOLA

October 14, 2014

With the death of Mr. Thomas Eric Duncan shortly after his arrival from Liberia, West Africa, the Ebola crisis has burst onto millions of news screens, generating deep levels of fear and xenophobia.

The African term "Ebola," named for a river in Congo following the first known outbreak in 1976, evokes the fear and anxiety of the foreign, but it is a tropical disease best known as hemorrhagic fever. The virus causes internal organs and systems to break down and leads to massive bleeding.

To be sure, Ebola is a serious health concern, for it has a 70 percent mortality rate. But to beat back the fear, public officials have been playing down the threats posed by the virus, often armed with little more than hope and false confidence.

For politics, often more imagery than reality, is a poor barrier against the seriousness of viruses, disease and death.

This isn't about the Ebola crisis, it's about the American health care crisis, made possible by a flawed business model that prioritizes profit above all other things: even life itself.

Consider this: When Mr. Duncan first entered Texas Presbyterian Hospital, he was interviewed by a screener, prescribed antibiotics, and sent home. That screener was likely not a medically trained health care professional, but a receptionist, perhaps armed with a checklist to cover. Chances are that the worker was among the lowest-paid staff, unless one considers the janitorial workers.

This business model, one followed by most institutions in America, is now exposed as ineffective, dangerous and the least health-conscious one possible.

That was a business decision, driven by the bottom line of money, not life.

Similarly, the recent crisis has exposed how vulnerable nurses are in this system, for the business perceives them as less valuable than doctors. Hence, they are paid less, trained less, protected less and worked more.

Who spends more time with ailing patients—doctors or nurses? Who has the closest physical contact with patients?

But according to published accounts, nurses had their necks exposed, and when they complained, they were told to use tape to protect themselves.

This is a system that protects profits and prestige, not people!

For doctors get the most protection—nurses, the least.

When this latest Ebola outbreak first struck West Africa, the U.S. mobilized soldiers to go there.

Cuba, which has advanced biotechnical medical experience with tropical diseases, sent more than 1,000 doctors, to help heal people.

Cuba, little, socialist Cuba, has sent more than 135,000 health care professionals to 154 countries, more than the UN's World Health Organization (WHO).

Their Latin American Medical School in Havana trains thousands of poor medical students, from all over the world—*for free.*

Not much of a business model.

But one hell of a human model.

GODDARD
COMMENCEMENT SPEECH

October 2014

Dear fellow Goddardites:

Students; graduates; parents; professors. I thank you for your kind invitation to join you in voice today.

I've been away from Goddard College perhaps longer than most of you have been alive.

I last walked on campus during the late 1970s.

But although it was undoubtedly quite a long time ago, it still sits in memory, and sometimes even visits in dreams of the funky atmosphere that suffused the campus like a cloud of exhaled marijuana smoke.

What really moved me however was the green life—the abundance of grass, trees standing like ancient sentinels, the majestic mountains of Vermont, which possessed a beauty that was, to a guy from the city, simply breathtaking. I remember with crystal clarity walking through the woods back to our dorms (Third World Studies) and feeling pure rapture in the presence of those trees. How many centuries had trees stood on this earth? My mind looked back to Indians who must've trod through these very woods, my steps touching the ground that once crunched under their moccasined feet. Not only have the surviving remnants of their once-great numbers been banished from the land of their fathers, but the reverence with which they held their lands, their collective embrace of Mother Earth, has been banished as well.

That living immensity, more sacred than anything built by man, has never left me, and rises up like a phoenix whenever I think of the campus.

But, of course, what really matters here is not my experience—but yours. This is your commencement, and as such, I will dwell on the world that you are about to enter into, inhabit, and true to Goddard's founding ideals, hopefully transform. As we all know, Goddard is rightly famous for its nontraditional teaching methods and focus.

Here, students stand at the center of the educational endeavor, and they are urged and expected to follow that vibe in their hearts—that which gives them passion—to determine not just what they will study, but how those studies can have impact and meaning in the larger society. This ain't a cookie-cutter school.

Goddard, deeply influenced by the ideas of John Dewey (1859–1952), strives to reach that happy and singular medium between the teacher and the taught, with one exploring with the other how best to achieve a meaningful resolution to questions that arise in the life of the mind.

Quoting Dewey, "Education is not preparation for life, it is life itself."

Dear Graduates, never have words such as these been truer than the hour that is upon us. For the nation is in deep trouble, largely because old thinking, both domestically and globally, has led us into the morass that the nation now faces, which may be encapsulated by references to place names that ring in our minds: Gaza; Ferguson; and Iraq—again!

These are some of the challenges that abide in the world, which it will be your destiny to try to analyze and resolve. As students of Goddard, you know that these challenges are not easy, but they must be faced and addressed.

The Brazilian scholar Paulo Freire, in his groundbreaking *Pedagogy of the Oppressed*, posits the power of literacy to transform psychology, to deepen and broaden one's place in the world. Moreover, when one seeks to interrogate one's radical beliefs, it draws one deeper into contact with the meaning of social change and social transformation. *One* is changed, the prerequisite to social change.

Goddard, because of its size and orientation, has given students the time and attention to find the focus to answer questions that few other places have even dared to entertain. In many ways, it is issues such as these that make Goddard, Goddard. Questions of power, of politics, of race, of gender, of place; questions about where one stands in the world—and how to move, act, interact in a world awash in complexity. Essentially, how does a young person (or for that matter, even an older one), looking at the vast, wide world with a quiet sense of terror, have a voice amidst that monstrous din? How does s/he find that voice that can create space, to think, to be—to grow?

We know that it must come from that place within: that which moves you; that which stirs you; that which is your truest, deepest self. Goddard, unlike most such institutions of higher learning, quietly asks that you listen to and interrogate that voice, and when appropriate, amplify it. For, who knows, within that deepest *you* may dwell the very voice that is silently resonating within the nation, if not the world, itself!

Here, social change and social transformation form the raison d'être of Goddard.

We need new questions for the world of the 21st century, but more important, we need new answers. We live in a world where massive wars can be launched by rumors and innuendo. Where the material interests of corporations are superior to the interests of working people (and remember: corporations are people!); where the ecological threats to fresh water supplies, clean air and the environment in American cities pose challenges that seem beyond our ken.

Did I not say that we need new thinking?

The present social, political, ecological and global course is, to the say the least, unsustainable.

Perhaps some of you new graduates of Goddard will think up ways to forestall some of the challenges facing the living and generations unborn.

I noted earlier my reverie in the woods of Goddard. That exquisite freshness in the wintry air, the nighttime respiration of hundreds of magnificent evergreen trees, has refreshed my mind even when miles—and decades—away from Goddard's sweet, cool ground. Our cities, built during the heights of the industrial age and now engulfed in post-industrial ennui, badly need a greening. Areas should be set aside where children and mothers can breathe and remember air loaded with freshness delivered by green life, not air-conditioned.

Think of the myriad of problems that beset this land, and strive to make it better. That's Dewey's vision—and Goddard's.

Let me say something that I've never said before: when I came to Goddard, I was intimidated. Although teachers and adults told me that I could do the work, I rarely believed them. I felt woefully unprepared.

But guess what? Goddard gave me confidence, and I never lost that feeling.

When I returned to Goddard—many years later—I was a man on Death Row, with a date to die. I was able to transfer credits for continuing education, and my final paper utilized the writings of Frantz Fanon and Ignacio Martín-Baró to examine the concepts of both, in liberation psychology and liberation theology.

Only at Goddard. Only at Goddard!

Goddard reawakened in me my love of learning. In my mind, I left Death Row to travel to France, where Fanon studied psychiatry, and on to Blide Hospital (north of Algiers) where he practiced and later joined the Algerian Revolution. By studying Martín-Baró, I traveled to El Salvador, where he worked as a priest and psychologist, teaching literacy to peasants, when the nation groaned under military terror supported by "El Norte"—the U.S. Empire.

Who were these figures? Fanon was born in the Caribbean island of Martinique, then a colony of France. When he witnessed oppression of the Arabs in Algeria, he felt compelled to join the Revolution on the side of what he called, "The Wretched of the Earth." Ignacio Martín-Baró was among six Jesuit priests, a housekeeper and her daughter slain by the U.S.-trained Atlacatl Battalion, a notorious Salvadoran death squad.

Goddard allowed those trips abroad (if only in the mind), and I thank the school—and many of my friends and alums there—immensely, for opening a door closed for decades.

Goddard allowed me to really study what interested and moved me: revolutionary movements. And through that doorway, history, psychology, politics and, of course, economics.

In one of the most repressive environments on earth—Death Row—Goddard allowed me to study and research human liberation and anti-colonial struggles on two continents: Africa and Latin/Central America.

I thank you for that grand opportunity.

For you graduates, your studies, visits to lands beyond your own, were done to give you both insights and confidence to work in the world, to try to create social change.

Your job isn't how to "get a job"; it's to make a difference!

I thank my friends at Goddard for inviting me back. If it's done for you half of what it's done for me, I assure you, you will have been well served.

Now, take what you know, and apply it in the real world. Help be the change you're seeking to make!

I thank you all!

—Mumia Abu-Jamal, B.A., Goddard
1996
M.A. (Humanities), California State
University, Dominguez Hills, 1999

10 REASONS WHY
MUMIA ABU-JAMAL
SHOULD BE FREED

By Johanna Fernández

1. MUMIA ABU-JAMAL IS INNOCENT.

Mumia has been wrongfully imprisoned for over three decades, charged with the 1981 murder of police officer Daniel Faulkner in Philadelphia. He spent the first 28.5 years of his imprisonment on Pennsylvania's death row. **In 2011, his death sentence was confirmed unconstitutional by the U.S. Supreme Court, and he is now serving a sentence of life in prison without parole.** Early in the morning of December 9, 1981, while driving his cab, Mumia happened upon the arrest of his brother, Billy Cook, by a police officer. Mumia stopped his car to see what was going on. In the events that followed, Mumia was shot in the chest by police officer Daniel Faulkner. Officer Faulkner was subsequently shot and killed by someone else. Mumia has maintained his innocence since his arrest. At trial he stated: "I am innocent of these charges that I have been tried for, despite the connivance of Judge Sabo, Prosecutor McGill and Tony Jackson [his defense attorney] to deny me my so-called right to represent myself, to assistance of my choice, to personally select a jury of my peers, to cross-examine witnesses, and to make both opening and closing arguments. I am innocent despite what you 12 people think, and the truth shall set me free!"[1]

2. THE PRESENCE OF A FOURTH PERSON AT THE CRIME SCENE WAS CONCEALED AT TRIAL.

On the night that Officer Daniel Faulkner and Mumia were

shot, four people were present at the crime scene: the officer, Billy Cook, Mumia and another person. Four witnesses reported seeing someone fleeing the crime scene. When Cook was stopped by Officer Faulkner for an alleged traffic violation, he was driving home from work, with another person in the passenger's seat. That person is believed to have been his business partner, Kenneth Freeman, with whom he owned a newsstand in downtown Philadelphia. In fact, within hours of the shooting, a driver's license application found in Officer Faulkner's shirt pocket led the police directly to Freeman. But **the presence at the crime scene of a fourth person was concealed at trial by the prosecutor, Joe McGill, and the trial judge, Albert Sabo.** The presence of that fourth person was acknowledged by prosecutor Joe McGill during Billy Cook's trial, which concluded before Mumia's began. Former *TV Guide* reporter and independent crime-investigation journalist Patrick O'Connor argues convincingly in his book about the case that it was the fourth person, Kenneth Freeman, who killed Officer Faulkner.[2] Amazingly, this key exculpatory evidence was hidden from the defense and jury during Mumia's trial.[3] Three years after Mumia's trial, Kenneth Freeman was mysteriously found dead in a parking lot, bound and gagged with a needle in his arm.[4] The coroner reported heart failure as the cause of death.

3. BILLY COOK, MUMIA'S BROTHER, LIVES IN FEAR.

Billy Cook has acknowledged that there was a fourth person at the crime scene in two affidavits, but on the advice of his attorney he did not testify at Mumia's trial.[5] For his presence at the crime scene, Cook was tried for resisting arrest and aggravated assault of a police officer, and sentenced to six months to one year in prison. The two witnesses against him, a prostitute named Cynthia White and a motorist, Michael Scanlan, were two of the core prosecution witnesses in Mumia's trial a couple of weeks later. The judge in Billy's trial made it clear that he considered White untrustworthy, if not an outright liar, and convicted Cook on the thin thread of Scanlan's testimony alone. This may explain the relatively light sentence he received for the alleged assault, during an event that resulted in a policeman's death. On appeal, Billy got probation. Five days after Faulkner's death, **the newspaper kiosk co-owned by Billy Cook and Kenneth Freeman was burned down**, and police openly suggested that they had something to do with it.[6] Given Kenneth Freeman's suspicious death, thought by many to have been a police murder, Billy Cook's concern about his personal safety is hardly surprising. Cook reports being under constant surveillance and a target of intimidation by the police. He says that he lives in fear for his life "every day."

4. 15 OF THE 35 POLICE OFFICERS INVOLVED IN COLLECTING EVIDENCE IN MUMIA'S CASE WERE CONVICTED OF EVIDENCE TAMPERING.

In 1979, prior to Mumia's trial, the Department of Justice filed an unprecedented lawsuit against Philadelphia's mayor and 18 top city and police officials. Its conclusions? That the police department's behavior—which included shooting nonviolent suspects, abusing handcuffed prisoners, and tampering with evidence—"shocks the conscience."[7] The officers who arrested and later brutalized Mumia came from a precinct of the Central Division, which was under yet another federal investigation for police corruption at the time of Officer Faulkner's death. The latter investigation was overseen by the U.S. Attorney's Office in Philadelphia, with the approval of the U.S. Department of Justice under President Ronald Reagan. As a result, **over one-third of the 35 officers involved in Mumia's case, including the top officer at the crime scene, Inspector Alfonzo Giordano, were subsequently convicted of rank corruption, extortion, and tampering with evidence to obtain convictions.**

5. MUMIA'S TRIAL WAS A COLOSSAL MISCARRIAGE OF JUSTICE.

According to a 2000 Amnesty International report, the trial **"failed to meet international standards safeguarding fair trial proceedings."**[8] The four pillars set in place to guarantee a fair trial—a fair judge, material evidence, a jury of one's peers, and the right to counsel worthy of the name—were all broken in Mumia's case. 1) In a jaw-dropping illustration of judicial bias, Judge Sabo was heard say to another person in the anteroom of his court, **"I'm going to help them fry the nigger."** Court stenographer Terry Carter testified in an affidavit that she overheard the remark by Judge Sabo, referring to how he was going to instruct the jury. Distinguished among his peers for sending more people to their execution than any other judge in the United States, Sabo earned a reputation as a "hanging judge," and the overwhelming majority of Sabo's victims were black defendants. 2) In a city where 40% of residents were African American, only two black people sat on the jury. 3) Mumia's court-appointed attorney, Anthony Jackson, repeatedly asked to be recused because he did not feel equipped to properly represent Mumia, but the judge refused to grant his request. 4) **Mumia was convicted in the absence of hard evidence.** The police failed to conduct the routine test on Mumia's hands to determine if he had fired a gun, and a critical fragment of the bullet retrieved from Officer Faulkner's body was somehow lost in the coroner's office. Nonetheless, Mumia was convicted of murder in the first degree.

6. THE POLICE MANUFACTURED A FALSE CONFESSION TO CONVICT MUMIA OF A CAPITAL CRIME.

The prosecution pegged the murder on Mumia based on the perjured testimony of two witnesses who said that Mumia confessed to the shooting at the hospital. These statements were made more than two months after the shooting and were contradicted by the testimony of Dr. Anthony Coletta, who was with Mumia from the moment he entered the hospital. Dr. Coletta said that Mumia was barely conscious and in a state of shock, and that due to the trauma produced by Mumia's bullet wound and the beating he had endured at the hands of the police, Mumia was incapable of speaking. In addition, the police report written on the night of the incident by the officer assigned to Mumia at the hospital, Gary Wakshul, states: **"The Negro male made no comment."**

7. THE NEWLY DISCOVERED POLAKOFF PHOTOGRAPHS SHOW THAT POLICE LIED AND DESTROYED WITH EVIDENCE.

The first photographs of the crime scene were taken by Pedro P. Polakoff, a Philadelphia freelance photographer. Polakoff immediately called the police and prosecutors to give them the photographs, but the police never responded. Polakoff assumed that Mumia was guilty and forgot about the issue. In 2006, the rediscovered photographs were studied by Dr. Michael Schiffman of Heidelberg University in Germany. The photos show that the police lied and destroyed evidence. For example, **officer James Forbes, who testified in court that he had properly handled the guns allegedly retrieved at the crime scene, is photographed holding the guns with his bare hands, destroying all potentially significant fingerprints.**

8. MUMIA'S APPEALS HAVE CONSISTENTLY MET WITH SHOCKING BIAS IN THE COURT SYSTEM.

One of the most outrageous examples of malfeasance in the U.S. appellate system was observed in Mumia's case, when Judge Sabo insisted on coming out of retirement to hear Mumia's 1995 Post Conviction Relief Act Hearing—a hearing on judicial and prosecutorial violations in the very case over which Sabo had presided 13 years earlier. In brief, **Judge Sabo himself was head of the review evaluating charges against**

him that he was biased. In permitting this, the Pennslyvania judicial system violated logic, ethics and elementary morality.

The political influence of the Fraternal Order of Police on this case has also blocked Mumia's relief in the courts. The FOP has a well-oiled lobbying infrastructure in the U.S. Congress and Senate, and locally it wields influence over judges, prosecutors and local politicians. In a bizarre intimidation gesture, the FOP maintains a website list of hundreds of citizens who have spoken out for a new trial or release of Mumia.[9]

In 1998, Mumia's attorneys made a different move: they filed an appeal to his conviction in the Pennsylvania Supreme Court. At the same time, they filed a petition requesting that the court's Chief Justice, Ronald Castille, remove himself from the panel overseeing the case, citing his close relationship with the FOP. **Although the police organization had helped fund his bid for the Pennsylvania Supreme Court and honored him as "Man of the Year," Justice Castille responded stridently that he would not step aside,** and noted that five of the seven judges of that Pennsylvania Supreme Court were supported by the FOP. It is no surprise that the court did not find one single error in the court proceedings and thus denied Mumia the right to a new trial.

When Mumia's attorney's appealed the PA Supreme Court's decision in federal district court, that appellate body was required by a series of new regressive states' rights laws to accept as fact the evidence and legal findings previously presented in the lower courts. One such legislation was Bill Clinton's Anti-Terrorism and Effective Death Penalty Act (AEDPA) of 1996. It forced federal judges to accept the often tampered-with and falsified evidence manufactured by the police, upon which the lower courts depend in making their rulings. Hence **the federal appeals judge was prevented from assessing claims that Mumia had ineffective counsel at trial, that witnesses were intimidated by police, and that evidence of his confession was fabricated by police.**

In 2007, a hearing in the Third Circuit Court of Appeals offered Mumia the best opportunity for relief in the form of new trial. Mumia's legal team presented evidence supporting the "Batson Claim," which grants a new trial to defendants who can prove discrimination in jury selection. Based on the 1984 Supreme Court decision *Batson V. Kentucky*, the claim sets a very low bar for proof of racial bias, stating that if the defendant can prove racial bias in even a single instance, the courts must grant a new trial. The legal team demonstrated that the prosecutor in Mumia's trial used 11 out of 15 peremptory challenges— the right to eliminate jurors without cause—to remove African Americans from the jury pool.

In a shocking 2-to-1 decision that overturned its own precedents, the Third Circuit Court voted against granting Mumia a new trial based on the Batson Claim. The sole dissenting judge, Thomas Ambro, wrote that the decision "goes against the grain of our prior actions." In language revealing his frustration with the double standard applied by his colleagues, Judge Ambro added, "I see no reason why we should not afford Abu-Jamal the courtesy of our precedents. . . .Why we pick this case to depart from that reasoning I do not know."[10]

9. MUMIA HAD LONG BEEN A POLITICAL DISSI-DENT AND A TARGET OF STATE SURVEILLANCE.

It is well documented in declassified FBI memos that the Philadelphia police, in consultation with COINTELPRO (the federal government's Counterintelligence Program), had for many years tried to peg some criminal act on the former Black Panther and radical journalist Mumia Abu-Jamal. At the time of his arrest, Mumia had been a thorn in the side of the establishment and a target of the state due to his relentlessly critical radio journalism on police brutality and corruption in City Hall, and his friendly reporting on the radical naturalist organization MOVE.[11] One of the least-known facts of the case remains that the investigation of Officer Faulkner's fatal shooting involved the Philadelphia Police Department's Civil Defense Unit, the local police arm of J. Edgar Hoover's COINTELPRO. Vastly expanded in 1967 when Frank Rizzo became Police Commissioner of Philadelphia, **the COINTELPRO-linked unit helped produce a 700-page surveillance record of Mumia. In 1973, the same unit collaborated in the failed attempt to pin a double murder on Mumia,** who beat the frame-up with an airtight alibi. At the time the Governor of Bermuda and his aide were killed, Mumia had been working for the Philadephia telephone company.[12] When the Philadelphia police found Mumia in the middle of a crime scene in 1981, they did everything in their power to frame him.

10. THIS IS NOT JUST ABOUT MUMIA.

From the hangings of the Haymarket martyrs in the late 19th century to the execution of Julius and Ethel Rosenberg in 1953, the U.S. state has historically sought to make an example out of those who challenge its power. Mumia's incarceration is a potent example of the state's relentless persecution and punishment of Black Power–era activists for their formidable challenge to Northern racism and police terror. The ideological attack on black radicals and Civil Rights movement workers during the 1960s stirred up a racist, moral panic around crime and linked it to black activism. This was the scaffolding on which the modern edifice of mass incarceration was built. Deployed first against black dissidents, the politics of "law and order" was later extended broadly to warehouse, contain and control communities of color, considered disposable by neoconservative politics and conveniently blamed for the growing crisis of urban deindustrialization. During the late 1970s and 1980s, in the face of economic crisis and U.S. imperial decline, the criminalization of poor black and brown youth and the demonization of immigrant communities were also used by politicians to scapegoat and blame a sector of American society for the growing problems facing the nation.

Mumia's case is a global symbol of the entrenched racism and repression of the U.S. court system. **Exposure of the ongoing gross injustices that continue to keep Mumia imprisoned for over three decades would open up a much larger conversation in the mainstream about the crisis of mass and political imprisonment in the United States.**

In the 1990s, an international movement kept the state from executing Mumia. Today, the fight to free him continues to be bound up in the fundamental right to protest and to fight for a better world. Freeing Mumia, and the many others who were imprisoned as a result of their work in the cause of freedom during the 1960s—NOW, while they are still alive—is one of the most important moral assignments of our generation.

Endnotes

INTRODUCTION
1. WWDB expressly asked Mumia not to mention MOVE, and WPEN, the soft rock station at which he worked under the name William Wellington Cole, fired him for "failure to commit to the station's mission." WPEN praised his talent simultaneously with letting him go; the station suggested that the quality of his voice was suited for a network like New York's CBS News. (Interview with the Editor. See also Terry Bisson, *On A Move: The Story of Mumia Abu-Jamal* [North Farmington, PA: Litmus Books, 2000], pp. 144–149).
2. For more on the bombing of the MOVE house, see "Let the Fire Burn: The MOVE Bombing 29 Years Later," PBS (May 12, 2014), www.pbs.org/independentlens/blog/let-fire-burn-fallout-29-years
3. Examples include: Eldridge Cleaver, *Soul on Ice*; Malcolm X, *The Autobiography of Malcolm X*; Russell Maroon Shoatz, *Maroon the Implacable: The Collected Writings of Russell Maroon Shoatz*; George Jackson, *Blood in My Eye*; Marshall "Eddie" Conway, *Marshall Law: The Life and Times of a Baltimore Black Panther*; and Austin Reed, *The Life and Adventures of a Haunted Convict, or the Inmate of a Gloomy Prison*, a recently discovered 19th-century manuscript.

CHAPTER 2
1. *The Judge's Letter* by John Africa, MOVE founder, pp. 11–12.

CHAPTER 4
1. *The Judge's Letter* by John Africa, MOVE founder

CHAPTER 6
1. *Time*, May 27, 1985, p. 18.

CHAPTER 7
1. The Black Bottom was Philadelphia's African American neighborhood.

CHAPTER 16
1. Eleanor Bumpurs was an African American woman who was killed by New York City Police on October 29, 1984, when the authorities were called to her apartment to settle an eviction dispute. The NYPD shot the emotionally disturbed Ms. Bumpurs with two rounds from a 12-gauge shotgun. www.nytimes.com/1985/04/13/nyregion/state-judge-dismisses-indictment-of-officer-in-the-bumpurs-killing.html

CHAPTER 18
1. DW = Death Watch, for suicidal prisoners
2. Restricted Housing Unit, commonly known as "the Hole"

CHAPTER 21
1. Joseph H. Berke, *The Tyranny of Malice* (New York: Summit Books, 1988).

CHAPTER 25
1. James Baldwin, in a 1965 debate with William F. Buckley at the Cambridge Union Society, Cambridge University.

CHAPTER 26
1. Quoted in *Turning the Tide*, vol. 12, no. 4 (winter 2000), p. 1.
2. Larvester Gaither, "Lynching and Police Powers in Texas," in Joy James, ed., *States of Confinement: Policing, Detention, and Prisons*, (New York: St. Martin's Press, 2000), p. 193.

CHAPTER 31
1. *Washington Post National Weekly Edition*, May 22, 2000, p. 9.
2. Ibid., p. 8.

CHAPTER 34
1. *The Haldeman Diaries: Inside the Nixon White House* (G.P. Putnam, 1994), p. 53.
2. *New York Times*, April 3, 1997. See www.nytimes.com/1997/04/03/us/former-philadelphia-prosecutor-accused-of-racial-bias.html

CHAPTER 36
1. Israel Shamir, "The Failed Test," in *Socialist Viewpoint*, June 2001, pp. 31–32.

CHAPTER 38
1. *Los Angeles Times*, August 4, 1996
2. Ibid., p. 2

CHAPTER 40
1. Howard Zinn, *A People's History of the United States* (New York: Harper & Row), pp. 386–7.
2. Randolph Bourne, *The State* (Gloucester, England: Dodo Press).

CHAPTER 42
1. *New York Times*, November 8, 1991. See www.nytimes.com/1991/11/08/world/bush-challenges-partners-in-nato-over-role-of-us.html
2. Michael Ignatieff, "Barbarians at the Gate?," *New York Review of Books*, February 28, 2002, pp. 4–6.

CHAPTER 43
1. Pete Hamill, "A Savage Disease Called New York," *New York Post* (April 23, 1989)
2. *Columbia Journalism Review*, Jan.-Feb. 2003.
3. *Haley v. Ohio*, 332 U.S. 596 (1948)

CHAPTER 45
1. See www.house.gov./mckinney/news/pr020626.htm

CHAPTER 47
1. H.P. Newton, *Revolutionary Suicide* (New York: Writers and Readers Pub., 1995), p. 113.
2. Quoted in Clayborne Carson, *Malcolm X: The FBI File* (New York: Carroll and Graf, 1991), p. 226.
3. Quoted in Ward Churchill and Jim Vander Wall, *The COINTELPRO Papers* (Cambridge, MA: South End Press, 1990/2002), p. 96.

CHAPTER 49
1. Quoted in Celucien L. Joseph, *Haitian Modernity and Liberative Interruptions: Discourse on Race, Religion, and Freedom* (Lanham, MD: University Press of America, 2013), p. 33.
2. Quoted in Paul Farmer, *The Uses of Haiti* (Monroe, ME: Common Courage Press, 1994), p. 61.
3. Farmer, p. 79.
4. Cited in Ralph Pezzullo, *Plunging Into Haiti: Clinton, Aristide, and the Defeat of Diplomacy* (Univ. Press of Mississippi, 2006), p. 81.

CHAPTER 51
1. Quoted in Philip S. Foner, *The Life and Writings of Frederick Douglass* (1950), pp. 118, 362.

CHAPTER 52
1. James Loewen, *Lies My Teacher Told Me* (New York: Touchstone, 1996), pp. 25-26.
2. Loewen, p. 25.

CHAPTER 53
1. *USA Today*, January 29, 2004, p. 1A.
2. William Rivers Pitt and Scott Ritter, *War on Iraq: What Team Bush Doesn't Want You to Know* (New York: Context, 2002), p. 10.

CHAPTER 54
1. Quoted in Derrick Bell, *Silent Covenants: Brown v. Board of Education and the Unfulfilled Hopes for Racial Reform* (New York: Oxford Univ. Press, 2005)

CHAPTER 55
1. Ian F. Haney Lopez, *White By Law: The Legal Construction of Race* (New York Univ. Press, 1996), p. 42.

CHAPTER 56
1. *The Spark*, May 17–June 6, 2004, p. 4. http://the-spark.net/np727402.html
2. *New York Times*, December 7, 2003.

CHAPTER 57
1. Richard Cloward and Frances Fox Piven, *The New Class War* (Cambridge, MA: South End, 1982/1985), p. 13.
2. Clara Nieto, *Masters of War* (New York: 7 Stories, 2003), p. 329.
3. Nieto, p. 330.

CHAPTER 59
1. Sources: Alvaro Michaels, "Chavez calls for struggle against imperialism," in *Fight Racism! Fight Imperialism!* (Aug.-Sept. 2004), p. 10.; Tom Paine, *Rights of Man* (Mineola, NY: Dover, 1999).

CHAPTER 60
1. www.legislature.state.al.us/codeofalabama/constitution/1901/ca-245806. htm

CHAPTER 62
1. Mumia Abu-Jamal interview with Lynne Stewart, April 25, 2005. http://archive.prisonradio.org/LynneStewart.htm
2. Andrew P. Napolitano, "No Defense," *New York Times* (online), February 17, 2004: www.nytimes.com/2005/02/17/opinion/17napolitano.html

CHAPTER 63
1. Seymour Hersh, *Chain of Command: The Road from 9/11 to Abu-Ghraib* (New York: Harper Collins, 2004).
2. Hersh, p. 43.

CHAPTER 64
1. William A. Schabas, *The Death Penalty as Cruel Treatment and Torture* (Boston: Northeastern University Press, 1996), p. 69.
2. From *Callins v. Collins, Certiorari. Denied*, 114 S.Ct. 1127, 1135 (Blackmun, J., dissent, 1994). *When a higher court denies an appeal to review the decisions of a lower court.

CHAPTER 65
1. *The Montgomery Bus Boycott and the Women Who Started It: The Memoir of Jo Ann Gibson Robinson* (Knoxville: Univ. of Tennessee Press, 1987)

CHAPTER 66
1. From pressworldcantwait_la@yahoo.com
2. Derrick Jensen, *Walking on Water: Reading, Writing and Revolution* (White River Junction, Vt.: Chelsea Green Publ., 2004).

CHAPTER 68
1. Frank Donner, *The Age of Surveillance: The Aims and Methods of America's Political Intelligence System* (New York: Knopf, 1981), p. 153.

CHAPTER 69
1. Marty Glaberman, *Punching Out* (Chicago: Kerr, 2002), pp. 14–15.

CHAPTER 70
1. Frank Donner, *The Age of Surveillance: The Aims and Methods of America's Political Intelligence System* (New York: Knopf, 1981)
2. From Alexis de Tocqueville, *Democracy in America* [2 vols.] (New York: Bantam Classic, 2004), orig. pub. 1835.

CHAPTER 71
1. Lawrence Britt, "Fascism Anyone?" in *Free Inquiry* (Spring 2003), p. 20. See www.secularhumanism.org/library/fi/britt_23_2.htm. Also, see the author's discussion of COINTELPRO in *We Want Freedom: A Life in the Black Panther Party* (Cambridge, MA: South End Press, 2004).

CHAPTER 72
1. Michael Eric Dyson, *Come Hell or High Water: Hurricane Katrina and the Color of Disaster* (New York: Basic Civitas, 2006), pp. 144–145.

CHAPTER 73
1. Kristian Williams, *Enemies in Blue: Police and Power in America* (Brooklyn, NY: Soft Skull Press), p. 121.

CHAPTER 74
1. From Kuwasi Balagoon, et al., *Look for Me in the Whirlwind: The Collective Autobiography of the New York 21* (New York: Vintage, 1971), p. 219. The "Panther 21" became a popular slogan for organizing around the indictment and arrest of 21 members of the New York chapter of the Black Panther Party, all of whom who were later acquitted by a jury despite false charges of bizarre bomb plots to destroy the Bronx Botanical Gardens and other such targets. One of the accused was the then-pregnant mother of rapper Tupac Shakur, Afeni Shakur.
2. Frantz Fanon, *The Wretched of the Earth* (New York: Grove Press, 1966). (Trans. by Catherine Farrington of *Les damnés de la terre* [Paris: François Maspero, 1961]).
3. Bobby Seale, *Seize the Time: The Story of the Black Panther Party and Huey P. Newton* (New York: Vintage, 1970), p. 25.
4. Kathleen Neal Cleaver, "Back to Africa: The Evolution of the International Section of the Black Panther Party (1968–1972)," in Charles E. Jones, ed., *The Black Panther Party [Reconsidered]* (Baltimore: Black Classic Press, 1998), p. 214.
5. Fanon, p. 174.
6. Fanon, p. 76.
7. Huey P. Newton (with the assistance of J. Herman Black), *Revolutionary Suicide* (New York: Writers and Readers, 1995), p. 111. (Original, New York:

Harcourt, 1973.)
8. Cleaver, p. 214.
9. Fanon, p. 141.

CHAPTER 76
1. Cited on BlackPast.org. See www.blackpast.org/primary/gary-declaration-national-black-political-convention-1972

CHAPTER 77
1. Ken Belson, "Vacant Houses, Scourge of a Beaten-Down Buffalo," *New York Times*, September 13, 2007.
2. Manny Fernandez, "Housing Takes Bigger Bite of New Yorkers' Incomes, Census Data Shows," *New York Times*, September 13, 2007.
3. Quoted in Eric Mayes, " 'Gentrification'—There Go the Neighborhoods," *Philadelphia Tribune*, September 14, 2007.

CHAPTER 78
1. Ryan Nissim-Sabat, "Panthers Set Up Shop in Cleveland," in Judson L. Jeffries, ed., *Comrades: Local History of the Black Panther Party* (Bloomington/Indianapolis: Indiana Univ. Press, 2007), pp. 111, 89, 144.

CHAPTER 79
1. WL 284060 (July 24, 2008)
2. Prosecutors are also known as Assistant District Attorneys (ADAs).

CHAPTER 81
1. Steve Palmer, "Capitalist Crisis-USA: Goodbye Wall Street," in *Fight Racism! Fight Imperialism!* (London) Oct.-Nov. 2008, p. 3.

CHAPTER 82
1. Cited in Robert Fisk, *The Great War for Civilisation: The Conquest of the Middle East* (U.K.: Fourth Estate, 2005).
2. William R. Polk, *The Arab World Today* (Cambridge, MA: Harvard Univ. Press, 1991).

CHAPTER 83
1. Frantz Fanon, *The Wretched of the Earth* (New York: Grove Press, 1966). (Trans. by Catherine Farrington of *Les damnés de la terre* [Paris: François Maspero, 1961]).
2. Frantz Fanon, *Toward the African Revolution* (New York: Grove Press, 1969)

CHAPTER 84
1. *Legal Intelligencer*, February 3, 2009, and February 4, 2009.

CHAPTER 85
1. "Urgent Action Alert: 6 Prisoners Assaulted in the Camp Hill SMU on Inauguration Day," Human Rights Coalition, Fed Up! chapter (February 17, 2009), posted at http://phillyimc.org/en/urgent-action-alert-6-prisoners-assaulted-camp-hill-smu-inauguration-day}

CHAPTER 86
1. Mary Frances Berry, *Black Resistance: White Law* (New York: Appleton-Century-Crofts, 1971), p. xi.

CHAPTER 88
1. Zinn, p. 110.

CHAPTER 89
1. A Supreme Court precedent that grants relief to defendants who prove that in their case the jury's verdict was reached in the presence of improper instructions given to them, by the judge or prosecutor, on the rules governing their decision making.

CHAPTER 90
1. C.L.R. James, *The Black Jacobins: Toussaint L'Ouverture and the San Domingo Revolution* (New York: Vintage, 1989).
2. James, p. xvi.

CHAPTER 91
1. Mumia Abu-Jamal, *Faith of Our Fathers* (Trenton, NJ: Africa World Press, 2003).

CHAPTER 93
1. "In Memory of John Carter," *The Movement* (official newsletter of the Human Rights Coalition, Phila.) #151, Summer 2012, p. 47.

CHAPTER 94
1. Mumia Abu-Jamal, *Live from Death Row* (New York: Avon, 1995).

CHAPTER 98
1. *Balzac v. Porto Rico* 1922, 258 U.S. 298; pp. 310–311

CHAPTER 99
1. Jonathan Kozol, 2005. *The Shame of the Nation: The Restoration of Apartheid Schooling in America* (New York: Three Rivers Press, 2005), pp. 18–19.
2. Gary B. Nash, *The Unknown American Revolution* (New York: Penguin, 2005)

CHAPTER 100
1. Bamford, James, *The Shadow Factory: The Ultra-Secret NSA from 9/11 to the Eavesdropping on America*, (New York: Doubleday/Random House, 2008), p. 113.

CHAPTER 102

1. Michael Eric Dyson, *I May Not Get There With You: The True Martin Luther King* (New York: Touchstone, 2000), p. 195.

2. Mumia Abu-Jamal, *We Want Freedom: A Life in the Black Panther Party* (Cambridge, MA: South End Press, 2004), p. 159.

3. Dyson, 208–9.

4. Angela D. LeBlanc-Ernest, "The Most Qualified Person to Handle the Job: Black Panther Party Women, 1966–1982," in Charles E. Jones, ed., *The Black Panther Party Reconsidered* (Baltimore, MD: Black Classic Press, 1988), p. 309 [citing Bobby Seale, *A Lonely Rage: The Autobiography of Bobby Seale* [New York Times Books, 1978]).

5. Abu-Jamal, p. 164.

6. Dyson, p. 84.

7. Howard Zinn, *A People's History of the United States* (New York: Harper Collins, 1980–2003), p. 404.

8. Additional source referenced in writing this piece: David E. Garrow, *Bearing the Cross: Martin Luther King, Jr. and the Southern Christian Leadership Conference* (New York: Harper Collins, 1986).

CHAPTER 105

1. Howard Zinn, *Howard Zinn Speaks: Collected Speeches: 1963–2009*, edited by Anthony Arnove (Chicago: Haymarket, 2012).

APPENDIX

1. Mumia Abu-Jamal trial transcript, July 3, 1982, pp. 14–15.

2. Patrick O'Connor, *The Framing of Mumia Abu-Jamal* (Chicago: Lawrence Hill Books, 2008), p. 9.

3. O'Connor, *The Framing of Mumia Abu-Jamal*.

4. This occurred on the night of the infamous MOVE bombing of May 13, 1985. See pages *xxvi–xxvii* and chapter 6 of this volume for a full account of the fire-bombing, by the Philadelphia police, of the MOVE organization's residence, which killed 11 people and incinerated 61 homes in the African American neighborhood of Powelton Village.

5. Billy Cook went public with this statement in the acclaimed film *In Prison My Whole Life*, by Marc Evans, which features Alice Walker, Noam Chomsky, Mos Def, Howard Zinn and Snoop Dogg, among others.

6. O'Connor, *The Framing of Mumia Abu-Jamal*, pp. 18–19.

7. Philip Taubman, "U.S. Files Rights Suit Charging Philadelphia Police With Brutality," *New York Times*, August 14, 1979, D14; see also Amnesty International, *A Life in the Balance: The Case of Mumia Abu-Jamal* (February 17, 2000), www.amnesty.org/en/library/asset/AMR51/001/2000/en/0987a185-dfd3-11dd-8e17-69926d493233/amr510012000en.pdf, pp. 4–5.

8. Amnesty International, *USA: A Life in the Balance*.

9. www.fop.net/causes/faulkner/projamal.shtml
10. Quoted in Dave Lindorff, "The Politics of Death," *Counterpunch* (June 30, 2010). www.counterpunch.org/2010/06/30/the-politics-of-death

Acknowledgements

In the 1990s, Mumia Abu-Jamal came dangerously close to being executed, first on August 17, 1995, and again on December 2, 1999. Had it not been for the international movement that mobilized in the streets to save his life, the world would know less today of the quiet power of the person behind the writings in this collection. The highest thanks, therefore, goes to the people, families, communities, and networks that form the movement to free Mumia—one of the longest-standing and most dedicated of the post–Civil Rights movement era. This movement has survived and thrived thanks to the 24/7 leadership and insurgent tenacity of Pam Africa and the International Concerned Family and Friends of Mumia Abu-Jamal.

Within the United States, the movement includes an array of committed individuals and organizations, including the late Safiya Bukhari; Mark Taylor and Educators for Mumia Abu-Jamal; Suzanne Ross and the Free Mumia Abu-Jamal Coalition (NYC); Noelle Hanrahan and the Prison Radio Project; Mumia's music instructor, Sister Bariki Hall; the Committee to Save Mumia Abu-Jamal; attorney Martha Conley; Tameka Cage; the late David Demarest; Anthony Monteiro; the late Leonard Weinglass; Clark Kissinger and Refuse and Resist; Rachel Wolkenstein; the Partisan Defense Committee; Craig Gordon and Bob Mandel of Oakland Teachers for Mumia; Jeff Mackler and the Mobilization to Free Abu-Jamal/Northern California; Monica Morehead, Betsey Piette and Millions for Mumia/IAC; Keith D. Cook, Jamal Hart, and the Cook Family & Friends; and a new generation of activists in the Campaign to Bring Mumia Home, among many others.

Mumia always acknowledges that it is the power of love that enables him to keep on striving. Deep respect goes out to Mumia's family from everyone in the movement, for it is his family that has provided him love with unstinting faithfulness, in spite of all the obstacles that decades of imprisonment have presented. We especially salute the love and fighting spirit of Wadiya A. Jamal, Mumia's wife. From the moment of his arrest to the present, she has fought for Mumia's life, health and freedom. Since Mumia's imprisonment in 1981, several beloved members of his family have passed to the realm of ancestors—his mother, Edith Cook and his sister, Lydia Barashango. The whole family's spirit of struggle is embodied in the life of Samiya "Goldii" Davis Abdullah, the youngest daughter of Mumia Abu-Jamal and Wadiya Jamal. She passed on December 17, 2014. Samiya had been living with cancer for several years, during which time she finished a Master's Degree with honors in Psychology at the University of Pennsylvania and was working on her doctorate. Samiya was an accomplished artist who expressed the injustice of her father's case through her music and in speeches at public events. A voracious reader, she read the books her father sent to her from prison, and discussed them with him over the phone. As a child she visited him on death row. In his radio essay, "Goldii's Visit," Mumia describes that during one of her visits to prison she was so distressed by the partition that separated her from her father that she pounded with her little fists on the plexiglass and called out to her mother to "break it." Goldii's fighting spirit, and that of all Mumia's family, helps to power the words you find in these pages.

Mumia has written seven books from prison and is read around the world. Beginning with his best seller, *Live From Death Row*, his writings were published and remained in print thanks to the vision and tenacity of his literary agent, Frances Goldin. At 91 she remains one of the most ardent champions of Mumia's writings and freedom.

A movement that has been around so long and weathered ongoing attacks by the Fraternal Order of Police has necessarily experienced its share of internal friction. In the process of working through such tensions, my own life and world-view have been profoundly enriched by the courage and revolutionary spirit of Pam and Ramona Africa and the MOVE organization.

Internationally, the movement includes Carolina of Amig@s de Mumia de México; Mireille Fanon Mendès-France and the Frantz Fanon Foundation; Claude Guillaumaud and Jacky Hortaut with Le Collectif Français "Libérons Mumia"; Julia Wright and the Saint-Denis Mumia Committee; Michael and Annette Schiffman of the German Network Against the Death Penalty and to Free Mumia Abu-Jamal; Free Mumia Berlin; and Vrienden Van Mumia of Amsterdam Berlin, among many others. They have set the standard for keeping the goal of winning Mumia's freedom in its rightful place historically.

Ten years ago, Greg Ruggiero approached me about working on a book of Mumia's writings. I was hesitant, having then just recently met Mumia, but Greg persisted, and two years ago the idea took hold. I am grateful that he conceived of *Writing on the Wall* and worked with me to bring it to fruition. His creative mind, unflinching commitment to excellence, and visionary appreciation of Mumia's writings and their place in the American literary canon steered this project to completion. If this book sings, it does so because of Greg Ruggiero. But books, like movements, are collective efforts. The patient and brilliant editorial eye of Elizabeth Bell was indispensible.

Mumia has written thousands of commentaries since 1982. Over the years, several women have transcribed Mumia's writings and disseminated them electronically. The public is indebted to Sister Fatirah Aziz (also known as Litestar01), Sister Marpessa Kupendua, and the late Susan Burnett (the wife of Ali Bey Hassan of the Black Panther 21) who have been the quiet telegraphers of his words to the world.

Collecting Mumia's writings and selecting just over 100 that reflect the breadth of the subjects with which Mumia is concerned was a difficult task. Thanks go to Ria Julian, who was instrumental in this process. The contributions of Jeff

Camp, Sophia Williams, and Laura Gottesdiener were also in-dispensable—thank you.

My colleagues Mark Taylor, Heidi Boghosian, Chris Tinson, Jessica Millward, Nora Eisenberg, Michael Schiffman, and especially Victor Wallis read drafts of the manuscript; their careful feedback is testament to their love and regard for the literary prose and political acumen of Mumia Abu-Jamal.

MUMIA ABU-JAMAL is an award-winning journalist and author of two best-selling books, *Live From Death Row* and *Death Blossoms*, which address prison life from a critical and spiritual perspective. In 1981 he was elected president of the Association of Black Journalists (Philadelphia chapter). That same year he was arrested for allegedly killing a white police officer in Philadelphia. He was convicted and sentenced to death in 1982, in a process that has been described as an epic miscarriage of justice. After he had spent more than 28 years on death row, in 2011 his death sentence was vacated when the Supreme Court allowed to stand the decisions of four federal judges who had earlier declared his death sentence unconstitutional. He is now serving a life sentence without the possibility of parole. In spite of his three-decade imprisonment, most of which was spent in solitary confinement on Death Row, Abu-Jamal has relentlessly fought for his freedom and for his profession. From prison he has written seven books and thousands of radio commentaries (www.prisonradio.org). He holds a B.A. from Goddard College and an M.A. from California State University, Dominguez Hills. His books have sold more than 100,000 copies and have been translated into seven languages. www.bringmumiahome.com • www.freemumia.com • www.emajonline.com • www.mumiaabujamal.com

JOHANNA FERNÁNDEZ is a former Fulbright Scholar to Jordan and Assistant Professor of History at Baruch College of the City University of New York, where she teaches 20th-Century U.S. history and African American History. She is author of the forthcoming *When the World Was Their Stage: A History of the Young Lords Party, 1968–1976* (Princeton University Press). Fernández is the writer and producer of the film *Justice on Trial: The Case of Mumia Abu-Jamal* and she is featured in the critically acclaimed documentary about Mumia

RECENT AND FORTHCOMING IN THE OPEN MEDIA SERIES

Because We Say So
By Noam Chomsky

Under The Affluence
By Tim Wise

Narrative of the Life of Frederick Douglass, an American Slave,
Written by Himself
A New Critical Edition
by Angela Y. Davis

Border Patrol Nation
By Todd Miller

Spying on Democracy
Government Surveillance, Corporate Power, and Public Resistance
By Heidi Boghosian, with a foreword by Lewis Lapham

A Power No Government Can Suppress
By Howard Zinn

Dying To Live
A Story of U.S. Immigration in an Age of Global Apartheid
By Joseph Nevins, with photography by Mizue Aizeki

The Meaning of Freedom
By Angela Y. Davis, with a foreword by Robin D.G. Kelley

The Speed of Dreams
Selected Writings 2001–2007
By Subcomandante Insurgente Marcos
Edited by Canek Pena-Vargas and Greg Ruggiero

City Lights Books I Open Media Series I www.citylights.com